T0331229

It's All Analytics, Part III

Professionals are challenged each day by a changing landscape of technology and terminology. In recent history, especially the last 25 years, there has been an explosion of terms and methods born that automate and improve decision-making and operations. One term, called "analytics," is an overarching description of a compilation of methodologies. But artificial intelligence (AI), statistics, decision science, and optimization, which have been around for decades, have resurged. Also, things like business intelligence, online analytical processing (OLAP) and many, many more have been born or reborn. How is someone to make sense of all this methodology, terminology?

Extending on the foundations introduced in the first book, this book illustrates how professionals in healthcare, business, and government are applying these disciplines, methods, and technologies. The goal of this book is to get leaders and practitioners to start thinking about how they may deploy techniques outside their function or industry into their domain. Application of modern technology into new areas is one of the fastest, most effective ways to improve results. By providing a rich set of examples, this book fosters creativity in the application and use of AI and analytics in innovative ways.

It's All Analytics, Part III

The Applications of AI, Analytics, and Data Science

Scott Burk & Gary Miner

Routledge
Taylor & Francis Group

A PRODUCTIVITY PRESS BOOK

First published 2024
by Routledge
605 Third Avenue, New York, NY 10158

and by Routledge
4 Park Square, Milton Park, Abingdon, Oxon, OX14 4RN

Routledge is an imprint of the Taylor & Francis Group, an informa business

© 2024 Scott Burk & Gary Miner

ISBN: 978-0-367-35970-6 (hbk)
ISBN: 978-1-032-55224-8 (pbk)
ISBN: 978-0-429-34397-1 (ebk)

DOI: 10.4324/9780429343971

Typeset in Garamond
by Apex CoVantage, LLC

Contents

Acknowledgement

Jackie, here we are again. Thanks for all your support!

Scott Burk

Bios of Authors

Scott Burk, Ph.D is founder of It's All Analytics (itsallanalytics.com) where he advises companies on creating the optimal data, AI and analytics architecture to maximize their objectives. He stays active by writing and teaching as well. He is the author of five books on AI, data science and analytics including the It's All Analytics Series, the Executive Guide for AI and Analytics and Practical Data Analytics for Innovation in Medicine. He currently teaches in the MS of Data Science program at CUNY and has taught at Baylor and Texas A&M. He has held executive and VP roles as well as hands on positions in startups to Fortune 50 enterprises.

His experience is primarily in solving difficult AI, statistical and analytical problems at companies such as Texas Instruments, Dell, Paypal, EBay, Overstock.com, healthcare companies and many others. Scott has a bachelors in biology and chemistry, master degrees in finance, statistics and data mining and a PhD in statistics. Data has been the thread that has tied his professional experience together.

Scott resides in Central Texas.

Reference - he is the senior author of the ITS ALL ANALYTICS series of books, the 3rd of 4 in the series released in June, 2022 (https://www.routledge. com/The-Executives-Guide-to-AI-and-Analytics-The-Foundations-of-Execution/ Burk-Miner/p/book/9781032007946#) and July 2020 (https://www.routledge. com/Its-All-Analytics-The-Foundations-of-Al-Big-Data-and-Data-Science-Land scape/Burk-Miner/p/book/9780367359683?source=igodigital#) and September 2021 (https://www.routledge.com/It-s-All-An-alytics---Part-II-Designing-an-Integrated/Burk-Sweenor-Miner/p/book/9780367359713).

His authors page with more details is found at: https://www.amazon. com/Scott-Burk/e/B08FG8677J/ref=aufs_dp_mata_dsk.

Gary Miner, Ph.D., received a B.S. from Hamline University, St. Paul, MN, with biology, chemistry, and education majors; an M.S. in zoology and population genetics from the University of Wyoming; and a Ph.D. in biochemical genetics from the University of Kansas as the recipient of a NASA pre-doctoral fellowship. He pursued additional National Institutes of Health post-doctoral studies at the University of Minnesota and University of Iowa, eventually becoming immersed in the study of affective disorders and Alzheimer's disease. In 1985, he and his wife, Dr. Linda Winters-Miner, founded the Familial Alzheimer's Disease Research Foundation, which became a leading force in organizing both local and international scientific meetings, bringing together all the leaders in the field of genetics of Alzheimer's from several countries, resulting in the first major book on the genetics of Alzheimer's disease. In the mid-1990 s, Dr. Miner turned his data analysis interests to the business world, joining the team at StatSoft and deciding to specialize in data mining. He started developing what eventually became the *Handbook of Statistical Analysis and Data Mining Applications* (co-authored with Drs. Robert A. Nisbet and John Elder), which received the 2009 American Publishers Award for Professional and Scholarly Excellence (PROSE). Their follow-up collaboration, Practical Text Mining and Statistical Analysis for Non-structured Text Data Applications also received a PROSE award in February of 2013. Overall, Dr. Miner's career has focused on medicine and health issues, so serving as the 'project director' for *Practical Predictive Analytics of Medicine* fit his knowledge and skills perfectly. Gary also serves as VP & Scientific Director of Healthcare Predictive Analytics Corp; as Merit Reviewer for Patient Centered Outcomes Research Institute that awards grants for predictive analytics research into the comparative effectiveness and heterogeneous treatment effects of medical interventions including drugs among different genetic groups of patients. Dr Miner has taught on-line classes in 'Introduction to Predictive Analytics', 'Text Analytics', and 'Risk Analytics' for the University of California-Irvine, and other classes in medical predictive analytics for the University of California-San Diego. Since retiring in 2016 from Dell Software as Senior Analyst-Healthcare Applications Specialist for Dell's Information Management Group. Dr Miner has continued to write books, including the ITS ALL ANALYTICS series (2020; 2021; 2022; and 4th expected 2023 or 2024), a 2nd edition of the popular 2009 HANDBOOK OF STATISTIAL ANALYSIS & DATA MINING APPLICATIONS (2019), and completing in 2022 this 2nd edition of the 2015 'BIG MEDICAL BOOK' (e.g. it weighs about 8 pounds, makes a 'good doorstop' !!) which was released in April of 2023 (https://www.elsevier.com/books/practical-data-analytics-for-innovation-in-medicine/miner/978-0-323-95274-3). Additionally, a 3rd edition of the 2009 "Data Mining Handbook" is currently being written for Elsevier-Academic Press with an expected release date sometime in 2024.

His authors page with more details is found at: https://www.amazon.com/Gary-D-Miner/e/B003CRRAI8/ref=aufs_dp_mata_dsk.

Preface—Basis for This Book and the Series

I think the danger with using the term "trilogy" is that it sets up particular expectations in the reader's mind.

—Alastair Reynolds

The authors have been collaborating and working on this series for several years. We met while working together in the software and technology sector. Each of us has backgrounds in statistics, machine learning, analytics, healthcare, and business. We noticed that while the products and solutions in the artificial intelligence (AI), data science, and analytics space offered tremendous value, there was a great deal of confusion and anxiety. We identified three major difficulties:

1. Lack of data and analytics literacy
2. Organizations were not designed to succeed in a data-driven world
3. Lack of understanding how AI and analytics could transform the business process

Data and Analytics Literacy

We noticed a lot of "reinventions" of methods that existed for years, meaning that in this "reinvention" many of the same concepts acquired "new names," thus adding to confusion, especially when attempting to communicate among different disciplines. It is difficult for a committed, full-time data scientist to keep up with the "jargon du jour" and to navigate the sea of changing terminology, and thus separate the truth from the hype. For a business analyst, financial analyst, product marketer, or any professional that uses analytics to serve them in their job, it is virtually impossible to know "the truth from the hype" unless they maintain a very close look at what is going on in the data analytics field; today they need either a "special employee position" whose job is to keep up with the field, or hire a consultant whose specialty is keeping abreast of analytic terminology changes and can guide the organization in all phases of its data analytics.

The first book of the series explores many different domains: AI, machine learning, data mining, big data, business intelligence (BI), visual BI, statistics, analytics, and more. When researching and drafting the book we found hundreds of types of analytics.

Analytics come in many different forms and methods of classifications. For example, there are business function analytics, like marketing analytics, financial analytics, customer analytics, retail analytics, and call center analytics, just to name a few. Then there are industry classifications— sports analytics, healthcare analytics, government analytics, public policy analytics, and life science analytics. Then there are analytics based on the outcome or objective, like descriptive analytics, diagnostic analytics, predictive analytics, and prescriptive analytics. You also have analytics based on the type of data being analyzed—big data analytics, text analytics, geospatial analytics, audio/speech analytics, video (content) analytics. There are hundreds of others, and they use a variety of AI, machine learning, and visual methods across everyone. It has become clear that "analytics" is the overarching term, and that is why this series is named *It's All Analytics!* In fact, we said in the first book:

> In the end, you shall see, It's All Analytics! We have witnessed companies of all sizes and industries gain tremendous value from applying analytic methods and technologies. We know there are companies of all shapes and sizes that are beginning their journey. We know many others that have deep roots, but in an applied area and cannot see the "big" picture and know of technologies outside their immediate application area. We know there are those that struggle with a constant changing sea of terms and technology. We know some fear, what they do not know, what they are not doing, what they should be doing. Everyone is moving at a million miles an hour and companies are worried they might lose their advantage in a competitive market and need to do something quickly with analytics or

expand with some nascent technology. However, it is time to take a step back. To survey the landscape and synthesize. With pause, we can view the analytics domain holistically.

Therefore, the first book is about data and analytics literacy, i.e., speaking the same language, even if at only an elementary level across all functional domains and data usage. We answer the following questions and many others:

- What are processes, data, and models?
- How does traditional BI differ from visual BI?
- How does machine learning differ from AI?
- Has the age of statistics passed us?
- What is causation?
- What is technical debt?
- What is big data?
- What is data mining?
- What is data science?
- Where does computer science, management/decision science, and operations research fit in?
- What are the hip, the hype, the fears, the intrigue, and the reality of data-driven methods and technology?

DATA AND ANALYTICS BASIC FLUENCY OFFERS LARGE REWARDS

Gartner is an independent analysis firm that reports on the technology sector. They phrased one need for this subject in several comments on their website, including the need for members of an organization to speak the same language. Kasey Panetta (2019) stated this clearly: "[Our need is to] . . . [c]hampion data literacy and teach data as a second language to enable data-driven business." She continued by stating:

"Imagine an organization where the marketing department speaks French, the product designers speak German, the analytics team speaks Spanish and no one speaks a second language. . . . That's essentially how a data-driven business functions when there is no data literacy."

She points out that in 2020 half of all organizations lacked the data literacy skills needed to achieve business value.

And Valerie Logan, Senior Director Analyst, Gartner, points out another important fact (see Panetta, 2019), that the:

"prevalence of data and analytics capabilities, including artificial intelligence, requires creators and consumers to 'speak data' as a common language, . . . Data and analytics leaders must champion workforce data literacy as an enabler of digital business and treat information as a second language."

Designing an Integrated System for Organizational Success with Analytics

We have worked with hundreds of companies across industries. From healthcare to energy, from life sciences to semiconductor manufacturing, from insurance to e-commerce, the list goes on and on. While there are many that have been highly successful, we see many with gaps in readiness to successfully execute with analytics to their full capacity. Other organizations were not at all designed to succeed in a data-driven world. We identified three major foundational gaps within these organizations. We lay out three foundations for success in this book.

1. Organizational design for success
2. Data design for success
3. Analytics technology design for success

We dive deep across these three pillars and explore design considerations. We answer the following questions and many others:

- What organizational structure is best for our business?
- What data security, privacy, and ethical considerations should we consider?
- How can we make our operations data more available to decision-makers?
- What business processes can we automate with AI?
- How do we keep our data consistent, meaningful, and useful?
- What are the basics of a good data design?
- What data might be available that we are not tapping into at the present moment?

- How do we effectively communicate analytics results?
- What technologies do we need to deploy models quickly into production?
- How do we minimize the risk of creating models that are not successfully implemented?
- How do we maintain model utility over time?
- What data governance and model governance processes and technologies should we employ?
- Should we build, buy, or outsource?

How Are Organizations Using AI and Analytics?

There is no "one size fits all" in AI and analytics. At least, if it is done correctly. As we will soon see not everyone needs sophisticated mathematical machinery or expensive computer technology to be successful in their industry. We have interviewed dozens of people across industries. There are different analytical needs across different industries. Some industries may use human-assisted analytic (human in the loop) methods, meaning that the decisions are still made by humans but their human intelligence is augmented using various data-driven techniques. Other industries are using fully automated methods where an action is automatically taken with no real-time human oversight. Each industry is different in what they need to be successful.

Here are some examples of the needs of different industries: Machine algorithms outperform radiologists (i.e., the human doctor) overall in pattern recognition. They are more accurate, less expensive, and extremely

> Would you want machines to make all your medical diagnoses?

efficient. However, the algorithms are only as good as the images they are trained upon, and radiologists have extensive knowledge that the algorithm does not. Furthermore, the radiologist may have seen edge (unique) cases that the algorithm has not or vice versa. In any case, it is normally agreed that a human in the loop of the decision process is preferred for these cases. The machine algorithm can vastly improve the efficiency of the clinicians, but most people would like a human involved in the decision process.

In national defense, who would ever want machines to be independently responsible for determining if a nuclear warhead should be launched? For nostalgic moviegoers, see the movie *War Games*. However, for companies like Amazon, it makes total sense for an algorithm to serve a recommendation for an additional product to an online customer. For insurance companies the auto adjudication process could be handled by an algorithm. For a manufacturer, automatic rejection or acceptance of products coming off an assembly line by visual AI makes perfect sense.

Those are examples across industries where needs and practices vary. Within-industry people are at different maturity levels. Some companies are small and have not invested much in analytics. Or they may be large and based on their unique strategy it does not make sense for them to invest great amounts in AI and analytics. Some companies want to get more data savvy but are just getting started. Others have been at it a long time and it is part of their cultural DNA.

Usage varies across industries. Usage varies across businesses within an industry. There is no one size fits all for AI and analytics. That is why we cover business use cases in this book across industries and across data and analytics maturity levels. We know there is great opportunity to assist decision-making with data. We know that there is a fantastic opportunity in acting based on data. We hope this book helps you identify an appropriate course of action for your organization.

Reference

Panetta, Kasey (2019, February 6) A Data and Analytics Leader's Guide to Data Literacy. *Gartner*. www.gartner.com/smarterwithgartner/a-data-and-analytics-leaders-guide-to-data-literacy/

Chapter 1

Introduction

"Some people want it to happen, some wish it would happen,
others make it happen."

—*Michael Jordan*

1.1 Introduction

This is the final book in the three-part series ***It's All Analytics***.

The first book in the series clears up all the hype surrounding data-driven technologies that are produced by academics, software companies, and consultants that is continually propagated in various forms of the media. It covers the foundational terminology—process, data, models, business intelligence (BI) and visual BI, machine learning and data mining, AI, data science, big data, cloud data, statistics, causation, prescription, operations research, management science, engineering, optimization, and more. In a nutshell it is a data science and analytics literacy guide. Its purpose is to get data users and consumers speaking the same language.

The second book discussed three pillars for designing a successful data-driven organization. These are organizational design, data design, and AI and analytics technology design. It covers the technical design for data systems and analytic systems. It discusses policy, procedures, and cultural and human organization to maximize analytics effectiveness.

Now that we speak the same data and analytics language and have organizational structures capable of driving business results we need to determine what programs and projects to pursue to gain a return on these investments.

DOI: 10.4324/9780429343971-1

This third book is meant to help organizations understand what is being accomplished across industries using data so they can translate similar ideas into their companies. Furthermore, it expresses these proven business use cases within an analytics maturity model. Some companies are just getting started (nascent) and other companies are advanced, even visionary. Furthermore, there are companies where different departments span all levels of analytics maturity model stages. It is very useful for departments and companies to understand their capabilities before proposing AI and analytics project plans.

In the preparation of this book, we have conducted interviews with dozens of industry leaders across the globe. These leaders represent multiple industries. They represent staff level, managerial, director, and C-suite positions. Backgrounds of these professionals include heavy technical backgrounds as well as more business-centric backgrounds. We have used these interviews to structure the use cases we present in this book illustrating analytics maturity and industry applications. We also provide simple stories, vignettes on a more personal level that were inspired by these interviews.

You learn from others, and I (Scott) was very fortunate to speak with well over 100 professionals, industry leaders, and business owners. We would like to thank the following people for their time to speak with us across four continents and 12 countries. We present their names and affiliations at the time of the interviews:

Stephen Usmar, Founder and CEO, Firstname Limited NZ
Gilbert Eijkelenboom, Founder, MindSpeaking.com
Crystal Yin, General Manager of Growth, Domino Data Lab
Hugo Shi, Founder, Saturn Cloud
Todd Rutherford, President/CEO, Process Point Energy Services
Mike Jay, Insights and Analytics Specialist, Serial 1 Cycle Company
Hossam Zaki, PhD, Global Head of Pricing Analytics Electrification
    Products Division, ABB
Doug Bryan, AI Strategist, Dataiku
Ali Barnard, Account Based Marketing, Snowflake
Carleton Jones, Services Sales Executive—Healthcare and Life Sciences,
    Microsoft
Jim Overdahl, PhD, Partner, Delta Strategy Group, former Chief Economist
    U.S. Securities and Exchange Commission and former Chief Economist,
    U.S. Commodity Futures Trading Commission
Joe Toner, VP of Fraud Risk, Money Lion

Balaji Jayakumar, PhD, Co-Founder and Chief Operating Officer, MaxQ

Dean Langfitt, VP of Sales & Marketing, New Innovations

Benjamin Kim, MHA, Senior Value Engineer, TIBCO

Josh Lemaitre, Founding Member, Thomson Reuters Labs

Marwān Êl Kharbīli, PhD, AI Guild, Former Gartner Director, Germany

Beth Spears, Business Development Consultant, Smile CDR Inc.

Carol Maginn, Healthcare Data Strategist, Teradata

Marylou Buyse, MD, CMO/SVP, Neighborhood Health Plan of Rhode Island

John Held, Management Consultant/Senior Director, Alvarez & Marsal

Anonymous, Business Intelligence/Analytics Manager, Texas Instruments

Matt Uekert, Operations Data Manager, Baylor Scott & White

Nathan Piccini, Marketing Manager, Data Science Dojo

Rick Jansky, Director Deal Strategy & Execution, Splunk

Pramod Singh, PhD, Chief Analytics Officer, Vice-President of Data Sciences and Analytics, Yodlee

Leo Skazhenik, Customer Engineer, Google Cloud

Kurt Janson, Account Director of High Tech Enterprise Sales, Salesforce

John Cromwell, MD, Associate Chief Medical Officer, Director of Surgical Quality & Safety, University of Iowa Hospitals and Clinics

Shi Zhong, PhD, Data Scientist, Google

Anonymous, Senior Vice President and Chief Information Officer for a Global Manufacturer

Melinda Holt, PhD, Associate Dean, College of Science & Engineering Technology, Sam Houston State University

Jim King, PhD, Director at M.Sc. in Information Systems, University of Mary Hardin Baylor

Eric Phillips, Director, Data Solutions Stambaugh Ness

Angela Waner, Senior Product Manager, Federal Contractor

Bill Inmon, CEO at Forest Rim, Bestselling Author, Father of Data Warehousing, Denver

Tobias Zwingmann, Data Scientist, Author, Germany

Reeto Mookherjee, PhD, SVP of Data Science, GoodRx

Danny Stout, PhD, Director of Forecasting and Analytics, Biolife at Takeda

Anonymous, VP, AI, Data Analytics, Cloud and IoT, Global Semiconductor Company, Singapore

Jim Sterne, President, Target Marketing of Santa Barbara

Bahadir Aral, PhD, Senior Director, Enterprise Machine Learning, Macy's

Mike Ibarra, Senior Enterprise ISV Manager, Oracle

Peter Evans, Strategic Technical Pre-Sales Evangelist, Tableau Software

Francisco Arroyo, Multivendor Support Specialist, IBM

Muhammad Ali, Director of Marketing Sciences, INNOCEAN USA, Los Angeles

Tony Smith, Data Science and Analytics Professional for the Retail and Performing Arts Industry

Joe Leyva, Vice President of Global Partners & Alliances, Zilliant

Anonymous, Chief Data & Analytics Officer at a Global Technology Services and Consulting Company in India

Karan Nisar, ML Engineer, Weights & Biases

Justin Fickle, Senior Account Executive, Infrastructure Operations and Cloud Strategies, Gartner

George Hamby, Senior Account Executive, SAP

Kinshuk Dutta, Head of Worldwide PreSales for Data Management, TIBCO

Geoffrey M. Pofahl, Data Science Leader & Educator, Arizona State University

Anonymous, Former Governmental Director, State of Texas

Kjell Carlsson, PhD, AI Strategist & Evangelist, Domino Data Lab

Alex Fly, Founder and CEO, Quickpath

Brandym Morelli, Founder and Head of Digital Strategy, Tilt Metrics

Kristen Prater, District Manager, MOD Pizza

Joe Nipko PhD, Head of AI/ML, FormBio

Shawn Rogers, Analytics Strategy, Thought Leader, Industry Influencer, and Marketing Executive

Rod Arends, Enterprise Account Executive | Data Science Strategy & Solutions, TIBCO

Wade Walker, Managing Director, Analytics & Information Management Strategist and Architect, IDM

Rajiv Bhattarai, Sr. Analyst-Operations Planning and Performance, American Airlines

Aurelie (Lily) Giraud, Data Scientist and Product Data Manager, Subai, Denmark

Venu Gopal Lolla, PhD, Senior Manager, Analytics Development, TIBCO

Chris Gengo, VP Enterprise Operational Improvement, Care Source

Lou Bajuk, Head of Product and Community Marketing at RStudio, PBC

Ray Hall, Senior Product Manager, Change Healthcare

Avraham Adler, Partner—Structured Solutions, McGill and Partners

Mark Layne, President, Decision Excellence Inc.

Elliot Layne, Doctoral Student, McGill University Canada

Craig Digby, Territory Sales Manager, Digga USA

Jeff Tanner, Former Dean, Old Dominion University

Michael Kramer, CHCIO, CTO/VP (Retired), Lifespan

Ranjan Ray, Solutions Architect, Fivetran

Aryl Kohrs, Director and Principal Technology Strategist, Psyncopate

Jeremy Melville, Senior Solutions Consultant, TIBCO

Vinoth Manamala, Senior Data Scientist, TIBCO Software

Steve Tao, Analytics Lead for Sales Excellence, Accenture

Mark Kroto, Senior Manager, Sales Executive for Strategy & Analytics, Deloitte

Saul Garza, Sr. Manager Enterprise Data Enablement, Vail Resorts

Tricia Cross, Senior Clinical and Operations Analyst, Behavioral Health Group (BHG)

Samson Teklemariam, Vice President of Clinical Services for a Behavioral Health Group

Xingchu Liu, PhD, CDAO | SVP, Enterprise Data Analytics & Technology, Macy's

Kenji Wong, Director of Product Management, NCQA

Jay Patkar, Principal Solutions Engineer, MuleSoft

Alireza Shalehi, PhD, Senior Researcher in Medical Science, RISE Research Institute of Sweden

Adam Sroka, PhD, Director, Hypercube Consulting, Scotland

Brian Anderson, Head Global Partners, Socrates AI

Carol Renne, Business Development, Forest Rim Technology

Joe Reis, CEO, Ternary Data

Robert Scott, CTO, Eon Collective

Ed Kelly, Data Consultant, Texas Secretary of State (Chief Data Officer, State of Texas, Retired)

Brett Dixon, Associate Director, Digital Nexus, KPMG

Ross Leher, CEO and Chairman, WAND, Inc.

Patty Watkins, Managing Partner, VP of Sales, MORE Sales Advisors

Tony Drake, Senior Partner, The 12 Group

Dave Rapien, Associate Professor, University of Cincinnati Carl H. Lindner College of Business

Samson Onyekachukwu Anene, Strategic Account Executive, John Snow Labs

John Salazar, General Manager, RedPort Applied Analytics

Juan Sequeda, Principal Scientist, data.world

Paula Furnace, World-Wide Digital and Channels Leader (previous), IBM

1.2 Why You Should Read This Book

"You either need to be a leader or a very fast follower—or you are going to be toast."

—Clare Lunn

Every organization is trying to capitalize on the promise of data and analytics. Organizations that invested in AI in the last several years that did so without great consideration and planning have wasted some money. However, organizations that are not investing in AI in the coming few years without great consideration and planning will never catch up. That is the reason we wrote this book and the series. Now is the time.

Often the best way to learn is through experience. You can learn a great deal by making mistakes, correcting them, and then moving forward. However, if you can learn what others are capitalizing on, you can often avoid mistakes and sometimes move to the head of the line. This book speaks to what has not worked for several organizations and what is working now. It presents ideas from people that are just getting started, the explorers through the veterans, the innovators. You can learn how organizations are using AI and analytics that are like yours.

> Making mistakes may be the best teacher. But if you can learn from others' mistakes, wouldn't you prefer that?

In this book, we offer real-world stories corroborated by our 50+ years of combined experience to leapfrog your efforts against your competition. We recommend that you do not only look at use cases similar to those in your industry, but look at innovations across industries. In our experience that is where the most fruitful applications exist. For example, Scott (author) took innovations he learned in manufacturing and process control at Texas Instruments and applied them to digital marketing at Overstock.com. This application greatly improved the efficiency for evaluating campaigns and creative content.

DO NOT OVERTHINK IT: A FEW SMART QUESTIONS AND THE RIGHT DATA

We often hear "keep it simple." And it is true that simple is best. However, we are often lured into big, audacious, sexy concepts. I had a chance to meet up with my good friend Bahadir Aral, PhD, and he reminded me of something that I know. People read too much, they think about the complex problems rather than the simple ones, and it is often the simple problems that provide the highest payoff. He has a long history of solving both simple and complex problems. Having worked with Bahadir, I know how bright he is and I have seen him attack very complicated problems with elegant solutions. However, when we spoke he offered a few core problems that if you get right in the retail space, you will do well. He works for Macy's; several of my old colleagues are there now. And they are doing great work with great results. In August 2022 Macy's reported nine consecutive quarters of beating and/or meeting earning expectations!

One of the things Bahadir said was, "it is not big data, it is right data." That is so important. More data with no information (signal) does not help solve the problem at all. He then listed some core questions in retail that AI and analytics can solve, as well as some lessons he has learned along the way. These are questions that retailers need answers to:

- What should I sell?
- How much I should I carry?
- Where should I place what?
- Price leadership? Price matching?
- Do you have competitor information or not? What can you do with it?
- Assortment problem—what product attributes matter most?
- What is not selling? How do I respond?
- Should I white label (private labeling)?
- What are my competitive differentiators?
- How should we monitor our website?
- Did you arrive via search engine?
- Are you a loyal customer that came directly to our site?
- How much inventory should I hold?
- What are my lead times for various products, product lines?
- Where are my risks?
- What are my holding costs?

These are not convoluted questions. They are straight forward, one dimensional. However, if you know the answers to them you are well on your way to be successful in retail. He told me that most of the answers require art, as well as data and models. You must know how the nuances of the business, the way the data is collected and the way to apply the math and data science to achieve meaningful answers.

1.3 How This Book Is Organized

This book contains 10 chapters. This first chapter sets the stage and outlines more specific needs and purposes of the book.

Chapter 2 covers various data and analytics maturity models used by industry organizations and analysts. It then defines the process we use in the book and provides descriptions of five levels we use to define organizations using data and analytics for improved decision-making—explorers, novices, practitioners, leaders, and innovators.

Chapter 3 describes AI and analytics lessons learned and uses for explorers. This includes how explorers get started and what lessons they learn in navigating the data and analytics field. It also includes what use cases and methods they are investigating, which ones they determined to be the most beneficial.

Chapter 4 describes AI and analytics lessons learned and uses for novices. It explains what novices have done to move from explorers to a new level of analytics maturity. What lessons they learn in navigating the data and analytics field. What use cases and methods they are investigating, which ones they determined to be the most beneficial.

Chapter 5 describes the experiences and lessons learned for practitioners. We explain how they matured to this level and the various industries that dominate this level of analytics maturity. It includes the challenges they faced and what use cases and methods they are successfully deploying.

Chapter 6 covers the next maturity level, leaders. These are organizations that are thriving in the AI and analytics space. Typically, they also have the scars and war stories of the uphill battle they faced to get to this level over a period of years.

Chapter 7 covers the highest level of data and analytics maturity, the innovators. These organizations have progressed through all the previous levels and typically have been applying data-driven techniques for decades.

Chapter 8 covers methods for the organization to follow to do a data and analytics readiness. It covers why an assessment is important and the steps you should follow in doing a self-assessment and some suggestions if you want to outsource the assessment. The goal is evaluating your strengths and weaknesses to minimize loss of financial and people resources.

Chapter 9 includes some additional real stories faced by people in various organizations.

And chapter 10 wraps things up and offers pointers in getting started or moving up the maturity continuum.

We use vignettes throughout the book. These are gray boxed stories and examples. We have done this in the entire series and have been told by our readers it is helpful. You may skip these without loss of continuity. They are meant to break up the reading and supplement the main story lines.

Let's dive in.

Chapter 2

Data and Analytics Maturity Models

"Knowledge comes, but wisdom lingers. It may not be difficult to store up in the mind a vast quantity of facts within a comparatively short time, but the ability to form judgments requires the severe discipline of hard work and the tempering heat of experience and maturity."

—*Calvin Coolidge*

Data and analytics maturity is a topic that has grown in importance over the last several years. Why? Technology companies are interested in offering a broad array of solution platforms to address the spectrum of the capability to address important business problems. The more they can understand where a prospect is on this continuum the better they can target a match between the products and services they offer to what a client would need.

While there is not a perfect 1:1 correspondence, in general the more time a company has spent in data-driven technologies, the higher it correlates with the upper end of the continuum. Subsequently, it correlates to a higher level of difficulty of business problems they can solve with these technologies. However, there are exceptions, with some companies making very rapid advances and others that are slow to mature.

In this chapter we cover a few maturity paradigms described in the business press, social and corporate media. Research and analyst firms such as Gartner and TDWI (The Data Warehouse Institute), as well as professional organizations such as INFORMS, all have some version of maturity

DOI: 10.4324/9780429343971-2

assessment. At the end of this chapter we will define our own maturity model that we use in this book, which categorizes organizations into one of five levels of maturity—explorers, novices, practitioners, leaders, and innovators. We will use these levels as the basis of Chapters 3–7.

A CONVERSATION WITH A STRATEGIC TECHNICAL EVANGELIST

The timing of my conversation with Peter Evans was a bit surreal. Queen Elizabeth II had just passed away a few days prior, and I knew Peter was from England and had served in the Royal Navy, so we spoke about it. I learned that Peter had met her twice, and he shared some interesting stories. It is amazing the connections that people have and how a brief conversation can yield so many interesting details.

Peter said the interesting thing in current business usage was the fact that rather than data being used by a single stream it is used in a multiple operations stream. It is having a significant impact on the way people think and plan. They are seeing

> . . . the key to unleashing the true power of AI and analytics . . .

things in a different light and using data in different ways. Moreover, people that have traditionally not used data to perform their work are realizing the benefits of utilizing data-driven technologies.

This is lowering the barrier to entry for everyone and is the key to unleashing the true power of AI and analytics. However, it is difficult. First, people must get the data, which is not huge for someone properly trained in data acquisition technology or someone who is "in the data" all the time. However, most people have many tasks to take care of every hour. They are not technologists. Then someone in the decision support systems, augmented intelligence platforms or whatever system, needs to access. Many people expect common capabilities in what they find on their cell phones and banking systems, and also what they see in their company IT systems. For the initiated, hard-core data scientists, this is not a problem. However, for the average Joe user this is a major obstacle, as their cell phone apps, banking systems, and their company IT software generally do NOT have "common capabilities."

We live in a consumer world where many of the answers we desire are one click away via our cell phone or Web browser. In many corporate systems the answer is unattainable for many. If we want to democratize data, if we want to enable a new generation of data scientists called citizen data scientists, we have to close this gap.

Subject matter experts (SMEs) should understand the business, they should be responding to the business needs. That is where their time needs to be spent. We need to enable SMEs with the data and analytics to answer most of their questions/needs. We can then send the remainder to hard-core data scientists to help answer.

There are several different maturity models available, but one of the most popular comes from *Competing on Analytics* (Davenport & Harris, 2017), which is illustrated in Figure 2.1

In the maturity model (Figure 2.1), the y-axis denotes the relative competitive advantage an organization may achieve by deploying the different categories of analytics—progressing from reactive to prescriptive analytics.

Maturity = capability, maturation, development, sophistication, advancement, fitness, readiness

Greater competitive advantage may be achieved as one moves up the y-axis. The x-axis illustrates the broad

Analytic Maturity

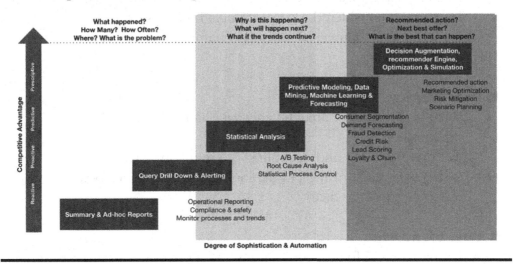

Figure 2.1   Analytic maturity model.

Source: Adapted from Davenport and Harris *Competing on analytics* © 2020, David E. Sweenor.

categories of analytic techniques associated with the analytic types. Reactive analytics are like looking in a rear-view mirror of an automobile; these typically include summary statistics and ad-hoc reports. The degree of sophistication, complexity, and automation increases as one moves from left to right on the x-axis.

One of the falsely drawn conclusions of Figure 2.1 is that one must progress up the maturity curve in a stepwise manner, like ascending a staircase. In other words, many organizations originally interpreted this to mean that they needed comprehensive reporting and dashboards before they could use predictive analytics, forecasts, or optimizations. However, this isn't necessarily the case. We have seen many organizations use various combinations of these different elements without fully exhausting all of the opportunities for an analytics category that is lower on the maturity scale. The key, as previously mentioned, is to understand the business decision to be made (and ensure it is in alignment with corporate strategic goals) and map the analytics functionality that needs to be in place to support the decision process.

Additionally, when assessing an organization's analytic maturity, there are also a few other elements to consider that are beyond the technology realm. Namely,

- **Organizational commitment**
  - Does the organization treat data as a critical business asset?
  - Is analytics considered a core strategic business process?
  - Is there an executive sponsor and champion assigned to the projects?

- **Data literacy**
  - What is the level of analytic and data literacy within the organization?
  - Are there training and upskilling programs in place?
  - What percentage of the population has access to dashboards and reports to analyze data?

- **Data foundation**
  - Is there a solid foundation of data and a continuous data quality improvement program in place?
  - Does the organization trust the data and analytic results generated from the data?

■ **Usage and span**
  – How broadly and often are analytics being used to make everyday decisions?
  – Are the results trusted by the organization, or are they often overridden by intuition or "gut feel"?

2.1 Contrasting Some Analytics Maturity Models

Many companies have developed analytics maturity models. Some even go as far as assessing an organization by specific type of industry. Most models comprise five analytics maturity levels. However, no detailed description of the assessment process or criteria for placing an organization at a specific analytics development level are available for many rating organizations.

A paper by Karol Król and Dariusz Zdonek presents and summarizes selected features of 11 various organizations' analytics maturity models (see Król & Zdonek, 2020). It is the first ever such extensive review of these models. They say:

> Generally, the notion of "maturity" is very broad and means "fully developed", "perfected." A maturity model indicates a path to perfection. It is a guidepost for the development with strictly defined criteria and indicators defining the current and target state from specific reference values. Organizations reach analytics maturity through evolution, which includes integration, management, and use of various data sources at key decision-making points. This paper aims to review, characterize, and comparatively analyze selected organizations' analytics maturity models.

In their research, they cover:

1. Analytic Processes Maturity Model (APMM) by Grossman, R.L.
2. Analytics Maturity Quotient Framework by Aryng LLC
3. Blast Analytics Maturity Assessment Framework by Blast Analytics & Marketing
4. Data Analytics Maturity Model for Associations by Association Analytics
5. DELTA Plus Model by Davenport, T.H., Harris, J., and Morison, B.

6. Gartner's Maturity Model for Data and Analytics by Gartner, Inc.
7. Logi Analytics Maturity Model by Logi Analytics
8. Online Analytics Maturity by Cardinal Path
9. SAS Analytics Maturity Scorecard by SAS Institute Inc.
10. TDWI Analytics Maturity Model by TDWI, Halper and Stodder.
11. Web Analytics Maturity Model by Hamel, S.

The authors have seen others. For example, some professional groups like INFORMS (Institute for Operations Research and the Management Sciences) have their own. And Gartner, a large US technological research and consulting firm, has identified user-specific assessments, such as their Five-Stage Maturity Model for Supply Chain Analytics. Gartner is most known for its analytics ascendency model, which consists of four levels:

1. Descriptive analytics
2. Diagnostic analytics
3. Predictive analytics
4. Prescriptive analytics

However, most models you see for the analytics maturity path comprise five levels of maturity, where each level on this path moves the organization toward the solutions that allow soundly based decisions to be taken faster:

1. Descriptive analytics
2. Diagnostic analytics
3. Predictive analytics
4. Prescriptive analytics
5. Process optimization

Sometimes the last level is referenced as cognitive analytics rather than process optimization. And there is a difference, which we will describe soon. A visual representation is presented in Figure 2.2.

The evolution of the use of analytics in an enterprise is not linear in nature. The implementation of organizational changes may vary in terms of the order and intensity, depending on both an organization's specificity and the business context. In the implementation and development of analytics in an organization, openness to changes is paramount.

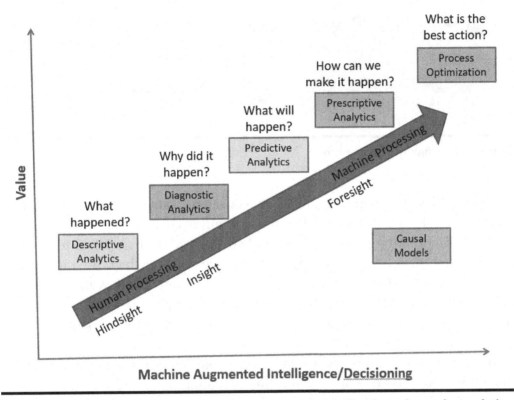

Figure 2.2   A visual reference of a generally accepted classification scheme for analytics.

2.1.1 Another View of Analytics Maturity

Another maturity level model has been adapted from other technology sectors, like Web Version 1.0. Some have adapted this model for analytics with three versions of analytics across a continuum. In the Analytics 1.0 era, enterprises used data warehouses and copies of operational data as the basis for analyses (Figure 2.3). In the Analytics 2.0 era, the focus was on Hadoop clusters and NoSQL databases. Analytics 3.0 makes use of new, "agile" analytics methods and machine-learning techniques that ensure a significantly quicker insight into data. Analytics 3.0 environment does not reject the existing concepts of analytics but integrates new technologies with the tools used so far.

Descriptive analytics enables learning about and understanding the reality through the characterization of data and the isolation of patterns that answer the question "what happened?," i.e., hindsight. It is the primary source of information for the management team. Descriptive analytics provides an answer to the question "What happened?" Diagnostic analytics provides an answer to the

Figure 2.3 Analytics continuum.

question "Why did it happen?" It is often considered equivalent to traditional analytics in which decisions made with a certain delay are dominant. This delay results from the need to collect and systematize data, and then to analyze and interpret them. Data are collected and processed at defined time intervals, hence the actions taken based on their analysis are carried out with a certain delay. Diagnostic analytics enables the detection of regularities and quantitative relationships between variables through the analysis of historical data.

Analytics architecture refers to the applications, infrastructures, tools, and leading practices that enable access to and analysis of information to optimize business decisions and performance. It supports all current analytics needs and strategically plans for future needs and initiatives. Many organizations start with descriptive and diagnostic analytics. Technologies on the data side that support these efforts are traditional files, network drives, RDBMS, ODS, Original Data Warehouse, OLAP. On the analytics technology side they are often accomplished with interactive business intelligence platforms, dashboards and visual business intelligence platforms, and statistical programs. It may include analytics that are embedded into functionally specific platforms for medical radiology, business finance, or similar departments. Successful implementation of descriptive and diagnostic analytics often leads the organization into a new direction of predictive and diagnostic analytics: optimization. These are often accomplished with data science, machine learning, and AI platforms.

ROI (return on investment) is a critical metric, and measuring analytics ROI requires good data as a baseline. It is important for business programs to have good financial metrics they can use to support or challenge the results of analytics and AI efforts. Most organizations support these metrics with a BI platform. **It is ill-advised for any organization to jump into an advanced analytics or AI program until they have the ability to consistently and accurately report business metrics—i.e., descriptive analytics must be in place prior to more advanced analytics.**

That is the reason most organizations start with BI and then jump into more advanced data-driven techniques and technologies.

Predictive analytics falls into the category of advanced analytics. It involves modeling as well as the preparation of simulations and forecasts. Both current and historical data are analyzed to gain an insight into what may happen in the future (foresight—what will happen technology: no/newSQL, in-memory, DB and processing, early data lake). Predictive analytics is focused on forecasts and provides answers to the question "What will happen in the future?" It is aimed at predicting future events and trends. Predictive analytics "learns" based on experiencing data to predict the future behavior of individuals to make better decisions. In the predictive model, the system can "make decisions," allowing it to achieve the set objective based on a specific policy of action, i.e., previously adopted and delivered rules.

Prescriptive analytics uses machine learning to suggest actions to be taken to achieve desired results. However, to be done correctly, it requires an additional step that is too often not taken. That is, these suggested actions must be causative to the desired outcome. Not just correlative! In Burk and Miner (2020) they outline an example in a vignette titled "THE MOST MISUNDERSTOOD CONCEPT IN DATA SCIENCE TODAY"; this example illustrates a situation where a variable hides a true relationship. It is a simple five-variable model to predict obesity by measuring BMI (body mass index). However, there is a confounding variable that underlies the true relationship (see the following vignette, if interested).

PREDICTIVE MODELS VS. PRESCRIPTIVE MODELS—THEY ARE NOT THE SAME!

It is amazing how many articles written today describe prescriptive analytics as just a different business case of predictive analytics with no additional requirements from the data side or the modeling side. It is absolutely one of the least understood paradigms out here. **You cannot simply use observational data and a machine-learning algorithm and declare it to be a prescriptive model. No. We are sorry to be so contentious here, but there are hundreds of articles and references that imply you can without potentially serious consequences.** We have even had conversations with people that know that causation is not correlation but still think there are no requirement differences for answering the question "what is the probability this event will happen?" vs. "why did it happen?" or "how can we make it happen?" The following is a very simple example of why (there are many reasons) you cannot take a predictive model and then declare it as a prescriptive model. Consider a simple five-variable model to predict obesity by measuring BMI (body mass index). BMI is a weight-to-height ratio, calculated by dividing one's weight in kilograms by the square of one's height in meters and used as an indicator of obesity and underweight. Suppose we use the following five variables to predict BMI:

1. Gender (male/female)
2. Number of hours per week in the gym or fitness center
3. Amount of diet soda intake per week
4. Age
5. Geographic location (place of current residence)

Those five factors would do a decent job **predicting BMI** via a machine-learning model given that we can train the model correctly and with enough data. This model will likely generalize, meaning that it will predict BMI of individuals with future data (given ordinary, common assumptions). **Good predictive model—PASS!** Now, if you believe the many posts, articles, and misdirection out on the internet and in some books, you can use this model to **PRESCRIBE** actions to lower your BMI. **No,** you cannot relocate someone to Colorado or Hawaii and expect it to have a practical effect. Colorado and Hawaii states have lower BMIs on average due to culture and genetics—not geography. **Culture and genetics are confounding variables (they relate to location and BMI), and they are the causal mechanisms NOT geography. Good prescriptive model—FAIL!** This is just one reason a predictive model may not be prescriptive.

This example is simple and straightforward; moving someone from Mississippi to Colorado will not likely change his or her BMI, at least in the near term. It is much more difficult to understand the underlying associative mechanism in medical models; therefore, practitioners must be careful and understand the difference between association and causation.

For those interested in a richer, more technical explanation, you can see Chapter 25 Predictive Models versus Prescriptive Models; Causal Inference and Bayesian Networks in (Miner et al., 2023).

Prescriptive analytics supports the decision-making process with the aim to automate the actions taken. It provides an answer to the question "What actions should be taken?"

The word "optimization" is overused these days. Process optimization in data science is very strict and mathematically defined if used correctly. A mathematical construct is created, including an objective function, goals, and constraints. The objective function states whether we want to maximize or minimize this target (decision) variable. This is optimization. Constraints cannot be violated, and goals are penalties to the objective function. We then search for solutions that maximize or minimize our function and do not violate our constraints. The solution that has the highest or lowest value of the objective function is the optimal solution.

Cognitive analytics leverages artificial intelligence (AI) technologies, such as machine and deep learning, and high-performance data analytics to automate decisions using a human-like analysis or augment human decisions through a partnership with smart machines. This level of maturity involves a natural interaction-based man/machine collaboration, where human experience is augmented with smart machines to offer breakthrough insights for businesses.

A final note is that as the level of maturity rises, the cost of the analytics program also rises. This is normally multifold as the license and subscription for the IT systems, the support of these systems, as well as developer job positions; an example is provided in the following gray box.

DATA MANAGEMENT FOR ADVANCED ANALYTICS IS A TEAM SPORT

In a survey conducted by Philip Russom, Senior Director of TDWI Research for Data Management, in 2018, an interesting question came up that applies directly to data management for advanced analytics:

The people who contribute most to the design and implementation of data management focused on analytics have job titles such as "Data Engineer", "DataOps", "Data Architects", and "Data Analysts". Additionally many other people in other job titles contribute. A snapshot of these job titles and proportion given to this task is captured in the following diagram (Figure 2.4). There are a number of positions involved and there are a number of "catch all" buckets in the table below. From this we think you, the reader, can determine that data management for advanced analytics is a team sport.

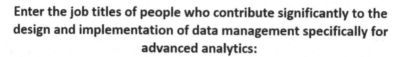

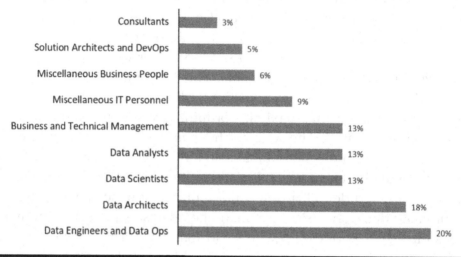

Figure 2.4   Roles supporting design and implementation for data management specifically for advanced analytics.

2.2 Assessment Practices

An assessment of an organization's analytics maturity can be carried out in a variety of ways. Traditional methods of measuring analytics capacities include self-assessment, qualitative interviews, and quantitative studies. However, a traditional approach to the assessment of analytics capacities has certain limitations, mainly due to the lack of an opportunity to verify them using what is referred to as the "depth and width" of analytics capacity.

Many self-assessment tools are online and are usually carried out using a survey checklist. They enable an assessment as to whether specific technologies and analytics tools have been implemented. They often cover a few dimensions that assess their maturity. Some are organizational and knowledge based, others are technically based.

Most of these assessments do not enable an assessment as to whether a particular organization uses them fully to make business decisions, and whether they affect the organization's activities. In turn, qualitative interviews with the management can be anecdotal and selective in their scope. Moreover, studies conducted in this way may not reveal differences in analytics maturity that occur between various groups of employees.

Analytics maturity can be described as the evolution of an organization to integrate, manage, and leverage all relevant internal and external data sources into key decision points. It means creating an ecosystem that enables insight and action. In other words, analytics maturity is not simply about having some technology in place; it involves technologies, data management, analytics, governance, and organizational components.

It can take years to create and instill an analytics culture in an organization. Analytics maturity describes how deeply and effectively the organization uses tools, people, processes, and strategy to manage and analyze data for the purpose of informing business decisions. Maturity models are used to guide this transformation process.

WE HAVE DATA! NOW WHAT?

We have data! Now what? That is the million-dollar question. Eric Phillips mentioned it when we spoke. Eric has a 20+ year track record of progressive leadership, strategy development, process improvement, consulting, and program delivery, implementing a wide array of business solutions and initiatives. We worked together at Baptist Health.

Eric said during his career he has seen this comment made over and over. People know they cannot do much without data. But what should they do once they have it? You would think the answer would be

> "Thinking about what you can do with data requires a mind shift. "

obvious, but it is not. Why? Because thinking operationally and getting the work done is very task oriented, it is very NOW oriented. Thinking about what you can do with data requires a mind shift. It requires you to take a critical assessment of where you are, how you do the work, and then reimagine how the work can be done. You must think outside the box. You must not forget your end objectives. These might be retaining your customers, providing the best care for your patients, or providing the best product at the lowest cost. However, you need to forget how you are currently trying to achieve these outcomes.

What if there was a genie that could foretell which customers were likely to leave your service? You could create that genie with your data and predictive analytics. Then you could create an action plan based on those likelihoods. What if you were to have a genie that could tell you the next best action you could take with a specific customer to reduce the probability that they will leave? You could create that genie with your data and prescriptive analytics.

However, if you are constantly in the operational whirlwind of the urgent you will never take time to think outside the box. To think strategically you must pause and move away from day-to-day tasks, the immediate. There is tremendous value in the data you have collected.

Recommended Reading:

- ■ We cover much of the dynamics of the immediate vs. the importance and developing executable AI and analytics plans in our executive guide. See Burk & Miner, 2022 in References.
- ■ Ryan Holiday, **Stillness Is the Key** (see references). Holiday draws on timeless Stoic and Buddhist philosophy to show why slowing down is the secret weapon for those charging ahead.

2.2.1 Analytic Processes Maturity Model (APMM)

The Analytic Processes Maturity Model (APMM) for evaluating the analytic maturity of an organization was developed by Robert Grossman (see Grossman, 2018). The APMM identifies analytic-related processes in six key process areas: i) building analytic models; ii) deploying analytic models; iii) managing and operating analytic infrastructure; iv) protecting analytic assets through appropriate policies and procedures; v) operating an analytic governance structure; and vi) identifying analytic opportunities, making decisions, and allocating resources based upon an analytic strategy.

Based upon the maturity of these processes, the APMM divides organizations into five maturity levels:

1. Organizations that can build reports
2. Organizations that can build and deploy models
3. Organizations that have repeatable processes for building and deploying analytics
4. Organizations that have consistent enterprise-wide processes for analytics
5. Enterprises whose analytics is strategy driven

The APMM is broadly based upon the Capability Maturity Model that is the basis for measuring the maturity of processes for developing software. The framework is based on common challenges that organizations face when developing and deploying analytic models:

- Problems obtaining the data necessary for building models.
- Problems deploying models into an organization's products, services, and operational systems.
- Problems quantifying the business value generated by models.
- Deployed models do not bring the business value that was expected.
- A lack of repeatability when building models.
- A lack of repeatability when deploying models.
- A lack of repeatability when testing and evaluating models.
- Difficulty integrating different models developed across an organization to meet the requirements of the organization as a whole.

There are also several common confusions that organizations face:

1. Not understanding the difference between reports generated from data and models built from data.
2. Not understanding the difference between models built from data and business rules.
3. Not understanding the difference between the outputs of models and the actions and business processes required so that products, services, and operations achieve a desired business goal.

The greater the analytic maturity of an organization, the more likely that it is for an organization to meet these challenges and not face these confusions.

2.2.2 Analytics Maturity Assessment or Delta Plus Method

Analytics Maturity Assessment (AMA) is a tool developed by the International Institute for Analytics (IIA), designed to examine an organization and to assess its capacity to apply corporate analytics. This framework comes from *Competing on Analytics* (Davenport & Harris, 2017), which is illustrated in Figure 2.1.

This assessment is carried out based on the DELTA Plus model and five analytics maturity stages. AMA allows an organization to be placed on the analytics development path through an assessment of its analytics capacities, analytics culture, and the capacity to use analytics tools. The DELTA model is based on five components relevant to the assessment of an organization's analytics maturity:

Data, **D** for available, high-quality data—in order to obtain valuable and reliable analysis results, data are required that are organized, integrated, available, and of a high quality.

Enterprise, **E** for an enterprise's orientation toward analytics management—it includes the development of analytics culture in the organization (analytical ecosystem), the designing and implementation of a strategy for analytics, and the adoption of analytics goals.

Leadership, **L** for analytics leadership—analytical organizations have leaders who make full use of analytics and steer the organization's development in such a manner that it makes use of the data analytics potential. It elevates the level of acceptance toward the analytics culture throughout the enterprise and streamlines the implementation of analytics initiatives.

Targets, **T** for strategic targets—analytics activities should be tailored to specific, strategic targets that should be in line with corporate objectives. The targets should be selected based on the organization's advantages and potential. Analytics initiatives should correspond (be considered equivalent) to business goals.

Analysts, **A** for analysts. Organizations employ staff with various analytics skills, both those using spreadsheets (analytical amateurs) and experienced data scientists (analytical professionals).

The availability of big data coupled with new analytics techniques such as machine learning have resulted in the DELTA model being extended to include two additional components:

Technology, **T**—An organization's capacity to implement and manage the infrastructure, tools, and technologies is becoming increasingly important. With the emergence of big data, artificial intelligence, data clouds, and open-source software, the development of an effective technological strategy for analytics is a key condition of success.

Analytics techniques, **A**—Falling costs of data storage, processing, and analysis, combined with widespread access to software, have resulted in the explosive development of analytics methods and techniques. At the same time, however, more traditional approaches to analytics, e.g., reporting, and visual analyses, are still applied.

The application of AMA and the DELTA Plus model enables an assessment of an organization's analytics maturity in seven dimensions. Depending on the scope of research, a full AMA is carried out based on surveys that may concern up to 33 unique competencies of the organization.

The rating of analytics maturity in the DELTA model takes the form of a score awarded on a scale ranging from 1.00 to 5.99 points. Each score represents a specific stage of analytics maturity Figure 2.5. Such an assessment indicates sensitive points that need to be improved.

In the DELTA Plus model, an organization is placed in one of the analytics continuum stages, which reflects the organization's analytics maturity:

Stage 1 **Analytically Impaired**. Organizations that are "analytically lagging" are managed based on intuition, have no formal plans of becoming more analytical, and their leaders use no data analytics.

Stage 2 **Localized Analytics**. Analytics or reporting in such organizations takes place in the "back office." It usually stays in the background of other activities and loses confrontation with the intuition-based management. Neither structures nor cooperation between particular units (management levels) in the use of data analytics are developed.

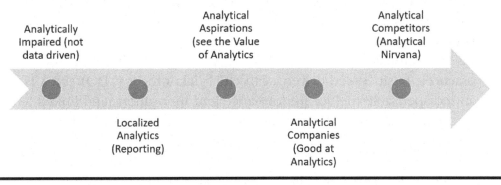

Figure 2.5   Analytics continuum—DELTA Plus model.

Stage 3 **Analytical Aspirations**. "Analytically ambitious" organizations recognize the value of data analytics and intend to make use of it to a greater extent. The progress they make, however, is slow and often insufficient.

Stage 4 **Analytical Companies**. Analytical organizations make effective use of data analytics. They are highly data-oriented, have analytics tools, and make extensive use of data analyses. At the same time, however, they are characterized by the lack of commitment sufficient to be able to fully compete in analytics or to use analytics strategically.

Stage 5 **Analytical Competitors**. These organizations use an analytics strategy that provides the basis for the operation of the entire enterprise. They use analytics skills to gain a competitive advantage.

2.2.3 Gartner's Maturity Model for Data and Analytics

Gartner's Maturity Model for Data and Analytics states an organization is placed in one of the five analytics maturity stages that are characterized by selected attributes (Figure 2.6):

Level 1 Basic—data are not exploited, D&A (data analytics) is managed in silos, people arguing about whose data are correct, analysis is ad hoc, spreadsheet and information firefighting.

Level 2 Opportunistic—IT attempts to formalize information availability requirements, inconsistent incentives. Organizational barriers and lack of leadership, strategy is still in the early stages, not business-relevant, data quality and insight efforts, but still in silos.

Level 3 Systematic—different content types are still treated differently, strategy and vision formed (middle stages), agile emerges, exogenous data sources are readily integrated, and business executives become D&A champions.

Level 4 Differentiating—executives champions and communicate best practices; business-led/driven, with chief data officer (CDO); D&A is an indispensable fuel for performance and innovations and linked across programs; link to outcome and data used for ROI (return on investment).

Level 5 Transformational—D&A is central to business strategy, data value influences investments, strategy and execution aligned and continually improved, outside-in perspective, CDO sits on board.

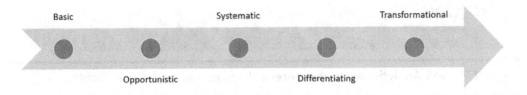

Figure 2.6   Gartner's Maturity Model for Data and Analytics. Based on (https://goo.gl/pAhfbt).

2.2.4 SAS Analytics Maturity Scorecard

SAS is a longstanding successful company in the data and analytics space, founded in 1972. The SAS Analytics Maturity Scorecard is prepared based on an analysis carried out in four dimensions:

1. Culture: decision-makers' use of data and analysis
2. Internal process readiness
3. Analytical capabilities
4. Data environment: infrastructure and software

According to the SAS Analytics Maturity Scorecard, an organization can be placed on one of the five analytics maturity stages (Figure 2.7):

Level 1 **Analytically Unaware**—decision-makers rely on perceptions, historical decisions, and non-validated beliefs. They have no defined data management or analytic processes to support insight development or business decisions. Organization has a lack of analytics skills or executive interest; considers historical reporting to be analytics. Furthermore, some projects have defined scope and objectives; inconsistency and duplication of software.

Level 2 **Analytically Aware**—decision-makers recognize benefits of analytics to support decision-making but do not leverage analytics consistently. Full benefits of analytics poorly understood, siloed, and ad-hoc activities, yet reasonable results.

Level 3 **Analytically Astute**—decision-makers adopt analytics for all decisions. Organization is characterized by common data management processes in place and use of datasets and analytics established for decision-making. Analytics capabilities are slow to change; analytics development is constrained, yet departments have own experts/plans.

Figure 2.7 SAS Analytics Maturity Scorecard—stages of analytics maturity.

Level 4 **Empowered**—decision-makers leverage analytics across the organization to support business decisions. Widely deployed data processes support specific business insights. Management supports analytics to bring business units into alignment.

Level 5 **Explorative**—decision-makers search for new ways to use advanced analytics to support business decisions. Processes around data enhancement and analytic methods to optimize resources are continually refining. Analytical capabilities: commits to innovative analytic use for future growth and draws on advanced analytics and advances in new techniques.

2.2.5 TDWI Analytics Maturity Model

The Data Warehouse Institute (TDWI) Analytics Maturity Model provides the methodology for measuring and monitoring the status of analytics implementation within the enterprise. It indicates the actions that should be taken to develop the organization's analytics culture. In the TDWI model, an analysis of the organization's analytics maturity is carried out based on 35 questions asked in five areas of analytics maturity: organizational, infrastructural, data management, analysis, and management. This analytics maturity model provides the methodology for measuring and monitoring the status of analytics implementation in the organization.

In the organizational area, the questions focus inter alia on the extent to which the organizational strategy, culture, leadership, skills, and financing support the analytics program. In the infrastructural area, the questions focus on the issues related to the advancement and accessibility of infrastructure for analytics applications.

In the data management area, the questions concern data quality, accessibility, and processing, as well as the company's data management method. In turn, in the analytics area, the questions are focused on the assessment of analytics culture and the extent to which analytics tools are used.

This analytics maturity model consists of five stages: nascent, pre-adoption, early adoption, corporate adoption, and mature/visionary. As organizations move through these stages, they should gain greater value from their investments (Figure 2.8).

Figure 2.8 TDWI Analytics Stages of Maturity.

Stage 1 **Nascent**—Organizations that are at the first stage most frequently use no analytics, except maybe a spreadsheet. Decision-makers do not invest in the development of analytics competencies, even though there are people working in an enterprise who may be interested in the potential of analytics. In these enterprises, decisions are made based on intuition.

Stage 2 **Pre-Adoption**—Organizations that are at the second stage begin the process of developing an analytics culture in the enterprise. This takes place in the field of training employees and forming an analyst team, and through the purchase of appropriate technologies. The management team recognizes the potential of analytics.

Stage 3 **Early Adoption**—In turn, in the initial implementation phase, organizations make use of analytics tools and software. However, they are still achieving proficiency in how to use them and searching for processes in which they could be used. The Chasm is a stage that symbolizes the obstacles and difficulties that an organization has to face on the analytics development path. At this stage, organizational solutions to ensure an opportunity to effectively use analytics are worked out.

Stage 4 **Corporate Adoption**—At the next stage, organizations are characterized by a high analytics culture and the democratization of analytics. Data analytics shapes the way in which the entire organization operates.

Stage 5 **Mature/Visionary**—Few organizations can be regarded as visionary in analytical terms. At this stage, organizations efficiently carry out analytics programs using a highly tuned infrastructure with well-established data management strategies. Due to the democratization of analytics, users have access to data so that they can explore them independently with no participation of IT.

2.2.5.1 Determining an Organization's Maturity Level

There are at least 20 different data and analytics maturity models. We have presented an overview of five. We presented the factors on which the models are based; however, the actual determination of scores by all these models is proprietary. A few offer online assessments that will return a score for you, but how the score is determined is proprietary. Other methods are more subjective based on open-ended questionnaires. We believe a closed-form calculation of a score is not optimal. There are just too many factors that come into play, industry specifics and individual nuances. Moreover, we believe that the business strategy and goals set the stage for the appropriate level of readiness, not solely the types of data being used or AI and analytics technology being deployed. The questionnaires available are largely focused on sponsorship and culture, data infrastructure, data and analytics technologies/tools, skills, and talent. They do not tie these to the goals and objectives of the organization.

2.3 The Analytics Model Moving Forward in This Book

We simplify this process greatly. We believe our approach is consistent with the maturity models outlined, but we did not do a full assessment of each organization. In fact, while we believe there is some utility in looking at maturity as it helps provide a structure for the reader, we have issues trying to suggest that individual use cases are consistent with the entire organization. In our experience an organization may have lines of business (LoBs) that are advanced in some areas, for example, finance, while other parts of the organization are just beginning to scratch the surface. Therefore, it is possible that one company may be at a lower level for one LoB and a higher level for another LoB.

We categorize the use cases across five levels of data and analytics maturity, and we separate each into a separate chapter. These are broad generalities that describe these levels. Each statement should be read with "generally speaking" in mind, as they are not absolutes.

2.3.1 Level 1 Explorers, Chapter Three

Explorers do not have established data and analytics programs in place. They do not have notable investments in data acquisition beyond the traditional needs of operations and administration. They are not improving their decision-making or taking better action based on data. They are running basic static reports and spreadsheets. These reports are not very informative in nature. They do not provide any correlative nature between inputs and outputs. Again, they are static and users cannot interact with them, drill down or across any dimensions of interest. There may be pockets of more savvy data users within the siloes of the organization, but these siloes operate independently and do not share information or methods and techniques. In a nutshell, everything they are doing with data is retrospective in nature.

However, explorers are beginning to get curious. They read or have heard stories about data-driven methodologies. They may be exploring some of these in various niche areas in the organization, but these are done in isolation. And there is not enough infrastructure or budget to carry on a great deal of analytics.

Explorers exist across many industries, and we highlight some of these (all smaller organizations) energy, manufacturing, construction, food and beverage, fashion, agriculture.

Where you are less likely to find explorers that are very dependent on technology, those that require very quick decision-making and those that do most of their business via the internet will be dependent on technology. Examples of those dependent on technology include such areas as fintech, e-commerce, commercial banking, and biotech and biomedical technology, and virtually any company outside the small to medium business (SMB) category, which we describe in Chapter 3. In other words, there are virtually no large companies that are explorers.

2.3.2 Level 2 Novices, Chapter 4

Novices are beginning to formulate and build their data and analytics programs. They are beginning to develop new strategies that include data-driven decision-making. They are beginning to think about how they can modify their operations using new techniques. They are looking at improved decision-making by supplementing human decisions with analytic techniques. They may be employing some outsourced or software as a service (SaaS) AI-assisted techniques like chat bots on their website. They are budgeting for education and technology and are hiring the appropriate talent.

They have some sort of visual BI tools in place. These may be functional or corporate in nature. They are using dashboards to accelerate and improve decision-making. These are interactive in nature where users can filter, drill down and across dimensions. They may have some corporate pioneers that are using machine learning to create predictive models. People within the organization are beginning to talk across functions and share stories about how their operations are improved with data usage.

Novices exist primarily in small and medium organizations with a few large organizations in this category. You find them in the public and private sectors. You are less likely to see novices very dependent on technology.

IT IS LONG-TERM VALUE THAT MATTERS! YET, WE SEE LEADERS CONSTANTLY MAKE SHORT-TERM DECISIONS!

I was fortunate and had lunch with a couple of great longtime friends, Matt and Justin. Everyone says, "we should do this more often" and then doesn't . . . well, Matt paid so I will probably be hearing from him—"we should do this more often and you can pay this time." Just joking, Matt is a great guy. He would not say that, that would be me.

We had a great lunch and caught up, but one thing that really came out was the short game that everyone is playing these days in IT and business in general. I believe there are many factors for it, but three come quickly to mind:

1. The budget cycle
2. Mandates from above
3. Lack of business understanding for leaders

The Budget Cycle

Operational expenses and strategic investments are subjects of the annual budget cycle. Which gets more weight? Near-term operational expenses and short-term capital investments. This leaves senior leaders in a myopic position. They focus on the short term. Their

> My friend Justin says, "There's nothing cheaper or faster than doing it right the first time."

tenure is focused on the short term. Therefore, they never do a return-on-investment calculation. **Moreover, they never consider the total cost of a project.** *This is where all the heavy costs live*—consumption of internal resources to cover knowledge gaps of consultants and system integrators, future costs of filling gaps in poor implementation, opportunity costs from missing the opportunity to do it right the first time, and much more. Stephen R. Covey and Chris McChesney do a great job of outlining the immediate versus the important in their book, *The 4 Disciplines of Execution*. Their point is directed toward the daily challenge, but the budget cycle could be seen as a near-perfect extension of this struggle.

Mandates from Above

This ties in heavily to the budget cycle, especially when businesses are faced with competing priorities with limited resources. The traditional way of handling this is from the top with mandates to functional groups without a full understanding of where the value is being produced. IT is a great example where it is seen as a true "cost center" and not a "value center." In general, anything that is seen as a cost center gets the biggest percentage cost-cutting mandates. Short sighted, limited thinking.

Lack of Business Understanding for Leader

Leaders in the United States often have a limited understanding of their core business. This seems crazy, but leaders have competing priorities, as everyone does. However, leaders have more degrees of freedom than the rank and file of where they spend their time. So they often get wrong what their priorities should be, where their time and effort should be spent. And their tenures are short, so they don't necessarily have to have intimate knowledge of "this" business. Herb Kelleher at Southwest Airlines knew where his time should be spent = success. Andy Grove at Intel knew = success. And version 2.0 of Steve Jobs did as well = success. I wrote about the necessary ingredients of execution and a very important ingredient was leaders' involvement in the details of the business (see reference).

2.3.3 Level 3 Practitioners, Chapter 5

Practitioners are actively developing strategies with data and analytics in mind. They have undergone some form of digital transformation, meaning they are reinventing some of their operational processes based on more innovative, transformative technology. Their percent of budget for human knowledge and technology that supports data initiatives is growing.

They have well-established corporate BI and visual BI programs in place. They are enhancing most of their decision-making process with some form of analytics, and they are taking some automated actions based on ML or AI. They are using dashboards to accelerate and improve decision-making across the organization. They have a few data scientists or savvy business users that can build machine-learning models. They have rapid deployment of models.

There is cross-pollination of ideas and methods relating to AI and analytics. People are beginning to speak the new language. They are becoming data and analytics literate.

Practitioners exist primarily in every size organization. You find them in the public and private sectors. You are less likely to see practitioners in very "low-tech" industries.

2.3.4 Level 4 Leaders, Chapter 6

For leaders, data-driven technologies are integral to their strategy. They have undergone major forms of digital transformation. They have reinvented much of their operational processes based on more innovative, AI, and analytics technology. The percentage of budget for human knowledge and technology that supports data initiatives is significant.

They are deeply engaging in three of the categories presented in Figure 2.2—descriptive analytics, diagnostic analytics, and predictive analytics—and they are likely doing some prescriptive analytics. The organization has data and analytics fluency. Analytics touches every profession inside the organization.

They have rich data pipelines both internally and externally. They are using the most advanced forms of technologies, such as AutoML, rapid deployment of models, DataOps, and ModelOps.

They are exploring the use of all forms of data, including unstructured and semi-structured data. They have a dedicated data science team as a center of excellence or some form of matrix organization or related community of practice.

Practitioners only exist in organizations that have committed to data and analytics for a period of time, established a data-driven culture, and invested a significant part of their budget to this purpose for people and technology.

2.3.5 Level 5 Innovators, Chapter 7

Innovators exhibit all the same characteristics as leaders with respect to strategy development. They are the top spenders for AI and analytics programs. They invest in formal education programs for staff, managers, and executive levels, including tuition. They also have associations with academic centers that are doing research and development of next-generation data technologies. They hire from top-tier data science and computer science universities programs.

They spend a significant portion of their budget on technology as well. They focus on creating an infrastructure that is elastic and rapidly scalable. They have corporate preferred technology but allow for learning and innovation with new tools as well to keep open minded to emerging technologies and providers. This allows for quicker innovation and job satisfaction for data engineers, data scientists, analysts, and developers.

These organizations have progressed through all the previous levels and typically have been applying data-driven techniques for decades.

References

Burk, S., & Miner, G. D. (2020). *It's all analytics!: The foundations of AI, big data, and data science landscape for professionals in healthcare, business, and government.* CRC Press.

Burk, S., & Miner, G. D. (2022). *The executive's guide to AI and analytics: The foundations of execution and success in the new world.* Productivity Press.

Covey, S. R., McChesney, C., & Huling, J. (2022). *The 4 disciplines of execution: The secret to getting things done, on time, with excellence.* Free Press.

Davenport, T. H., & Harris, J. G. (2017). *Competing on analytics: The new science of winning.* Harvard Business Review Press.

Grossman, R. L. (2018). A framework for evaluating the analytic maturity of an organization. *International Journal of Information Management, 38*(1), 45–51.

Halper, F., & Stodder, D. (2014). *TDWI analytics maturity model guide. Interpreting your assessment score.* TDWI Research, The Data Warehousing Institute.

Król, K., & Zdonek, D. (2020). Analytics maturity models: An overview. *Information: An Open Access Journal by MDPI, 11,* 142.

Miner, L. A., Miner, G. D., Burk, S., Goldstein, M., Nisbet, R., Walton, N., & Hill, T. (2023). *Practical data analytics for innovation in medicine: Building real predictive and prescriptive models in personalized healthcare and medical research using AI, ML, and related technologies* (2nd ed.). Elsevier—Academic Press.

Ryan Holiday. (2019, October 1). *Stillness is the key.* Portfolio Publishing.

Chapter 3

The Explorers

"The appeal of the wild for me is its unpredictability. You have to develop an awareness, react fast, be resourceful and come up with a plan and act on it."

—*Bear Grylls*

3.1 Introduction

In this chapter we discuss the experience of, AI and analytics use cases for, and lessons learned for explorers. As the name "explorer" suggests,

Explorers are adventurers.

these are organizations and professionals that investigate an unfamiliar area; they are adventurers. They are at the earliest phases of acquisition of data and understanding that data, and of finding the best methods to analyze that data. They are just getting started and they have many questions:

- How do we determine the need for using data to solve our problems?
- How do we even get started with data?
- What knowledge do we gain in navigating the data field? In the analytics field?
- What use cases and methods should we start with?
- What data are people in the industry using?
- How are they using it?
- What AI and analytics should we be preparing for in the next three to five years?
- Which techniques give the highest payoff or reward?

DOI: 10.4324/9780429343971-3

It is exciting to be an explorer. There is so much out there to learn and do. Let it be an adventure.

3.2 Some Characteristics of Explorers

The typical explorer is an organization that has been collecting data for years. They collect this data for basic operations like order fulfillment, customer contact, billing, and compliance. These organizations vary in size but are typically small to mid-sized. Small organizations are usually defined as organizations with fewer than 100 employees or revenues/budgets less than $50 million. Midsize enterprises are those organizations with 100–999 employees or revenues/budgets of more than $50 million but less than $1 billion.

While there are considerable differences in these organizations, we have identified some common characteristics:

1. The enterprise's orientation toward data-driven decision-making is typically low. The organization has been operationally oriented. Leadership is more concerned about maintaining the business rather than expanding the business. There may be signs of a fear of innovation and change in other parts of the business; one example of this fear can be a lack of investment in plant and equipment.
2. These enterprises have not made significant investments in data infrastructure. They are using operational data only, very little supplementary data, and therefore often lack the information needed to build meaningful machine-learning models.
3. Decision-making based on any formal data is made at the management level or above and is based on reports and spreadsheets. Reports are the least informative type of descriptive analytics. Managers often mistrust at least some of these reports. In these enterprises, decisions are made based primarily on intuition.
4. They are likely using some systems with ***"packaged" analytics***. This is generating interest in what analytics might be able to do for them.
5. These systems with ***packaged analytics*** might be growing a little frustrating as the users want to look at the data in different ways and find the software to be constraining. This is adding an unease with canned technology and a desire to break out and create custom analytics for the business.

6. Educational support is very limited and there is little cross-departmental knowledge sharing. The organization operates in functional siloes.
7. The reporting technology they have is from legacy systems or some older type of add-on reporting system or custom development. The sustainability of these systems is often fragile. Updates and modifications are expensive.
8. Knowledge of data and analytics is very low.
9. There is an unease that the business can continue with its current rate of technological innovation. Leaders may be hearing or reading about their competitors succeeding with analytics. There is a curiosity on what more investment and knowledge in data analytics can do for the organization.
10. They may have heard from newer hires the need for digital innovation and digital transformation.

3.3 Common Technology Employed by Explorers

Data technologies used by explorers mainly include operational client server or mainframe application systems. These are operational data stores used by these systems for elementary reports and some access methods for IT to tap into operational data. However, many explorers do not have such centralized systems on site. Their hardware may consist primarily of desktop PCs and maybe some shared network drives.

For analytics applications they are primarily using PC-based systems, with a few exceptions. The data consists primarily of spreadsheets and PC databases from which reports are generated. They may be dabbling with tools such as Microsoft Power BI, Google Looker, Yellowfin, or similar. They are using these tools in niche pockets and do not have broad, cross-functional use cases. Use of ML or AI is extremely rare.

Explorers are not using cloud technologies for moving or storing data in cloud repositories (databases). They may have some business and operational systems that are provided as software as a service (SaaS). These are likely to be hosted in the cloud. These systems may offer some packaged analytics.

Explorers started much of their data usage with PC spreadsheets (e.g., Microsoft Excel) or PC databases (e.g. Microsoft Access). As a natural extension there are many add-ins capable of applying various forms of analytics. For example, there are add-ins for forecasting, simulation, even AI and machine learning. These are natural extensions for spreadsheet users.

3..3.1 *Where Explorers Are Gaining the Most from Data and Analytics*

Likely the biggest gain explorers are getting from the use of data is the energizing effects that new learning and opportunity bring. They are catalysts to starting to reimagine the way you could conduct your business. It can re-energize companies that have operated under

> AI and analytics is a way to get people re-engaged and re-energized in more mature business models.

an existing business model for a long time, at times way too long. It can be a new leg up in basic business understanding and processes to support changing the business in changing markets.

It can be a recruitment bonus as students are learning more about technology and its potential. Younger professionals are more likely to gravitate and support the benefits technology can support. Interviewees are more attracted to companies that are open minded; adopting new technology is one of the most transparent forms of openness to change.

Finally, the early steps they take in analytics are often the most financially rewarding and transforming that they see. It is not uncommon for analytics to achieve orders of magnitude in the ROI. This should not be too surprising as many solutions are low-hanging fruit for businesses. Business models are often rethought and redesigned based on data. Even basic decision quality improvements can have a significant financial impact.

3.4 Healthcare Explorers

Healthcare is a very interesting industry when it comes to technology and innovation. In some ways it is on the forefront in AI, as we will see in Chapter 7, where we look at innovators with such applications as real-time clinical decision-making while the patient is on the operating table or the AI-enabled medical devices that can use AI to understand biological acoustic signals to predict downstream patient adverse events, improving patient outcomes, preventing hospital readmissions, and reducing the cost of care. In many other ways it falls far behind other industries in AI and analytics use, and technology adoption. This is especially true when comparative IT budgets are considered.

For example, most people would be surprised that at least 70% of healthcare providers still exchange medical information by
fax, according to federal officials, and some
providers, such as nursing homes and skilled
nursing facilities, rely heavily on the outdated
technology. This is shocking; the only industry on earth dominated by
fax machines.

> This is a shocking
> number, the only industry
> on earth dominated by
> fax machines.

Regulatory changes are on the way that will start pushing the healthcare
system away from the fax machine in the direction of "interoperability." (See
Chapter 6, the vignette "Mobile Healthcare in the Palm of Your Hand for the
Promises of Interoperability"). But the full replacement of the fax machine
likely won't occur until the design of health IT technology shows as much
concern for provider communication and care coordination as it does for
those of billing and compliance, analysts say.

Reliance on faxes is particularly strong in sectors of the healthcare system
where the adoption of electronic health records systems has lagged. This
includes the public health sector, which depended on faxed case reports
from providers in the early stages of the Covid-19 pandemic as local and
state health departments struggled to keep abreast of the rapidly spreading
disease. Much of this gap is due to funding where some sectors, including skilled nursing facilities and behavioral health providers, didn't receive
federal funds for EHR adoption that was provided through the 2009 Health
Information Technology for Economic and Clinical Health Act, known as the
HITECH Act.

We speak to additional gaps in EHR use in Chapter 5, "The Practitioners."
It is important to note that EHRs in their current form have not really lived
up to their original intent to improve patient care and clinical outcomes for
many medical practices. Faxes are still routinely exchanged between hospitals and healthcare providers outfitted with the latest EHR technology. This
is because EHR systems from different makers can't talk to each other.

The result can be absurd, according to Steve Posnack, deputy assistant
coordinator in the Office of the National Coordinator for Health Information
Technology:

> It's not at all unusual for a provider to print off records from an
> electronic health records system and fax them to another provider,
> who then faces the task of extracting the information from the
> faxed records for entry into the provider's own EHR system.

THE CASE FOR SOME SIMPLE (LOW-TECH) DATA-DRIVEN HEALTHCARE

We often equate high-tech and expensive healthcare as having better outcomes and results. Interestingly, high-cost, high-tech innovation doesn't always offer improvements. A multi-year study of almost 24,000 patients with kidney cancer by researchers at the Stanford University School of Medicine found that robot-assisted (AI) laparoscopic surgeries are associated with increases in operating times and costs compared with traditional (non-robot-assisted) laparoscopic surgeries. The clinical outcomes revealed no statistical differences for patients, including no differences in length of hospital stay.

One of the earliest and lowest-tech examples of data collection are checklists. Yet, safety checklists in operating rooms and intensive care units are essential as they appear to be effective tools for improving patient safety in various clinical settings by strengthening compliance with guidelines, improving human factors, reducing the incidence of adverse events, and decreasing mortality and morbidity.

3.4.1 Self-Improvement Is Often the Best Improvement—How Can Analytics Help?

Digital trackers PLUS user-friendly analytics inspire health enthusiasts of all ages and at all levels of fitness. Smart phones, physical fitness monitors, smart watches, activity trackers, pedometers are all great ways people can track their activity levels, and devices like pedometers have been around for decades. What is new is:

1. The increased variety of biometric data being tracked—distance, heart rate, pulse, oxygen, calories burned, sleep time, and more
2. Increased activities measured—steps, distance, floors climbed, active minutes, running, biking, elliptical and swimming, even golf, sleep time, and sleep quality
3. Geolocation data
4. The real-time nature of the data—tracking by seconds, minutes, hours, days, weeks. Any granularity of time that the user wants to see
5. Sun exposure

These devices can be motivating. Users find themselves wanting to outpace or outdo their historic measures. And there are ways companies are adding social psychology as well to improve. There are simple initiatives such as social media campaigns. And there are community boards where people can sign up with friends, colleagues, and family to essentially compete, or at least find shared goals and support one another.

The bottom line is that we are starting to see AI and analytics everywhere. We have been and will continue to be affected by them. The authors are curious about the impact of these easy-to-use analytics. We want to understand the following:

1. Are the analytics being tracked and the use of these devices having a positive impact on health? The results that we have read so far are mixed. More well-designed studies are needed. This is the type of study the US government should be supporting and funding to understand the impact. A study by Lisa Wu for Bloomberg (Wu, 2016) ranks the United States 50th out of 55 developed countries in the effectiveness of our healthcare system. The authors would like to see more practical spending by the US government, and investments on this type of research could have significant return of investment.
2. We are also curious if the analytics applications being added to many services show increases in the general knowledge level of those consumers. This ranges from billing information to the analytics credit card services are providing. Are they improving the understanding and use of analytics in general?
3. Does the increase in adding all these analytics into devices, reports, bills, and the like increase the interest level of most people? Does it make them want to learn and understand more? Does it increase their curiosity level?

3.5 Manufacturing Explorers

Explorers in manufacturing are beginning to investigate new techniques to improve product quality and reduce costs. Specifically, some of the questions they ask are:

■ How can we improve process capability to reduce variation of desired characteristics?
■ How can we improve process capability to reduce scrap and waste?

- Can we reduce manufacturing steps to improve efficiency?
- Can we alter our input mix to optimize our product?
- How can we reduce the number of product returns?
- What can we do to earn customers for life?
- How can we manufacture in the most environmentally friendly means?

Statistical analysis and basic manufacturing analytics can help the organizations formulate some basic answer to most of these questions. It is surprising how many small manufacturing companies are doing little to nothing with data outside of financial and regulatory activities. And to be fair, not every company needs to be sophisticated in their data and analytics (see the following gray box, Technology Must Serve the Need and Not Vice Versa). However, some basic things can be done with minimum time and effort to improve the answers to the previous questions.

3.5.1 A Mom-and-Pop Shop Learns Statistical Process Control (SPC)

A small fertilizer company has been in business for several years. They have grown steadily and have been successful in a regional market. They were looking to improve their manufacturing process. Originally, they had a manual fill process where the fertilizer was shoveled into bags, weighed, and then sealed. They then purchased some automated fill machines. These machines are very simple. They have two control mechanisms that adjust the fill speed and volume. The machines do not automatically weigh the bags; weighing requires a second step in the process. They have allowed a generous overfill rate, allowing anything that meets the minimum of 50 pound fill up to a 55-pound fill to move to the binding (sealing) process. If under 50 pounds they had to take the bags back and insure at least a 50-pound fill. Therefore, they were overly likely to overfill bags.

As prices increased, they understood that they either needed to invest in better equipment or change their operations in some way. They turned to statistical process control and spreadsheets. They had been using spreadsheets for years for their financing and general record tracking. Statistical process control would allow them to correctly calibrate the machines so that there was less overage and anticipate when their filling process started to drift and essentially tell them when the machine control needed to be adjusted. Essentially the data was telling the humans when to let the machine be and when to adjust it. Previously they had been "over control-ling" the process by making too many adjustments.

With simple spreadsheets and some calculations, they have avoided a very expensive capital investment in new machinery and are saving money by reducing their fertilizer overage by 40– 60%. They are also more likely to move into more advanced analytical methods.

TECHNOLOGY MUST SERVE THE NEED AND NOT VICE VERSA

Process Point Energy Services is a small but growing energy services company based in Texas. This interview (August 2022) was extremely enjoyable as I (Scott) am a longtime friend with the president and CEO, Todd Rutherford. Process Point is in a unique situation in that they do not have to look hard for business these days. First, they are in a very high-demand product market, second, they have few competitors in this market, and finally, they have established a great reputation. They serve the power generation, compression, production, and gas process-ing needs for the liquid propane gas (LPG) industry. Their major markets are Nigeria, Morocco, Tunisia, Egypt, Pakistan, Columbia, Peru, Ecuador, and Mexico.

During our conversation I once again realized that technology should not be a solution searching for a problem, but a solution to a specific problem. Process Point uses data in a variety of ways; however, it would not be considered a technology leader. Their business is supported largely by years of experience and expertise. They could receive value from some technological enhancements, and I am sure that will come in time. But, for now, these tech improvements would be an interruption in a thriving business. A business should not spend time looking for large technological innovation in this type of market. Most of the time should be spent acquiring new business and fulfilling orders. There will be a time in the future, when a more normal business cycle occurs, when reflection is needed, and efficiencies can be explored, to look at adding enhancements. For Process Point now it is time to strike out and reap the benefits of a hot market.

"Simplicity don't need to be greased."

—Billy Joe Shaver

www.processpointes.com

3.6 Retail Explorers

3.6.1 Small Plant Nursery Benefits from Marketing Analytics

A small nursery in Central Texas that has been in business for over 20 years has seen a lot of customers, and within the last couple of years they have invited their customers to provide email addresses for special mailings of special events. This was done manually until the customer list and time requirements grew to become unworkable. The company automated the process of contacting their customers on different events and specials with an email marketing software.

This software automates much of the manual processes the company was performing, and it also provided a look inside the power of analytics by offering the company visual dashboards. These visual BI tools are interactive and allow the business to learn from their data. It has helped bring together the email click-through traffic to their website and understand what is working and what is not. This has sparked new ideas on what to offer and track what is working and what is not.

The company is now exploring new ways to use data to understand their customers. They are wanting to gather data that ties purchases and particular items back to individual customers. The company has never been able to do this, but with the simple analytics provided by the email marketing software the company is energized and interested in gathering data in new ways to better understand their customers.

> The pandemic has wrecked existing business models. Change or perish.

3.6.2 Auto Parts Retailer Discovers Demand Forecasting and Inventory Management Analytics

The business mantra for years and years has been "reduce your inventory," "inventory is expensive," and "you should plan for just in time inventory and hold nothing in your warehouse." The pandemic has changed all of that. In fact, COVID has greatly complicated all the supply-chain notions of the past. With major bottlenecks, especially shipping from China, it is more important than ever to think critically about the way you hold and replenish inventory.

For a small auto parts retailer in Arkansas, inventory management was not in the top three critical business challenges they had faced until the pandemic struck. However, the resulting supply-chain crunch changed all of that. It suddenly became the #1 business challenge. This business receives most of its parts via distributors but does have other replenishment options as well. However, these direct channels often cost the business more money. The business quickly put together some decision considerations:

1. We do not want to be without certain products. We need to come up with a priority scheme for our product master.
2. We know certain parts are sourced offshore, and if there is another major event it could take months to get these parts. It is better to overstock these items.
3. We need to come up with a weighting scheme to balance days of supply vs $ for competing modes of sourcing—direct vs distributor.

The business tracked most of their product master in a PC database and did its analysis with spreadsheets. Management understood they needed more forecasting horsepower than they could assemble from their spreadsheet abilities. So, they acquired an Excel add-in that offered many forecasting abilities and allowed them to model and do scenario analysis based on different assumptions and market conditions. This has provided them with confidence that they are in a much better position to ride out future storms and supply-chain disruptions. They also have instilled confidence in data-driven decision-making and their ability to execute business priorities with them. They are actively discussing ways to meet other business challenges with analytics.

3.7 Energy Explorers

3.7.1 Green Energy Company Leverages the Power of Financial Simulation

This story is about a small Southern California company that installs residential solar panel systems with easy-to-use systems. The panels typically pay for themselves in utility bill savings, and the consumer continues to save money and use less fossil fuel–powered electricity. The company has grown considerably from 2016 to 2022 and is generating positive cash flow. The company started with just four people in one market and has grown to over 200 in seven years serving five locations.

The company started with PC-based systems and some cloud applications (primarily billing and accounting). They would rate themselves as "scratching the surface" in analytics doing spreadsheet analysis. However, one success story that they shared was using a spreadsheet add-in that allowed them to greatly improve their business expansion decision-making, where and when to expand. "It has taken a lot of uncertainty out of our decision process. We still know there are risks, but using this tool is much better to compare and evaluate different scenarios than before when we were just simply guessing and hoping" said a company founder.

One specific use case was to determine where new locations would be targeted and opened. The company had built financial spreadsheet models that contained various cost components (labor, material, and depreciation) as well as projected revenues. This has allowed them to project earnings with reasonable accuracy and stability. However, with new markets they knew the cost/revenue mix would be different in every potential location.

The software add-in allowed them to take their existing spreadsheets, add in the most likely data for new markets, and then run thousands of Monte Carlo simulations to see the entire distribution of potential earnings. Worst case, best case, and every case in-between. This allowed them to determine their new location using data and analytics and not just gut reaction or opinions. And, it has been very successful in the last two new markets they have entered, with actual margins being very close to the model projections. This has left them more confident and very curious about determining business problems they can tackle by expanding these new tools. It has also inspired several employees to further their education in an analytics certification program offered at a local university.

3.8 Financial Services and Insurance Explorers

3.8.1 A Small Credit Union Enters the Analytics Space

With self-service analytics via web services becoming so easy, almost anyone can use it. Case in point is a small credit union that wanted to better understand how its current and prospective customers might be using its website. Enter Google Analytics. We try to refrain from using a lot of specific platform or tool providers that are not available via open source, but it is hard not to mention Google Analytics, as it is almost one of a kind in the web analytics space. Google Analytics is a web analytics service that tracks and reports website traffic.

In one day, the credit union's IT manager and a loan officer were able to set up the system for their website. They are now using traffic sources to find out where their visitors and customers are coming from and can find which search terms visitors are using that led them to your website. And these searches are more than just Google Search. They are tracking more than 20 major search engines and searches from international search engines as well as searches from major websites. They also set up custom reports, which allows them to configure metrics based on click through–specific portions of their web page and internal website search functions.

The credit union is actively exploring ways it can employ other analytics tools. They want to figure out a way to cross-reference their social media and email campaign efforts with their web analytics.

3.9 Other Explorers

3.9.1 Smart Apps Enabling "Low-Tech" Industries from Farmers and Ranchers

3.9.1.1 AI-Enabled Smart App for Cattle Weighing

Personal note: I, Scott (author) have a small hobby farm with a few livestock. Cattle are new to us, and we didn't know how to weigh them; however, we found that there are formulas you can use based on a few measurements of a calf that will provide a reasonable estimate. However, our calves are not friendly like the ones you see on YouTube. They will not allow you to come up to them.

One day when we were driving back from the farm, I told my wife I had a great idea, use visual AI to estimate the weight of the calves. That way ranchers with many head of cattle could quickly assess the weights across their herd. I was proud of myself, until 15 seconds later she informed me that there was "already an app for that." She had her phone in hand searching as I was driving. I said, "see, I told you it was a good idea." I am sure it was a subconscious reference. In fact, I remembered afterward a podcast where the interviewee said that he had an idea for 1,000 new startups—just add AI to any existing business.

Agroninja beefie3d™ is a mobile application for cattle weight measurement. The innovative tool was developed to make the farmer's life easier. This smartphone app can weigh cattle with up to 95% accuracy through simply taking a picture. The Hungarian startup's technology hit the market the summer of 2022 and has expanded globally to eight countries—Greece, Germany, France, South Africa, Australia, New Zealand, Brazil, and the United States.

Prior to the launch, the Beefie3d team conducted more than 5,000 cattle weighing tests in its app and concluded a 95% accuracy rate. The technology aims to be a solution for the "risky, costly, difficult procedure of weighing cattle," according to Agroninja. These typical methods are stressful and occasionally harmful for both cattle farmers and their livestock. But the beefy app eliminates this stress by keeping everything contained to a smartphone. Farmers simply must photograph each individual animal. Results are delivered in less than half a minute without touching the animal or doing any special preparation.

> The technology aims to be a solution for the "risky, costly, difficult procedure of weighing cattle."

https://agroninja.com/

3.9.1.2 AI-Enabled Smart Apps for Plant and Animal Identification

Image recognition is a type of pattern recognition that machines do very well, in fact, much better than humans assuming a large collection of images to train models upon. Another simple AI technology based upon image recognition is plant identification. In fact, there are many applications in smartphones that are based on using the camera, sending the image to a cloud-based service that takes the data and runs it against an AI model. The model returns the result to the service request.

Examples—plant identification apps (there are many) and a bird identification app (https://merlin.allaboutbirds.org/, thanks to Dr. Marylou Buyse).

3.10 Challenges from Moving Explorers to Novices

There are many challenges explorers face in their desire to move to the next level in analytic maturity. Some of these are knowledge, some financial, some cultural. Some of these challenges are listed next, then in the following paragraphs are elaborated upon in more detail, and finally recommendations are provided.

The biggest challenges are:

1. Separating the urgent from the important
2. Separating AI and analytics hype from reality
3. Getting data right and consistent

4. Budget
5. People
6. Projects

3.10.1 Separating the Urgent from the Important

It is very easy for people to get caught up in the whirlwind of urgent things—ringing phones, answering email, responding to the boss, running through their to do list at the same time things are being constantly added. It is often very difficult for people to set aside time to think about ways to improve their work. They are too busy doing the work to take time to improve the process. We dedicate a large part of our book *The Executive's Guide to AI and Analytics: The Foundations of Execution and Success in the New World* to this problem (see Burk & Miner, 2022). There is one thing for sure, you are very likely to improve the quality or efficiency of your organization with providing dedicated time to work on it. Therefore, you should set aside dedicated time each week to this effort. We suggest four hours per week, and these must not be low-productivity hours when you are drained or thinking of other things, like late afternoons or Friday after lunch.

3.10.2 Projects

Projects may be the most important challenge. You need to translate the most important business challenges into a problem statement that can be addressed with AI and analytics. And this is somewhat circular to the other pieces that you are trying to put into place. The business challenges should not be that hard to list. What category do they call within? Typically, there are many, but they fall in a small number of categories, primarily three:

1. Improve something
   a. Improve customer service to increase revenue
      i. GOAL: Reduce customers going to the competition (preserve revenue)
      ii. GOAL: Reduce complaints (preserve revenue)
      iii. GOAL: Increase upsell or cross-sell (increase revenue)

   b. Improve catalog campaign
      i. GOAL: Increase product listings (increase revenue)
      ii. GOAL: Improve mail recipient targets (increase margin)
      iii. GOAL: Improve quality of customer experience

2. Increase efficiency
   a. Improve product quality to decrease cost
      i. GOAL: Reduce the number of returns (reduce costs)
      ii. GOAL: Reduce the amount of rework (reduce costs)

   b. Streamline production
      i. GOAL: Cut inspection numbers with sampling (reduce costs)

3. Reduce risk and uncertainty
   a. Reduce revenue risk
      i. GOAL: Reduce fraudulent payments
      ii. GOAL: Reduce credit default

   b. Reduce legal liability
      i. GOAL: Identify insecure contracts

There will be other problems and use cases, but more than 90% will fall in one of these three categories.

3.10.3 Separating AI and Analytics Hype from Reality

Explorers are just getting started and do not have much experience or knowledge of where to find good information. Software vendors are not typically good sources information for three reasons:

1. **Their primary interest is their financial interest.** This does not mean they are wicked or immoral. It is simply natural. Software vendors exist to develop, sell, and support their customers.
2. **They are biased toward their solutions**. AI and analytics is a huge field and given one very specific problem there are many methods to solve it. Commercial solutions offer a limited set.
3. **They are biased toward their solutions market.** This is a higher-level view of #2. Many commercial software platforms belong to a particular camp. For example, there are providers that look at every problem as a ML problem that they can solve. This is not the correct way to look at your business problems. You want to define your problems and then look for tools to help you solve them, and often you need multiple tools. You do not want to choose a "tool to rule them all" and then look for problems to solve. You know the old hammer and nail adage.

Are we against commercial software solutions? Not at all. In fact, both authors have worked for software companies. It is best not to define your AI and analytics program, or projects based on a vendor. You should instead pick some projects that are most likely to succeed and add value, then go after a software solution, open source or commercial to help you solve it. Software tools offer great leverage in solving problems. The primary benefit of commercial software is it often allows you to build faster with support that you may need. The disadvantage is the way they solve a particular problem is limited by their research and product development teams. Open source often requires more internal knowledge, which takes longer to develop solutions, but the ecosystems are huge, allowing many people to contribute to the knowledge base and associated libraries.

Should you use a consultant? Maybe. But you should be fearful of the same problems as using vendors. The simple truth is, it's a big world and there is only so much one person or a collection of people in one entity can know. Therefore, the best information is through knowledge. That means you can use consultants, but vet them carefully. Beyond the normal business checks, consider the following:

1. **Check for any software vendor biases.** Are they associated with a software company? Then every problem looks like a nail for that software company's hammer.
2. **Check for any other internal biases.** Once they do an evaluation or assessment is the next step in their business to provide services to complete the recommendation? You can see the bias here. You want someone that operates independently of their recommendation.
3. **Check for any other professional biases.** Very similar to #3, at the end of the consultant's evaluation are they going to hand you off to one of their recommended partners? That could be okay, but you need to know what biases are in play to make informed decisions.

What should you do? Look to broader education than just software and consulting. Even if you use either, make sure you independently educate yourself as well. How? Get some books and make a real attempt to get books that do not focus on a specific technology, especially commercial platforms. That is why in the first two books of this series, we did not mention any commercial platforms. The only technologies we mentioned were open source, and we kept this to a minimum. Books offer a broader, more independent, more rounded view than blogs and social media posts.

You can also join professional groups and analytics forums. You are look-ing for a breadth of ideas. Consider a university program for a certificate or degree. Do not go for a specific toolset but, say, a certificate in analytics and check the curriculum carefully. Most of these offer a broader, more indepen-dent, more rounded education versus Massive Open Online Courses (MOOCs) that are focused on learning a coding language or software platform.

3.10.4 Getting Data Right and Consistent

Data itself does nothing. However, without it there is no objective, rational decision-making. There certainly are no successful AI and analytics proj-ects. In math proofs, we say something is a necessary condition, but not sufficient to prove something. Meaning you need both conditions. Data is that necessary condition and then you need the proper analytics. So, you need to have some general ideas of the questions you are going to want to answer and start to collect that data. No, you do not have to be overly concrete, but if you are going to try to improve your customer contacts and make your marketing campaigns, then you need to start collecting as much data as you can on every customer interaction and your market in general. If you are wanting to improve internal operations based on the processes you currently follow you want to collect that data (the following vignette might be helpful).

CONSISTENCY OF DATA AND PROCESS IS PARAMOUNT

We have said in the first two books in the series that data reflects a process or a set of processes which by definition is a system. When we automatically collect data with a sensor or machine the data collected is consistent assuming the sensor or machine is recording properly. If we are collecting data from a website there is data that is highly con-sistent, such as web logs and order entry. When we begin to record a lot of human-generated information the data can become very messy very quickly. People may have different naming conventions, some may update the records consistently, and some may not update the records at all. Some may be very good at recording only certain fields or records consistently and omitting others. Data based on human entry can be very non-informative if not done with great care.

This was an insight I was reminded of when George Hamby and I spoke. At first my mind went to the first problem—inconsistent data entry. But George brought up something just as important, if not more important. That is, you have another source of error if people are not following the same process. That provides two layers of error or lack of information and it is multiplicative.

This is a very important point that affects all analytics professionals at all levels. IF you plan to use the data you are collecting for process improvement you have to make sure you are monitoring the same process and collecting data in the same fashion to make that data informative and actionable.

3.10.5 Budget

Budgets are always a set of competing alternatives. There are hard numbers as well as politics associated with budgets. First and foremost, before you start any analytics project you must determine the measure of its effectiveness. Even softer goals like improving customer satisfaction can normally be quantified back to dollars using some simple finance and economics. If you need help check out *How to Measure Anything: Finding the Value of Intangibles in Business* (Hubbard, 2010).

Track your successes for the quantitative side of the budget decisions and start conversations with others in the organization to gather strength on the political side. Are the projects you are competing with tracked with good metrics and quantified to dollars spent?

3.10.6 People

People are the key to any data-driven success. If your organization needs to become more AI and analytics focused it needs to determine the capabilities of the people currently on the train and who you need to board the train moving forward. Surprisingly, the most important criterion is not that you currently have current analytics, mathematical, or technical people on board. The most important point is that you have people with three qualities:

1. An open mind
2. Willingness to change
3. Ability to learn

That's it. You can work around almost anything else as long as you have patience. As with most things that add significant value, it takes time to get your people right to support your program.

3.11 Conclusion and Next Steps for Explorers

We have covered a great deal of information in this chapter. We covered characteristics of explorers and technologies they are employing. Explorers are just getting started with AI and analytics, and they show interest in investigating and moving to the next level. Their venture into analytics tends to be PC based, using spreadsheets and databases, but they are also exploiting the power of add-ins for simulation, forecasting, and visual BI. They are taking advantage of AI and analytics that are packaged with other tools, such as digital marketing and analytics, as we have seen with email marketing and Google Analytics.

It is exciting to be an explorer. There is so much out there to learn and do. They have the most potential to gain from data-driven decision-making.

> "Adventure is worthwhile." —Aesop

They should do their best to do it right.

1. Leadership support and sponsorship
2. Curiosity and creative thinking
3. Education in every way possible!

References

Burk, S., & Miner, G. D. (2022). *The executive's guide to AI and analytics: The foundations of execution and success in the new world*. Productivity Press.

Hubbard, D. W. (2010, April 12). *How to measure anything: Finding the value of "intangibles," in business*. Wiley.

Wu, L. (2016, September 26). *U.S. Health-care system ranks as one of the least-efficient*. Retrieved from www.bloomberg.com/news/articles/2016-09-29/u-s-health-care-systemranks-as-one-of-the-least-efficient

Chapter 4

The Novices

"We arrive at the various stages of life quite as novices."

—*Francois de la Rochefoucauld*

"The expanse of the ocean is seldom seen by the novice with indifference."

—*James F. Cooper*

4.1 Introduction

In this chapter we discuss experiences, AI and analytics use cases, and lessons learned by novices. Novices are entering the next level of analytics maturity. They have had a few successes under their belt and are hungry for more. They are expanding their scope of interest, they want to learn more, they want to apply analytics in more areas of the organization, and they want to learn and apply new analytic techniques. Some of the questions they may be starting to ask may look like:

- Should we separate our analytics budget out of our IT budget? How would that work?
- Should analytics be a formal part of our strategy planning session this year?
- What systems on our IT requirements list include analytics as part of the platform?
- Should we centralize any analytics function?
- Should we name someone to be our analytics head?

DOI: 10.4324/9780429343971-4

- How do we make our analytics program more formal?
- Should our vendor selection and requirement documents include something about analytics?
- How are we to expand our data-driven success at this point?
- How do we expand knowledge of our "data champions" to other parts of the organization?
- Should we offer financial incentives/reimbursements for educational programs we approve?
- Would informal programs like brown bag lunch-and-learns help share knowledge?
- Should we target some professional conferences this year for data and analytics?

The organization is full of questions, with many members filled with excitement and others fearful of change. Changing the organization into a data-driven organization changes the company culture as well. It requires an open mind and an openness to trying new ideas. It also requires some mental flexibility and the dedication to learn some new skills. With easy-to-learn and applied techniques and technology, this is easier than ever. Not everyone has to have deep technical skills; you will not need an army of mathematicians or data scientists.

4.2 Some Characteristics of Novices

The typical novice is an organization that has been collecting data for years. However, they may just be beginning to collect the right data for analytics. Data collected for basic operations often lacks information to answer important questions. It may allow the business to track financial numbers and keep up with regulations and compliance, but it tends to be retrospective and is much more "what happened" and not "why it happened."

> It is not the amount of data collected that is important. It is the amount of information in the data collected that matters.

Now they are moving forward and beginning to collect the right data. They may be accessing publicly available data or even purchasing data to make up for gaps in resources of meaningful, actionable data. There is more external data available today than ever. Accessing it can be a great way for novices to bridge the gaps.

Novice organizations vary in size, but like explorers are typically small to mid-sized. Small organizations are usually defined as organizations with fewer than 100 employees or revenues/budgets less than $50 million. Midsize enterprises are those organizations with 100–999 employees or revenues/budgets of more than $50 million but less than $1 billion.

While there are considerable differences in these organizations, we have identified some common characteristics of these organizations:

1. The enterprise's orientation toward data-driven decision-making is rising. The organization has seen some successful results using analytics. Leaders are beginning to buy in. The organization is getting more curious. "Pockets of innovation" are beginning to materialize. A few people are beginning to see that their career possibilities can be enhanced with analytics, they can shine with their current company and at the same time rise in marketability and job opportunity.

2. At the same time, there may be friction within the organization as some people want to stay with the methods that they see as having been historically successful. Sometimes, these gaps between the early adopters of innovation and analytics may be between younger and older employers. There are many exceptions, but in general, younger workers are more open to change and innovation. These are cultural shifts. Successful adopters recognize and plan for these shifts.

3. These enterprises are making more investments in data infrastructure. They have been historically focused on only operational data. They are beginning to realize that data reflects processes and to improve processes they must acquire that data. They are making the investments required to make this happen, or depending on the industry, they may find that some of this data is available for purchase.

4. They are expanding the usage of systems with packaged analytics. What may have started with one functional analytics app is now expanding to new functions. These functional analytics are becoming requirements in purchase decisions for new systems moving forward. In fact, the analytics included in new systems and new platforms may constitute the key features in the selection process.

5. While the number of packaged analytics might be growing, it is likely that there is frustration growing with some of the more closed analytics packages in some of these apps. Closed analytics means that there are very few options for the organization to alter or adapt the types of systems. What was exciting at first when the new systems came on board

are now growing frustrating as users are becoming savvier and wanting to do their own thing, build their own dashboards. The request for purchase (RFP) process for selection is ruling out any of these closed analytics systems that do not allow for users to create custom dashboards and supplement analytics for the business.

6. Desire for "from the ground up" analytics, BI and dashboard platforms. Once users are educated and have success, they do not want to be constrained in the way dashboard and analytics are displayed and used. As they get more educated, they become sophisticated in their appetite to alter views and navigation of those views. This is a natural progression to control the analytics process. There are many fully functional visual analytics platforms, and most of these tools offer a path beyond simple analytics into advanced analytics and ML. This does not mean they will do away with embedded analytics, they will just want additional tools.

7. For novices, educational support is growing, and there may be the beginnings of cross-departmental knowledge sharing. The organization is beginning to break down functional silos.

8. Knowledge of data and analytics has grown and is beginning to accelerate.

9. Leaders are hearing and reading about their competitors succeeding with analytics. There is a curiosity on what more investment and knowledge can do for the organization.

4.3 Common Technology Employed by Novices

Data technologies used by novices include operational client server or mainframe application systems with operational data stores and potentially some functional data stores as well, like a financial data mart. These serve the function of a department or small group of the organization. However, it could be a very visible and important division. Organizations often start their first data mart to support finance. If the organization moves to the next analytics maturity level, the progression and timing of this evolution will depend on the successes of this department.

Technology for novices includes a mixture of centralized and decentralized systems. The centralized systems could be hosted in a data center or by subscribing to a cloud application provider (software as a service, SaaS). Systems that affect the majority of the organization are typically centralized. Examples might include a time and attendance system or an enterprise resource planning system (ERP). Decentralized systems could be installed locally within a department on a client server, PC based or by subscribing to a cloud application provider.

Analytics applications include the technologies mentioned for explorers—spreadsheets, PC databases, reporting, and visual BI and dashboard tools. The organization is likely to have a presence of all these tools somewhere within the organization. Their IT tools that have some sort of embedded analytics tools are growing. They may be experimenting in some ML or advanced analytics tools. Examples of these are ML and simulation tools for spreadsheets, open-source coding systems such as R and Python, and possibly some dabbling in commercial AI systems.

4.4 Where Novices Are Gaining the Most for Data and Analytics

Novices are taking their exploration to the next level, and they are beginning to intensify their relationship and dependence on data to make decisions and take actions. This is the natural progression in the second stage of analytics

> Learning new things offers excitement; the creative process offers excitement.

maturity. It is an exciting period, but also a period fraught with doubt and uncertainty. Learning new things offers excitement; the creative process always offers excitement. These two elements of discovery are at a peak for novices. They are investigating, trying out new things, and this is exciting. At the same time there is some anxiousness. With this anxiety people in the organization might be asking:

- Are we doing this right?
- What is the downside if we are misreading this?
- I found some data problems; can I believe this dashboard?
- We are changing so fast, how can I keep up with the new lingo and technology?
- They want me to do everything I have been doing and add in this new stuff, how can I?
- Sharon has been a data ninja, are we going to be able to keep her satisfied?
- If Sharon leaves, can we fill the void? No one know what she knows.
- Paul does not want to change his department; can he not see the opportunity here?

- Do we have the right talent in place to evolve in data-based decision-making?
- Should we outsource the analytics process and platform development?
- I read that open source is free, why are we paying a license for this system?
- What should our security and privacy concerns be with this data?
- What are the challenges we face that data are more suitable to solve?
- Do we now have a hammer and are just searching for nails?

So, one big initial gain is excitement and anticipation, sprinkled with a bit of apprehension. For some organizations this reinvigorates and energizes the staff with a new feeling of purpose. For others, it might be a bit overwhelming to add on something else to an already full work week (see Section 3.10.1 in the previous chapter). It is leadership's job to create the right working environment where culture is changed in a positive manner rather than a negative one.

UNIVERSITIES ARE ALSO ON AN ANALYTICS MATURITY CONTINUUM (KING)

During my interviews for this book, I spoke with several higher-education professionals across many different universities, some private, some state supported, some large, some small. One thing that I discovered was an interesting parallel between education and industry. Just as many businesses find themselves somewhere along the analytics maturity continuum, wondering what they should do next, the same thing is happening with universities. Everyone knows they need to get on the analytics train. Some have been riding it for a long time. Others are just beginning and they are trying to figure it out.

For universities just getting started it might be best to offer AI and analytics certifications (see "Higher Education Is Bridging the Gap and Addressing Professional and Industry Needs" at the end of this chapter).

For universities that are farther along and want to offer specific AI and analytics courses, there are other options. First, they could have each department customize their AI and analytics courses within their programs for students that will graduate from their specific department. The benefit of this approach is that the courses can be highly customized. For example, a computer science department can offer

AI computer vision or deep learning courses. However, this paradigm might not scale well.

There are ways to achieve economies of scale. They can be very effective if done properly. If carefully planned, universities should consider some method of consolidating efforts within a central location of the university. One way of doing this is the creation of an institute that is created by departments and schools working together. This was my experience at Baylor University.

The leadership of Baylor realized that several departments and schools were offering undergraduate and graduate courses in statistics. They believed there was a better structure that could support these needs and they wanted to combine efforts. Second they wanted to offer new graduate degrees in statistics and offer industry concentrations. They created an Institute of Graduate statistics that offered master's and doctorate degrees. It was made up of three organizations—the department of mathematics, the business school, and the department of psychology. I was fortunate to be part of the first cohort of students in that institute.

The university later created a fully dedicated department of statistical science and broadened the program tremendously. So Baylor evolved its structure as the needs changed and the related programs. Certification programs plus the three models that Baylor adopted over time allows four models. Universities can start slowly and adopt new models as they grow and mature.

The second big gain is value added by objective decision-making. There are volumes of publications that can assist with this—trade magazines, business, and news reporting—that when used correctly can help drive data-driven technologies that will gain positive organizational results. They can reshape operational workflows, improve efficiencies, and drive down costs. They can also enhance customer experiences and increase revenues and margins. They can reduce business and liability risks while offering consistent and sustainable business results.

Finally, as we have said, these programs can be a recruiting bonus as students are learning more about technology and its potential. Younger professionals are more likely to gravitate and support the benefits technology can support. Interviewees are more attracted to companies that are open minded, and adopting new technology is one of the most transparent forms of openness to change.

4.5 Healthcare Novices

4.5.1 Medium-Sized Physician Group Gets Boost in Revenue Cycle Management with Analytics Platform

Revenue cycle management (RCM) is a major concern for providers. Gaps in coding, billing, authorization, and recovery can cost the practice much needed revenue. A poorly defined and effective process can reduce patient satisfaction and goodwill. Simply defined, RCM is a financial process that enables organizations to identify, track, collect, and manage incoming payments for services provided. The RCM process plays an essential role in maintaining financial viability and providing exceptional service.

Physicians and other healthcare practice groups need efficient and effective RCM processes and systems. At a minimum they need these systems to:

1. Connect systems and data
2. Manage collection, revenue, and reconciliation of data
3. Provide efficient mechanisms to communicate and engage consumers

AI and analytics can impact revenue leakage and recovery and maintain customer satisfaction by addressing four processes:

1. Document and coding improvement
2. Denial management and recovery
3. Claims integrity and processing
4. Patient financial experience

A medium-sized physician practice in Texas has increased their revenues with no decline in customer experience by adding a new revenue management system that is augmented with meaningful analytics. In fact, analytics components and related user functionality were the defining characteristics for the choice of the platform.

The system allowed for more efficient and effective front-end revenue cycle process and management. This allows front office staff to more clearly and accurately inform patients of their financial responsibility before services are rendered. This staff is also able to automate insurance eligibility, authorizations, and medical necessity prior to receiving services.

Then successful middle revenue cycle operations allow for a foundation of accurate and validated documentation to support appropriate clinical coding. That coding supports appropriate billing, reimbursement, and medical necessity determinations. Workflow automation supports staff in the process, and it also allows for interoffice collaboration.

Expert guidance and AI-enabled clinical content, rules, and guidelines increase revenue for the physician group. They are yielding much higher cash flows based on this multifaceted approach. They have streamlined staff due to these efficiencies, error reductions, and revenue integrity despite changing payment models.

On the back end the system improves claim integrity and simplifies claim processing. It leverages payer-specific rules, necessary attachments, and prior patient claims data that can ensure revenue integrity by identifying certain-to-deny claims prior to submission. It removes unnecessary costs on claim processing.

The practice has seen a higher collection rate in accounts receivables, higher estimate capture of fees for visits compared to historical rates. It has allowed the practice to embrace analytics to perform root cause analysis. Since they had success in perform this analysis in RCM they are not looking for other methods to identify business and process and other bottlenecks that are harming the business. They have experienced a very positive return on their analytics initiatives and are dedicated to reinvesting some of those returns in additional AI and analytics projects.

SELF-CARE AND IMPROVED HEALTH WITH CONTINUOUS GLUCOSE MONITORING

Casey Means, MD, is a Stanford-trained physician, chief medical officer and co-founder of metabolic health companies, and associate editor of the *International Journal of Disease Reversal and Prevention*. Her mission is to maximize human potential and reverse the epidemic of preventable chronic disease by empowering individuals with tech-enabled tools that can inform smart, personalized, and sustainable dietary and lifestyle choices. Dr. Mean's perspective has been recently featured in leading newspapers, magazines, and podcasts. She has held research positions at top US universities.

She offers some intriguing advice on healthcare technology that is simple but impactful to health. Some of the most expensive, more pervasive, and possibly the most avoidable related diseases are related to insulin and the metabolic cycle. Particularly, diseases of diabetes. NOTE: that is diseases, diabetes is not a single disease.

In an interview with Lewis Howes, Dr. Means said:

> "It is hard. That is why I'm excited about technology that helps people eat better, because **continuous glucose monitoring** can be life changing." Of course, it's not like I want to walk around and see everyone being a cyborg with technology on their arm. I'm actually a very crunchy granola person. I'm not the most tech savvy person. I want to just be in the back country unplugged. That is my ideal. However, the cards are stacked against us so monumentally in the ways we've talked about. The past 50 to 100 years, the human body has had to be bombarded with all these external signals. That it's never had to deal with the tens of thousands, hundreds of thousands of years of evolution. It's breaking our bodies. We have broken bodies by and large in America, as evidenced by the fact that **six in 10 American adults have at least one chronic disease**. **We're breaking.** Those cards are stacked against us. Of course, there's governmental factors. There's all this stuff. There's food marketing, our school lunches for kids are awful. In the face of that modern reality, we have tools to empower ourselves, to make decisions that are better. I think this is very important. Ideally, you could use these tools to gain awareness, to gain learning, to gain knowledge of how to eat and live in a way that keeps your blood sugar more stable."

Dr. Means wears one of these devices. She reports that individuals respond differently to various foods and knowing how your particular body is critical to your health. "Put a blood sugar monitor on your arm and eat the oatmeal and see what happens. Maybe for you, your blood sugar stays quite stable and you don't have a big spike."

Data can improve decision-making at all levels. Physicians can offer more informed decisions and take better actions with data. But so can individuals with personalized data unique to them. There is nothing more powerful than "this is how this affects you today!" rather than "this is how this affects millions of people on average over a long period."
www.levelshealth.com/blog/author/caseymeans

4.5.2 *Fetal Ultrasound and Estimated Weight Accuracy*

One of the most important reasons for prenatal visits is doing an ultrasound examination to estimate fetal size and development. If the fetus is too small, there may be a problem with the placenta or with the fetus. If it's too big, the mother could have gestational diabetes.

However, measuring the uterus or estimating fetal weight manually is not foolproof because many factors can affect the examination, such as the mother's weight and height, the thickness of the uterus, the size of the placenta, and the amount of amniotic fluid. Ultrasound measurements of the fetus's head, abdomen, and upper thighbone provide a more accurate way to determine size.

But unlike weighing the baby on a scale after birth, even the best ultrasound measurements aren't 100% reliable. There is no method of checking fetal size before delivery that can provide more than an estimated fetal weight.

A clinic in North Texas found this to be true. While generally useful and within a low margin of error, the clinic had a mother deliver a baby that was estimated to have an estimated fetal weight of nine pounds but the child was just six and one-half pounds at birth.

4.6 Manufacturing Novices

Data analytics doesn't operate in a vacuum. It is used to solve specific problems and to provide information about your operations to improve strategic decision-making. The best place to begin a manufacturing analytics project is with a targeted, focused implementation. Start with a specific problem you are trying to solve and get all the relevant stakeholders involved. Together, define the impact that problem has on the organization. You want to be as specific as possible with quantitative metrics that track your success of the project. After your initial pilot or proof-of-concept project, you can expand implementation from there either iteratively or with a planned plant-wide deployment.

The easiest way to demonstrate progress is via visual analytics. The human brain has adapted to quickly see patterns in data and changes in those patterns as well. The one caveat is to supplement your visual analytics with statistics to make sure the patterns you are seeing are valid and not just a pattern that seems to be true but in reality is not meaningful or repeatable.

A few simple ideas to get started are:

1. Use benchmarking and monitor progress
2. Consistently track key performance indicators (KPIs)
3. Create meaningful, configurable, and interactive dashboards
4. Enable the workforce where they work—desktop, tablet, and mobile

4.6.1 A Large Food Products Company Innovates with ML and Visual Dashboards

An established food products company has been successful for decades; it employs several thousand employees with manufacturing facilities across the United States and some international operations. The company grew into new markets from foodservice and retail to in-store bakery, deli, and prepared foods. Historically, its strengths were a reputation for customer service and some very smart acquisitions in the foodservice markets. These acquisitions were beneficial in two ways. First, it allowed them to gain market share and reduce regional competition. However, more importantly, it was able to buy packaging innovation and technologies that it could leverage across the company.

The company came to realize that it needed to work smarter outside of manufacturing and packaging, so it undertook an ambitious first step in AI and analytics. Some of the questions and project goals the customer wanted to focus on were:

1. Can we develop customer profiles? Meaning, can we identify customers that look and behave similarly so we can use this information so that our sales account representatives can more intelligently engage with the clients? The goal would be to maximize sales revenues, cross-sale, and upsell opportunities and to align with corporate sales initiatives.
2. Can we determine logical product pairs or sets of products across customers? Meaning that if a customer is interested in purchasing product A, what is the logical cross-sell opportunity for the sales representative to offer with it?
3. Combining #1 and #2, can we offer the next best action for a specific customer?
4. Can we deliver these results and supporting sales information via a mobile device? This would be easy to use, supporting our existing sales platform as well as geolocation data.

The company wisely prepared and funded the investment in a judicious fashion. The CEO and senior sales leadership were on board and developed the project plan and appropriate funding. There were informational sessions across all affected parties with opportunities to provide feedback to formulate the appropriate plan. A core oversight team had overall authority and budget control for the project, formulated and oversaw four more teams.

- A technology and implementation team that would select and coordinate internal and external resources. This includes vendor selection and the internal partners.
- The business advocacy team translates the business needs to the technology needs. This team would work closely with the technology and implementation team. This team would also persist to carry out measurements of success, KPIs that determine ongoing return on investment and evaluation of the program effort. They would also recommend future modifications and budget proposals.
- The education and rollout team responsible for developing, scheduling, and conducting education to all stakeholders. This training was very role specific in nature.
- The affiliated team which was a collection of all the teams plus anyone that was affected by the program. This was primarily used as an informational channel for the program.

There were two primary external components of the product. A systems integrator was selected to work with the technology and implementation team to develop:

1. ML segmentation and clustering algorithms to create customer profiles
2. ML association rule learning to product sets
3. Optimization algorithms to model lift for various actions
4. Ensemble modeling to combine results of one to three to determine the recommended action
5. Deploy models to the production system with the aforementioned AI intelligence on schedule
6. Map the sales system with geolocation to the database for predictions/scoring and refresh daily
7. Develop the model interface and make recommendations and supplemental sales information available for account executives upon request via a model application

The base application was available to a test market within nine months. It was tested and updated for the next six months. Expected results based on the test to control was over a 40% increase in revenue with a payback rate of 10 months, meaning the entire initial development and investment would be recovered in 10 months, which meant a huge success. The program was then rolled out to the rest of the enterprise. It has excited the entire organization about the possibilities of undertaking similar initiatives, and the program has the capacity to easily fund such initiatives.

FORTUNE GLOBAL 500 COMPANY—"DATA IS NOT A FOCUS, DATA IS NOT A SEXY TERM"

Some very large companies have not capitalized on data as much as they could. In fact, in a conversation (name, company anonymous) he said, "I was told data is not a focus, data is not a sexy term." This is a very successful manufacturing company, and while engineers have the data they need, much of the business does not. The company has a decentralized operations model where each territory runs its own distribution and sales operations and does not share information across the territories. While this leads to some benefits—autonomy, local control, and faster decisions—it can lead to gaps for cross-fertilization of ideas, scale, consistency, and synergy.

This is a cutting-edge leader in manufacturing that operates in over 100 countries, but for this executive getting data is a problem. He has a proven track record with other companies and knows he could drive more margin to the bottom line for this one. He says it has improved a bit and is hoping it will accelerate. I hope it does so that they can see what this individual can bring to the table before he tires of it and moves on.

4.6.2 Engineering and Construction Firm Uses Simulation to Improve Reliability

An engineering and construction firm based in Texas supports clients in the reliability, availability, and maintenance of their plant assets. Specifically, they are identifying facilities where asset failures can have significant consequences—financial and otherwise. Early identification of industrial process failure can save millions for the firm's clients. One method recently discovered by reliability engineers is data analysis and Monte Carlo simulation to predict and prevent failures.

Historically, the firm's reliability engineers working in client process plants have observed that failure rates can abruptly increase due to unintended and unrecognized changes in repair quality, or operating or process conditions. These failure rates were slow to be recognized, often only after several additional failures had occurred.

The firm's engineers recognized failure rate trends at the earliest point in the process so that failure trends could be immediately turned around. All new failures trigger an automatic analysis so that results with statistical significance are known prior to repair. This permits the data analysis to influence inspection and repair plans. This immediate and selective intervention of reliability degradation allows elimination of failures that otherwise would occur.

Historically, the failure time analysis methods the firm was using were slow to detect shifts in failure rates and required larger datasets than what are often available. New methods were developed using a spreadsheet simulation tool add-in. This allowed the firm to do powerful simulation using statistical modeling with much less data. This allowed for early detection of failure rate abnormalities by providing confidence bands around the "probability of failure." You can see the best case, the worst case, and most likely case of failure. This allows engineers to take deeper dives into the most likely and most expensive potential failures.

Simulation, a form of probabilistic analysis or decision analysis, is a very powerful tool, and there are hundreds of applications it can be applied to. Thousands of statistical Monte Carlo simulations can be performed in a matter of minutes. This allows engineers to model well-known industrial processes and study behavior across machines or environments. It also allows for scenarios or "what if" analysis all done within a simple spreadsheet environment.

4.7 Retail Novices

4.7.1 Family-Owned Grocery Chain Starts CRM Program

A mid-sized family-owned grocery store chain in West Texas had a data mart that had been collecting data for several years. The data collected was on store sales across the business. The only analytics performed were simple sales reports that were provided via the relational data mart's simple built-in BI tool (a simple BI system on top of a relational database management system). The business knew there was value in the data collected well beyond these retrospective reports.

A small team was put together to consider various proposals. The team consisted of business and IT people. Members of the team were allowed to research ideas and draw from whatever resources they could, professional and academic affiliations, trade and business press, whatever might be helpful. Through a series of biweekly presentations, they presented back to the team. The result was an overall goal to formalize a customer loyalty program.

The team understood that they should break down this program into a number of smaller projects and came up with a plan of action. The first project was a CRM system. The business was able to find a freemium service that allowed it to do some basic testing for no charge. Once the organization saw the benefit, it initiated an enterprise subscription. The platform was a cloud-hosted system modeled as software as a service (SaaS).

The next step the organization is planning is an enterprise service bus (ESB) architecture, which will allow them to collect data from more sources and enrich the system and to test a formal customer loyalty program.

4.7.2 Small Business Dream of Website and Internet Sales Happens

A small company in Cincinnati, Ohio, had two physical stores and sold antiques and art to the local market. The business had a simple website that was used primarily for information purposes—location, hours, basic categories of inventory they carried, but not specific items. They did not allow for any sales through the website and had no e-commerce in any other means or partners. While they had considered it, business was "good enough" and the store owners were satisfied. That is, until the pandemic hit.

They were forced to close their shop, and sales went to zero. Even once the lockdown was lifted, store traffic was a small fraction of the typical business. This prompted the owners to consider a new business model. The store turned to a proprietary e-commerce platform for online stores and retail point-of-sale systems. The platform offers online retailers a suite of services, including payments, marketing, shipping, and customer engagement tools.

The business found the platform took time to set up, but the process was not difficult. And the platform added some analytics and utilities that made the business more effective. "Had we known it would have been this easy and beneficial, we would have done this years ago," said one owner. The analytics the platform provided included finance reports,

> "Had we known it would have been this easy and beneficial, we would have done this years ago."

including taxes and payments, product analytics, real-time views of traffic and user activity, inventory, market, customer behavior, and more.

Having an online presence has opened the stores market far beyond Cincinnati. The firm has sold products to virtually every state. Obviously with a major change in the business model there are additional headaches. Shipping logistics, inventory management, and regulations have complicated things, but overall the jump to e-commerce has been worthwhile and sales are accelerating.

THE FUNCTIONALITY VS VALUE GAP

A company with a long, successful history knew they needed to innovate. To protect the parties, the company and interviewee remain anonymous. The company has been engaged in a niche market for 25 years. It was one of the first to offer informational products and then developed a mobile app. The market it serves was growing slowly, but the potential applications the company could provide were widening and the overall revenue potential was growing. The company knew it needed to expand its services to stay relevant and continue to grow. It has provided basic descriptive analytics since its inception. Data technology has improved over the years, but its analytics capabilities were lacking. It decided what it really needed was visual dashboards, an interactive visual business intelligence function.

A product manager communicated the desire for these functions with development. Development went off to research vendors and put out a request for purchase. It gathered information, selected a vendor, and embedded the product within its mobile app. When the product manager was informed that the new dashboarding capability would be available in the next release, she was very excited.

During a product review meeting she asked to see it. A developer opened the dashboard portal and said, "here it is." The product manager said, "Okay, so what can our customers do with it?" The developer responded, "Anything they want to. They have full functionality to build any dashboard they want, schedule, control access. They have access to every feature that our vendor offers, just as if you bought the vendor's software outright." The product manager replied, "There are not any dashboards constructed for our business cases? The customer must not only learn the tool, but determine what makes sense to view/monitor/control?

We have been doing this for 25 years. We are the experts. We are our customers' trusted advisors. *Where is the value in that to our customers?"*

Technologists often focus on features and functionality. They should. This is what they know better than anyone. Business and sales professionals focus on value—what value their product offers the customer. The failure here was not managing the project such that all parties aligned and communicated. You cannot overcommunicate. Make sure your teams work together.

4.8 Energy Novices

4.8.1 Small Electric Co-op Improves Inspections with Analytics

Energy production and distribution co-ops, also known as electric or utility co-ops, are prevalent in rural America and provide at-cost electricity to their members. These cooperatives keep the lights on for over 20 million members in the United States. Co-ops are small to medium-sized

> Cooperatives keep the lights on for over 20 million members in the United States.

businesses. One of these small co-ops in East Texas improved its operations and reduced costs with analytics by improving its inspection process.

This co-op is a small business with less than 100 employees and only four employees responsible for substation inspections. For decades, the process for substation monitoring, inspecting, and maintenance remained mostly unchanged and relied heavily on manual paper documentation. Central office personnel used these paper documents created by inspectors to generate work orders (again on paper) and schedule repairs. Based on the schedules of substation inspection teams, field reports often were delayed a week or more, which created opportunities for error and oversight.

The co-op realized it needed asset management software to track equipment life cycles and assist with maintenance requirements. The two primary goals of the system were:

1. Build efficiency into its process of transferring information, documenting inspection results, tracking equipment, visualizing trends, and reporting quickly.
2. It wanted a solution that was easy to use.

The selection of a web-based database management system achieved both objectives. It provided for efficient equipment tracking and scheduling. It significantly modernized the approach and enabled the utility to become increasingly proactive in its approach to inspections and monitoring. Inspectors are now using computer tablets with visual geolocation analytics to see exactly where the equipment is located. Inspector data entry is immediately loaded in the systems database.

Now that the initial phase of the project has been completed, the organization is looking for next steps. Since the data can be exported into spreadsheets or other applications it will be easy to add more values via additional analytics capabilities. Specifically, they have plans to assess performance trends and conduct statistical analysis on operating data, including but not limited to, transformers, breakers, regulators, and (automatic circuit) reclosers. They already have a more accurate understanding of key performance metrics. Operational insight helps them strengthen their reliability, increase member satisfaction, and support employee safety while also reducing its environmental impact and assuring full compliance with all laws and regulations.

4.9 Financial Services and Insurance Novices

4.9.1 Medium-Sized Bank Capitalizes on Workflow and Analytics

A medium-sized bank was facing high labor costs based on manual inputs and data verification in its feeding of data into a corporate financial planning and reporting system. They spent hundreds of hours each month doing manual entry and basic task work in spreadsheets. This included passing certain inputs from one team member of the process to another team member and then continuing the process to another person further down the chain consolidating pieces together into other spreadsheets. Similar processes were being undertaken elsewhere across the regional branches of the bank. The process was costly, burdensome, and error prone. The final stages of the process were to validate the operational branch information with the corporate-level mainframe system. When the systems did not agree, the audit process was carried out manually in spreadsheets. That was an additional, burdensome process.

The CFO identified this as a key project, assigned a cross-functional team that included the finance organization, IT, a business analyst, and an internal project manager, to look into this issue. The team contracted a vendor-neutral consultant. This consultant would receive a fixed fee for the engagement and would not receive any additional money from any software companies, system integration services, or anyone else. This made her advice as unbiased as possible in determining the proper technology stack and type of implementation. The bank invested in a workflow system that:

1. Allowed much of the data to be automatically consolidated
2. Sent notifications to users along the workflow when they had specific tasks to complete
3. Fed data into a visual BI dashboard system
4. Provided data-driven operational intelligence based on statistical forecasting methods

The entire process benefited from the automation and reduced manual labor. It also improved data accuracy and therefore reduced the number of audits and rework. However, the biggest gains came from the analytics and dashboard system. This system allowed users to quickly access:

1. Any variances that exist in the mainframe system and the corporate financial planning and reporting system.
2. Visual analytics into the expected values for key financial indicators tracked at each branch based on a "smart forecast" based on history. This along with #1, reduce the audit process to be reduced from hours to minutes.
3. The dashboards are providing great value in helping the business make operational and strategic decisions. Additionally, the system is open in nature, allowing users to create their own unique dashboard based on the data in the system.
4. It has allowed bank employees to add higher value to the organization, by freeing up their time from doing manual inputs to thinking about how they can better serve customers more efficiently.

Users of the system are very excited about having more high-value time to solve bigger challenges rather than moving data around and researching and scrutinizing errors made in the process. Employees are excited about a more rewarding career path doing higher-value work and being recognized for it. They feel their job worth and market worth has substantially grown. They want to learn more, do more, with analytics.

4.9.2 Medium-Sized Mortgage Company Cleans Data and Begins Forecasting

A medium-sized mortgage company in Oklahoma wanted to expand its data-driven activities from retrospective reporting to more actionable analytics. It had a list of projects it was considering, but it had a problem. Internal stakeholders had issues with data quality in its data warehouse. It decided that before any additional investment should be made in analytics it had to strengthen the quality of its data and more importantly the perception or belief in the value and credibility of the data.

The firm hired a systems integrator local to its corporate office and they developed a needs requirement document. They then opened a formal RFP (request for proposal) process and selected a quick interactive cloud-based data cleansing platform. This allowed the firm to open IT tickets on data issues. IT was able to quickly respond to the issues and within a few months the company's perception of data issues quickly turned from a vote of no confidence to highly confident. It was time to choose an analytics project.

The firm decided on two projects. They were different business cases, but very closely modeled in the same way with statistical and ML models competing for accuracy. These were time series modeling, neural networks, and queuing models. They modeled future revenue and receipts using traditional time series methods as well as more advanced machine learning techniques, neural networks, and queueing models. The second business case was forecasting staffing levels for the call center. While in the end the techniques turned out to be different—revenues and receipts were modeled with time series and the call center staffing model was determined to be a queuing model—they both performed well.

Now the selection of the next analytics project is underway, with great expectations.

4.10 Other Novices

4.10.1 Dallas Auto Body and Painting Company Forecasting Labor

An automotive paint and body shop in Dallas, Texas, had been tracking historical labor requirements in spreadsheets and creating some very simple forecasts for labor and resource requirements. But when the labor market tightened in 2021 they knew they needed to rethink what they were doing. They were losing business due to delays and wild variations of completion dates.

The solution was not very technical or difficult to initiate. They simply added a spreadsheet add-in tool to their existing spreadsheets that helped with supply and demand forecasting accuracy. They were able to hire and estimate completion times more accurately. They had happier staff, as workers had more consistent hours. They had happier customers because they delivered upon predefined completion estimates. Major win:

1. Employees happier
2. Customers happier
3. Simple solution

DATA AND ANALYTICS OFFER A RICH AND REWARDING CAREER

During my conversation with Mike Jay, I realized we have something in common that revealed itself. In fact, I bet it is something that many people who have had a lengthy career in data-driven solutions are able to say. They have worked in a variety of fields and worked on a broad set of problems. However, the thread that binds us is data.

Mike has a background that has spanned engineering, marketing, pricing, teaching, customer relationship management, and more. He has worked with a variety of data, AI, and analytics systems and has an MBA as well as an MS in engineering. Many industries, many technologies, many disciplines, many methods.

I have experienced a great career as well across many industries and functions, tools, and education as well. And one of the most rewarding things was to take something used in one industry and apply it to an entirely new business case, e.g., statistical process control at Texas Instruments to replace A/B campaign management in internet retail at Overstock.com. Mike and I both experienced this in our own career pathway; it is the creative brain hit when you can take something you know from something you have done and apply it to something new—a dopamine rush.

The great thing about data is that it is agnostic in its application. There are so many commonalities of structure and use you can apply the data trade from economics to engineering to marketing. It offers a great career journey and Mike said he enjoyed the ride.

> *"Things turn out best for the people who make the best of the way things work out."*
> Art Linkletter

4.11 Challenges from Moving Novices to Practitioners

Novices have some momentum and excitement within the organization. There is something new happening and when leadership sees the positive response of value created via ML and analytics, they are beginning to really get excited. This excitement is demonstrated with high fives, pats on the back, and possibly some out of the ordinary bonuses and raises to members of the organization that are creating this value.

This has an upside and a downside that leadership needs to be aware of. The positive side is the accolades combined with the positive feeling of contribution by members creating positive results with analytics makes these members want to do more, which is great! The downside with novices is that the whole organization has not bought into the analytics revolution. Not surprisingly, these hesitant members may feel left out. This may lead to the need to make organizational changes.

4.11.1 Team Changes May Be Required to Move to the Next Level of AI and Analytics Maturity

Change is difficult, that is nothing new. There are varying reasons for people not wanting to change. It could be educational in nature, and there are many ways to bridge those gaps (see the following gray box "Higher Education Is Bridging the Gap and Addressing Professional and Industry Needs"). People may not have a clue how analytics can improve what they do, and that is not their fault.

It could be that people have considered themselves successful doing the job that they have been engaged in for years. In other words, they do not believe change is necessary, there is no advantage for them or the organization to change the ways things are done. This could be a real challenge for leaders and the sooner they are identified, the better.

HIGHER EDUCATION IS BRIDGING THE GAP AND ADDRESSING PROFESSIONAL AND INDUSTRY NEEDS

Higher education is bridging the gap and addressing professional and industry needs in a changing world. Things are changing! Higher Ed is innovating for new industry challenges. This is the message I received when I spoke with Melinda Holt this week. Melinda and I went to graduate school together at Baylor University, and we are both strong believers in education. Melinda told me about Zeus and the Texas State University System.

Many people cannot afford the time and expense to enter a full-time university degree program. Massive Open Online Courses (MOOCs) are very targeted and good for some specific skills, but they do not allow for the breadth of material offered in university courses. Zeus bridges the gap. It was developed by top educators and industry leaders but is a certification program rather than a full degree program.

The mission of Zeus is to provide industry-leading skills, credentials, and educational opportunities to develop the Texas workforce. And the vision is to develop the best-qualified professionals by providing high-quality, industry-leading certifications of value for a low price.

By working in concert with industry, educators are preparing data scientists for the Associate Big Data Analyst (ABDA™) certification program. Companies like Cisco, Verizon, AT&T, Oracle, Deloitte, Accenture, and Infosys hire ABDA™-certified professionals. Data scientist has ranked within the top three best jobs in America for four consecutive years.

Data Science Pathways comprises 10 blocks and is a world-class data science course that is fully online, with bonus access to experienced professors from the Texas State University System, designed to create successful pathways to a degree, a certification, or even a fast-tracked career in this high-demand industry.

The final reason people are not adapting to analytics is their job function. Some functions are much more available to improve via analytics. It could be that staff are very acceptable to change, but at the current level of maturity of the organization, the time has not come or the data is not available for them to alter the way their job functions.

Leadership and management are both required, and leadership and management are very different. Stephen Covey is the guru on these differences and addresses these differences in several of his books, and we cover it in Burk and Miner (2022). In short:

1. Leadership (with the entire organization involved) needs to determine the strategy for the organization. The organizations that are successful will include data and analytic decision-making and AI-enabled actions in this strategy.
2. Management will need to take and execute this strategy. They will need to make the difficult decisions on how to handle staff.
   a. If staff are involved and contributing they need to be rewarded and encouraged to accelerate contributions.
   b. If staff are willing to contribute but do not know how they can do so, they need to be educated and encouraged.
   c. If staff are unwilling to change they need to be supported but encouraged to move on to other opportunities.
   d. If staff have job functions where data is not available to contribute to the next stage or there are other shortcomings, management needs to support them in the interim, as there will be a time in the future when the organization grows for virtually every function to benefit from analytics.

PRICING ANALYTICS—FRIEND OR FOE?

My friend and previous coworker Hossam Zaki told me about an executive that was responsible for global pricing at a large manufacturer. This individual was well versed in pricing analytics and pricing optimization. Yet, when this individual started at the company he was viewed as an auditor by many within the firm.

Originally he was the only real pricing expert in the company, a company of over 100,000 employees. He slowly started applying product and market segmentation to the pricing efforts of the firm. He gained executive support with one of the CFO's lieutenants who saw the financial impact that was being made. This finance executive started expanding the pricing analytics function. The firm now has over 25 pricing managers with the same objectives as the first. However, these people are now seen as saints instead of auditors. They are performing the same function, but with proven results in pricing optimization and analytics driving results to the bottom line that they do not have a negative perception.

4.12 Conclusion

We have covered a great deal of information in this chapter. We covered characteristics of novices and technologies they are employing. They are getting very excited by the accomplishments and changes they are making with AI and analytics. They are hungrier for more, and they need more education and support to move to the next level.

Chapter 5

The Practitioners

"Knowledge is of no value unless you put it into practice."

—Anton Chekhov

"In theory there is no difference between theory and practice.
In practice there is."

—Yogi Berra

5.1 Introduction

In this chapter we discuss experiences, AI and analytics use cases, and lessons learned from practitioners.

Practitioners are in the center stage of the AI and analytics maturity continuum. They have an established track record and an overall positive return on investment for their programs. They also have had several missteps or failures that have added to their knowledge and thus gained the ability to overcome future setbacks.

We will cover detailed characteristics of practitioners in this chapter, but briefly, let's differentiate them from novices and leaders. They have advanced in culture, knowledge, and technology beyond the novice stage. This is particularly exemplified in AI and analytics permeating much of the organization. These programs are not siloed or departmentalized. However, these programs are not necessarily in every fiber of the organization. It is not part of every process and is not yet grounded in the organization's thinking.

DOI: 10.4324/9780429343971-5

Another important point is that practitioners may have evolved to their final stage. Explorers and novices gain energy and momentum from the excitement of learning new things and feeling they are making new contributions with novel approaches in finding solutions. This momentum normally propels them into the next stage. However, once they arrive at the practitioner level they may have lost some of the excitement and drive to make it to the next level. This can be natural. There is nothing right or wrong about this. There are fewer leaders than practitioners and fewer innovators than leaders. Additionally, there may be a period of several years where practitioners stay at this level and then leadership changes or culture changes and they may move forward or even drop back.

Some quick hallmarks of practitioners:

■ They have an annual, dedicated analytics budget.
■ They have a corporate-level head of analytics.
■ Their AI and analytics strategy drive a significant part of IT strategy.
■ They have mature data pipelines and data infrastructure.
■ They have staff that has received specific training in AI and analytics.
■ HR is educated in specific data-related skill sets for recruiting and hiring.
■ The organization has received corporate education on legal and ethical uses of data.
■ They already have needed analytics in place or they are asking, "should we have some sort of matrix or overlay function for AI and analytics?"
■ They have specific KPIs that track results, particularly the financial success of analytics projects.
■ They offer financial incentives/reimbursement for educational programs.
■ They send staff to professional conferences for data and analytics.

As we eluded, the practitioner stage of maturity has a high level of inertia. Organizations that get here are likely to stay here without intervention. The natural energy and momentum that pushed the organization to this stage is likely waning. It will not be sufficient to push it forward without dedication and discipline. Nor does it have to; many successful organizations are right to stay at this stage. The organization can maintain the course, it can advance, or it can slide back into its previous state. It is up to leadership to determine and execute the correct strategy.

> "Discipline is the bridge between goals and accomplishment."
> —Novak Djokovic

TOP RECOMMENDATIONS FOR SUCCESSFUL DATA-DRIVEN ANALYTICS PRACTICES

I had a great conversation with my former colleague Shawn Rogers. Shawn is a marketing executive in the analytics industry and a former industry analyst. I asked him, "Based on the hundreds of conversations you have had with executives, what are the most important takeaways you could share with people wanting to make a difference with analytics?" Based on our conversation, here are some insights:

A Village

A successful data-driven analytics practice takes a village. You have to bring together people across the enterprise. You need business people, data and IT people, and analytics professionals all working together to make significant progress. You cannot compartmentalize all your analytics to a group of data scientists. That was part of the problem with the original formulation and job description of data scientists. These were the experts that were to go off by themselves and create value from data. While data scientists are great with all things data, often they do not know enough about the business. So, it is the alliance across these functions that creates synergy.

"Random Acts of Analytics Do Not Work"

I loved that quote from Shawn. He mentioned the need for an analytics center of excellence (ACE). This is an enterprise group that provides data and analysis services to business units and departments. Its mission is to enable the business to ask questions and get answers quickly using data. It also enables a function to coordinate the data and analytics projects in the most constructive way so people are not creating these "random acts of analytics." Finally it allows for a community of learning and sharing, thought leadership.

Another problem in isolated, decentralized analytics projects is a lack of action. The project starts but stalls because some unanticipated challenges are encountered. Because the charter of the ACE is analytics success they have an invested stake to make sure the projects succeed. There are success criteria developed as part of the plan. Projects must deliver specific improvements. These successes are quantified and communicated.

Bright Shiny Toys Become Part of the Ecosystem

We spoke about the last dozen years in technology and how many bright shiny toys that were going to revolutionize everything (example Hadoop) are now just part of the larger ecosystem. Businesses need to recognize them for what they are, potentially useful in the long haul, but they should not fear missing out because rarely does technology create new radical shifts that require immediate decisions. It is better to take time to fully research and determine if the organization will truly benefit.

5.2 Some Characteristics of Practitioners

> "Practitioner" means a full commitment to the pursuit and engagement to an endeavor, as Scott's (author) friend Frank Villamaria, MD, said: "We say we are practicing medicine because we never arrive at perfection, we are forever practicing, trying to get better."

In our maturity continuum we constructed for this book, we borrowed the term "practitioner" from medical practice. According to Barrie England:

> The word's earliest meaning was, in the OED's definition, "to pursue or be engaged in (a particular occupation, profession, skill, or art)". It is first recorded as such in 1421 and that is the meaning it continues to have when we speak of practising (BrEng spelling) law or medicine.

Practitioners, unlike novices, are dedicated as an organization to the pursuit and engagement of AI and analytics methods and practices.

The typical practitioner is an organization that has fully completed data pipelines that not only reflect the processes of the business but also contains data that is of the needed quality and value to be used in broad AI and analytics applications. This means that the data contains sufficient "information" (= sufficient to answer important questions).

Practitioners are moving beyond the question "what happened?" to the more valuable questions of "why did it happen?" and "what is going to happen?"

Practitioners, in addition to the data they are collecting internally, may be also accessing publicly available data, or even purchasing data, in order to be more agile and make better and faster decisions. They might not only be purchasing data, but also purchasing pre-built algorithms and models from marketplaces. An algorithm marketplace takes the app economy one step further. It allows algorithms and other software components to be brokered. These algorithms are not stand-alone apps but are meant to be used as building blocks within custom-tailored solutions.

Most practitioner organizations are mid-sized to large. There are some small organizations that are practitioners, but this is a minority of small organizations. So most practitioners are enterprises with more than 100 employees and/or revenues and budgets of more than $50 million.

While there are considerable differences among these organizations, we have identified some common characteristics of organizations that are working as practitioners:

1. The enterprise's orientation toward data-driven decision-making has arrived. The organization has seen many successful results using analytics. Leadership has firmly invested in the data-driven decision-making paradigm. Rather than localized departmental or pockets of innovation, the majority of the organization is involved in using data to improve their functions.

2. The organization has many people with AI and analytics titles, such as analysts of varying types—data, business, marketing, financial; BI developers, data scientists, analytics developers, AI engineers, data engineers, and DataOPS and MLOPs engineers, to name a few. In addition, there may be formal career ladders developing within the organization.

3. The organization has weeded out naysayers and the old guard that did not want to change the way they have always done it. Every new hire has a job description with some component of data included. *A data-driven culture has been established.*

4. Data-driven decision-making permeates the majority of the organization. There may be some hold out functions, but analytics applications run the majority of the enterprise.

5. Advanced analytics like ML and AI are present. There are parts of the organization that have moved beyond BI reporting and visual dashboards and are employing predictive (and potentially prescriptive) analytics techniques.

6. It is likely that some actions are taking place automatically. This is human-out-of-the-loop analytics. This means that processes that were normally controlled by humans have been replaced with algorithms and are now performed automatically.

7. Investments in data and analytics technology are significant. Also, the investment in people with the correct technical data skills are also significant.

8. There is opportunity for cross-pollination of data and knowledge. These opportunities might be in the form of an analytics center of excellence (ACE), an analytics community of practice, or some other form of "matrix organization" that allows data knowledge to be shared across work assignments or job functions. There could be less formal brown bag lunches or internal conferences for this as well. More about these and others in the next chapter, the leaders.

DUKE UNIVERSITY HEALTH SYSTEM TAKES DATA DEMOCRACY TO NEXT LEVEL

Duke Health has formed an analytics center of excellence (ACE). Their website states, "Analytics is the engine for excellence, growth, and innovation as Duke Health strives to be best-in-class for patient-centered care, care delivery transformation, and knowledge discovery. ACE provides various data solution offerings to our different customers across Duke." Their solution offerings include:

1. Reports and data
2. Accounts, access, and training
3. Population health analytics

The Duke Analytics Community started when four individuals came together who were all passionate about information accessibility. The group realized that they all unintentionally had information about analytics that the others did not. Through working together, they created a space for individuals to share analytical knowledge.

https://empowered.duke.edu/analytics-center-excellence-ace

5.3 Common Technology Employed by Practitioners

Practitioners are using data-driven technologies every day in their business processes. We can categorize them as mature in their data capacities. They support the majority of the organization with automated pipelines. However, what *may* distinguish them from leaders can be the lack of some of the following characteristics that the majority of leaders possess:

1. Use of data as a service (DaaS) and easy use self-service data access.
2. Use of streaming data—data that is being pushed in real time versus being pulled by batch or user queries.
3. Use of data diversity—rich formats that include structured, unstructured, and semi-structured data.
4. Use of forms of a semantic (meta) data layer.
5. Use of hybrid data environments that include data repositories across the cloud and an on-premises data center, and user environments that are enabled with some overarching data virtualization component.

Data governance is a must for practitioners, and it is embedded in the organizational structure and technology. There is some form of data governance technology in place, it may be at a platform level where master and reference are maintained within the system, or it could be at an enterprise level where all corporate data is maintained by a centralized system.

PER GARTNER

"Master data management (MDM) is a technology-enabled discipline in which business and IT work together to ensure the uniformity, accuracy, stewardship, semantic consistency and accountability of the enterprise's official shared master data assets. Master data is the consistent and uniform set of identifiers and extended attributes that describes the core entities of the enterprise including customers, prospects, citizens, suppliers, sites, hierarchies and chart of accounts."

Master data management is a critical requirement for practitioners. More advanced data management techniques are forthcoming in the next chapters, but at a minimum data quality and coherence that is preserved with IT to insure consistent and accurate data that is understood by all pertinent stakeholders.

This was supported by my colleague Kinshuk Dutta in a recent call. Kinshuk has been involved in master data management (MDM) and the related technology solutions for years. NOTE: MDM is a methodology and process as well as a technology. However, when most people hear MDM they think of technology; this is a mistake because no technology is worthwhile without the underlying processes and understanding of the business.

Practitioners often have a mixture of commercial AI and analytics platforms for analyzing and visually exploring data, creating dashboards, building ML pipelines, and managing these assets.

5.3.1 Work Your Strategy Roadmap Backwards

Andre Agassi is one of the best tennis players in history. One of his methods for preparation was to "work the goal backwards." This would look like the following:

1. I want to be the number one tennis player in the world.
2. To be a number one in the world I need to win the Grand Slam.
3. To win the Grand Slam I must win all four major championships in one year.
4. I must win the Australian Open, the French Open, Wimbledon, and the US Open.
5. To win the Australian Open I must qualify for the open by receiving ranking points.

He would continue to work back to what he needed to do in the present. He created a roadmap to his goals. This is a good plan for anyone developing a successful AI and analytics program. Work your goal/strategy backwards. We recommend that you develop a threefold strategy that is tightly coupled—a people strategy, a data technology strategy, and an AI and analytics strategy. More on this in the next chapter.

5.4 Healthcare Practitioners

Health and economic costs of chronic diseases and mental health consume 90% of the nation's $4.1 trillion annual healthcare expenditures per the US Centers for Disease Control and Prevention (CDC website, December 6, 2022). Six in 10 adults in the United States have a chronic disease, and four in 10 adults in the United States have two or more chronic diseases. These diseases have consumed the lion's share of healthcare budgets, and their prevalence does not appear to be declining.

> Six in 10 adults in the United States have a chronic disease, and four in 10 have two or more.

While healthcare organizations have traditionally focused on treating the complications of chronic diseases and mental health, advances in data and analytics can help clinicians and patients manage and slow the progression of chronic diseases to result in higher quality of life for patients and lower healthcare costs. Some focus areas where practitioners are using AI and analytics to reduce these cost burdens are:

5.4.1 Smart Medical Devices

We mentioned continuous glucose monitoring in Chapter 4. These devices allow for higher precision of insulin and diabetic medication administration. This saves a great deal of money, improves clinical outcomes, and increases patient satisfaction. It also reduces the number of critical events whereby diabetic patients might have to go to urgent care, the emergency room, or even have to be admitted to the hospital.

There are hundreds of smart, AI-enabled medical devices that are coming online every year. This will help reduce significant costs of other chronic disease categories such as:

- Alzheimer's disease and related dementia
- Chronic obstructive pulmonary disease
- Heart failure
- Hypertension
- Ischemic heart failure
- Atrial fibrillation

5.4.2 Time to Diagnosis

AI and analytics are being used to speed the time and accuracy of diagnosis and treatment. The faster an accurate diagnosis is made, the quicker treatment can be started, and it is common knowledge that the quicker a patient is treated, clinical outcomes are improved, cost of additional care is avoided, and quality of life and patient satisfaction increase.

Data and analytics create healthcare value by displacing the time at which providers and patients make interventions to improve healthcare outcomes and reduce costs. This healthcare value is created by strategic actions taken at specific points in time during the treatment process. These interventions have been statistically proven to displace later high-cost interventions in favor of earlier preventative procedures using four years of data on 45,000 patients (Thompson et al., 2020).

5.4.3 Electronic Health Records (EHRs), the Electronic Medical Records (EMRs)

We mentioned in Chapter 3 that the EHR is not commonly used as a tool for improving clinical care. Its primary purpose is billing and operations: "The health IT focus up until now has been on electronic medical records systems," said Will O'Connor, chief medical information officer at TigerConnect, a health IT company focused on collaboration. "But EMRs are really a billing tool more than a tool to help doctors and other providers."

THE ELECTRONIC HEALTH RECORD (EHR) IS FAILING TO DELIVER

During my interview process I spoke with several people, and it was shocking to hear the number of ways the EHR is failing to deliver. I spoke with multiple medical doctors that mentioned the lack of usefulness and insight provided. Healthcare has been slammed by the pandemic and personnel shortage, and the EHR does little to meet clinical needs. I spoke with a friend who is part of a major technology company, and she works in the healthcare space, but it was her personal story of her mother's care that was so sad and disappointing. If she had not been there to navigate and correct the care team, the outcomes could have been far worse. Another conversation with a data scientist talked about the care team having to circumvent the EHR.

Here are some major issues with the EHR:

1. Data is collected in the EHR but is fractured. Patients are seen in multiple facilities, but these facilities do not share information. The care providers at a hospital may have no idea what happened in a clinic or rehab center.
2. Data that is not collected in the EHR. There are many forms of data that have an impact on health that are not ever captured in the EHR. This may range from social determinants of health data to air quality, weather, and patients' location information related to disease and pollutant information.
3. Data is not provided in a form that is actionable. Healthcare givers do not have time to wade through mountains of information, even if it is available electronically. They need intelligent systems that can

recommend courses of action. The caregiver will have the option to take or neglect the recommendation. Nevertheless, AI and analytics can provide efficiencies in care management.

5.4.4 Using AI and Analytics to Determine Dental Group Practice Quality

A large national dental plan association providing coverage to millions of people in all 50 states had a very important quality initiative. It wanted to model the quality of dentists and their practices currently in their network. This would be the first step of a much larger quality strategy.

To model the quality of dentists across the network required initial discovery and analysis of dental claims. These summary statistics provided base information for the plan and helped to develop a claims stratification methodology. Then they wanted to create a predictive model that would take claim information and predict the quality of service provided. To build this model they would use a supervised ML method; this meant that the claim data and quality of service indicator variables would have to be fed into the ML algorithm.

The claim data was easy to obtain. However, there was no quality-of-care indicator in their database. This information had to be created by professional review and determination of adherence to appropriate medical practice across several episodes of care for a given patient. A statistical sample of a few thousand claims across several predefined strata were taken and reviewed. Professionals created an appended score to the claim data that measured the clinical quality of the dentist. This data was then used to train the quality model. The model was used to score new claims, and then a second manual review process validated the model results.

The model was put into production, and the plan is now creating scorecards based on the results. There is an ongoing small sampling taken each month to ensure model quality. Additionally, there is a process in place for dental practices to challenge scorecard results. These two mechanisms provide for continual learning and thus improvement of the system.

The plan hopes to use the model in the future for external reporting, vetting new practice groups and potentially formulating a quality bonus program (QBP) like the Affordable Care Act (ACA) that increases payments to practice groups based on a larger quality and satisfaction rating system. The goal of the program is to encourage practice groups to compete for enrollees based on quality.

FOUR MEDICAL USES! UNDERUSE, OVERUSE, MISUSE, AND OPTIMAL USE

Dr. Marylou Buyse is a physician and has been a chief medical officer for several health plans. We worked together at Scott & White Health Plan. During our conversation she categorized medical use in terms that were new to me, and I found extremely interesting. Data and analytics are important at every level. These medical uses are:

1. Underuse
2. Overuse
3. Misuse
4. Optimal use

This is what Dr. Buyse provided as a follow-up to explain these topics.

Managed care was organized among other reasons to save dollars by combating issues like overuse, waste, and even fraud. There are numerous examples of each of these with studies dating back to the '70s showing certain patterns of care that were clearly overuse. The classic example of this was a study showing that the hysterectomy rate in Boston was about four times higher than the hysterectomy rate in New Haven, Connecticut. Moreover, this was true even when normalized for population and severity. There is no medical or demographic reason for such a discrepancy, and this study was among the earliest of many demonstrating overuse and waste in the healthcare system.

Managed care organizations (MCOs) still seek to find and avoid both waste and overuse in the healthcare system. Analytics are key to identifying and addressing this.

An example of overuse at a large MCO found a significant increase in its outpatient department's surgical costs. Analytics showed it was due to general issue (routine) outpatient surgical procedures. Analysis by clinicians narrowed it down to either colonoscopy or upper endoscopy. As the MCO wanted to increase its colonoscopy rate to detect early colon cancer, it looked at upper endoscopy and found a large increase in upper endoscopy rates in specific GI groups. Upper endoscopy is a simple, short, affordable, and easy to do test with very few real indications. Certainly not as many cases as justified the number being done. The MCO considered how best to manage this and decided on a policy change to address this. Analytics showed the cause of the increase in one service affected the entire cost of outpatient surgery was affected almost entirely by a very large increase in upper endoscopy. Without careful analytics working with clinicians this would not have been detected.

Medical Underuse

In the early days of managed care there was much concern that with contracting focusing on avoiding overuse and waste that prevention and screening would suffer. The HEDIS (Health Plan Employer Data Information Set) dataset came into being and has been widely used in the industry for decades as a measure of quality of care being provided. Many of the measures are designed to make sure that underuse is avoided. A good example of underuse is colon cancer screening. The previous example showed that upper endoscopy was oftentimes overused. However, colon cancer screening, of which colonoscopy is the gold standard, is a clear example of underuse, as a HEDIS measured that health plans are encouraged to increase year over year. Many of the HEDIS measures are designed to correct underuse in the healthcare system. Many areas of prevention are underused, for example.

Medical Overuse Examples

- Milliman (actuarial firm)—Overuse, prior authorization (utilization management department, and claims review)
- Outpatient surgery higher than general issues, and overuse in endoscopy
- Milliman segments a list of cost categories—tightly managed, loosely managed, etc.

Medical Misuse Examples

- Medical errors (sponge in patient)
- Adverse events (post-op infection)
- Member complaints: Managed care organizations listen to and analyze medical complaints and look for patterns of repeated issues with a provider or facility. These include things such as rudeness,

lateness of the proprietor, as well as much more serious incidences. The MCO places the severity levels on these complaints, gets feedback from the provider or facility, and takes appropriate action.

Medical Optimal Use

Analytics are extremely helpful in evaluating each of these areas of overuse, underuse, and misuse. In most MCOs there is close collaboration between the leaders of the clinical area and the analytics area.

- Quality/HEDIS/HEDIS for 5% withhold in Medicare star rating
- Star rating—three things CAHPS (satisfaction, HEDIS, Administrative Measures)
- HOS—health outcome studies—(flu shots, illness due to tobacco use, etc.)
- Star—COMBO admin measures/HOS CAHPS
- Chronic—diabetes, etc. Feet, heart, low preventive screenings (HEDIS + reduce)

5.4.5 Some Ways Various Healthcare Professionals Are Using Textual Analytics

One of the great opportunities in AI and analytics is extracting information from unstructured data like text. Text is the bulk of data collected, estimated to be 80% in most organizations, and even 90+% in others. Virtually every healthcare role can benefit from using this type of information. For example:

> **Administrator's responsibility** for their healthcare facility in needing data to make decisions about the facility, including contracts with suppliers, cost of supplies/medications, staff efficiencies, and even patient sentiment.

In general, knowledge extraction can reduce administrative costs. An example would be improving efficiency and accuracy of billing by extracting relevant information from unstructured physician notes and appropriately assigned medical codes. Healthcare is full of code sets; these code sets provide varying standards for diagnoses and procedures. It is also full of acronyms, complex terminology, and inconsistency of terminology and format for the same characteristics. Extracting knowledge from text can add information, improve quality and efficiency, and thus reduce administrative costs and increase revenue.

Prior authorization is a utilization management practice used by health insurance companies that requires certain procedures, tests, and medications prescribed by healthcare clinicians to first be evaluated to assess the medical necessity and cost-of-care ramifications before they are authorized. Prior authorization can be an expensive, time consuming, and a tedious process. Leveraging information from physician notes using text mining can alleviate delays and administrative errors and thus can greatly reduce these costs and save time.

Patient Care within the healthcare facility needing care-type data that will help keep the focus on patient care; this includes patient outcomes, quality of care from physicians, nursing staff, technicians, staff, and providing what is needed for release debriefing of the patient.

Information extracted from physician notes, lab reports, clinical protocols, and discharge summaries can greatly improve the efficiency and quality of clinical care. This information, when placed in the proper hands across the patient journey, improves value across the entire care experience and improves patient satisfaction.

Automation of analysis of internal patient satisfaction surveys, various CAHPS (Consumer Assessment of Healthcare Providers and Systems) surveys and the CAHPS patient narrative, customer complaints or any unstructured data sources.

Health safety for the community needing data for outbreaks, including Covid, flu virus, mumps, etc.

1. Providers can improve patient safety by finding contraindications of prescription use with physician notes, lab reports, and more.
2. Compile and compare clinical guidance from public sources to define the most appropriate care guidelines for care delivery.
3. Compare and detect changes in clinical guidelines and lab reports.

Research within the healthcare facility needing data for grant submissions and eligible publication candidates. Text analytics can extract clinical concepts like diagnoses, procedures, and symptoms from electronic medical records (EMRs), patient discharge summaries, and lab reports. This supports medical education, expedites scholarly pursuits, grant submission, and other funding submissions.

5.5 Manufacturing Practitioners

Manufacturers face many challenges amongst fierce global competition and in the wake of the 2020–22 global pandemic that has created many additional challenges, some of these are:

- Need for more agile, flexible operations
- Easily accommodate mix shifts and new products
- The need to invest in quality and reliability
- Pressures to increase productivity while reducing cycle times and costs
- The need to maximize value obtained from factory equipment
- Complexity due to proliferation of products: more options, shorter life cycles, more complex products
- Global market, competition, and supply chains

5.5.1 Predictive Maintenance to Proactively Identify and Address Impending Equipment Failure

Research from McKinsey suggests that predictive maintenance generally reduces machine downtime by 30–50% and increases asset life by 20–40%.

HIGH-TECH SEMICONDUCTOR INDUSTRY STRUGGLES WITH DIGITAL TRANSFORMATION AFTER THE GREAT RESET

A colleague told me that the semiconductor industry in the United States is looking for its footing in a post-pandemic world. After a long steady series of predictable forces, things are rapidly changing. For decades the mantra has been to keep costs to a minimum, meaning margins are razor thin.

Virtually all efforts have been in cost reduction from offshoring as much manufacturing as possible to keeping antiquated IT systems that are bandaged together. Furthermore, this is an industry that prefers minimal risk and tends to not be very innovative beyond its engineering and design functions. Specifically, unlike other industries where hiring is often done outside the industry to spark new ideas and ways of doing business, semiconductor companies are less open to consider this practice.

In 2022 there were significant shifts that affected the industry:

1. A continued major chip shortage has hammered supply lines with automotive factories sitting on thousands of cars that are ready to go except for a few chips, so they sit idle, costing companies hundreds of millions in inventory and opportunity costs.
2. Geopolitical unease, with tensions raised between China and Taiwan and the United States.
3. A realization in the US government that there are great national security concerns by having most of its high-tech semiconductors produced offshore.
4. The cost of global shipping increased due to diesel and other fuel costs.
5. Passage of a new Chips and Science Act in Washington that authorized $250 billion in government subsidies for technology and science, and $52 billion of that is earmarked for companies and institutions working with semiconductors.

With all these changes, my friend, who has worked with several major semiconductor manufacturers, says it is time for them to embrace risk and change. In 2022 they saw their revenues and margins appreciate significantly, yet they cannot give up old ways of thinking. He says what they should be doing is investing in all their systems. But specifically enhancing their systems and staffing capability to

1. Predict demand across the supply chain with statistical and AI demand forecasting models.
2. Track current inventory with automated systems and visual dashboards. Enable internal operations, distributors, and end customers to see this information. When can orders be expected? Will it be complete or a partial shipment? Have this information feed back into #1.
3. Track bill of material (BOM) changes and do so automatically via a system and not by email. Have this information feed back into #1.
4. Prevent data lockdown and embrace cloud technologies! This is where every industry is headed (see "Executive has an Epiphany in 2011 on Compute, the Cloud and Open Source" vignette, page 222). There are security concerns, but these can be minimized with the right strategy and planning.

5. Invest more in customer relationship management (CRM) systems. Get closer to customers and understand their needs rather than assume they are still the same as yesterday or what you are thinking. Use data.

6. Use data for strategic planning and fab construction. There has not been a lot of fab construction in the United States for years. The data in the supply chains and CRM systems will be unbelievably valuable for determining strategic plans and fab locations.

Lao Tzu said, "If you do not change direction, you may end up where you are heading." And Amelia Earhart said, "The most difficult thing is the decision to act; the rest is merely tenacity. The fears are paper tigers. You can do anything you decide to do."

I hope the semiconductor industry will seize upon the opportunities presented in this current environment and transform the industry.

5.6 Retail Practitioners

Perhaps more than any other industry, retail has been disrupted by a shift to digital, leading to the shuttering of physical stores and the collapse of time-honored brands. The pandemic has only accelerated the need for innovation. Now, more than ever, retailers must adapt their business to be data-centric. Retailers must capitalize on emerging trends, overcome industry challenges, and drive success to attain and maintain market leadership. This requires an investment in intellectual and technology investments to support required AI and analytics proficiency.

Any medium-size or larger enterprise has to be at or above the practitioner level. Retail is one of the most competitive industries that exists. Some detailed use cases for retailers include:

- In-store inventory management
- Fraud detection
- Customer retention
- Loss prevention
- Customer service
- Retailer–supplier collaboration
- Next best action

- Personalized marketing
- Supply-chain optimization
- Last mile fulfillment
- Demand forecasting
- Store performance
- Customer journey management
- E-commerce

SUCCESSFUL RETAIL PROFESSIONAL BREAKS INTO ANALYTICS FOR THE PERFORMING ARTS

I had an interesting call with Tony Smith. Tony and I met several years ago in the pricing science/pricing analytics area, and we have kept up with each other. Retail analytics has been Tony's main focus for many years. He has a great track record of providing value to his clients. He has an established career in marketing and pricing analytics for the retail space. However, Tony has had a lifelong interest (passion may be more apt?) for the arts. He was a music major in college, and he has been involved in the arts his entire life.

After three decades in retail data, Tony began applying his established analytics knowledge to the arts. A new, exciting venture. He has been loving it. He sent me a picture of him at Carnegie Hall, very incredible!

We have seen example after example in this book—a currency that transcends organizational size, industry, and function. That currency is data. Knowledge of data can take you into all sorts of interesting places. It has for Tony!

5.7 Telecommunication Practitioners

The telecommunications (telecom) industry has always been a big user of data, especially data involving math and engineering. The mathematics that supported analog switches and digital switches for decades have linear and mathematical programming at their core. These same disciplines, plus route optimization and other forms of mathematical optimization methods, are at

The global data analytics market is projected to reach USD 684.12 billion by 2030, growing at a CAGR of 13.5% (Valuates Reports) (CAGR means compound annual growth rate).

the heart of many AI methodologies, including ML algorithms and beyond. Telecom now benefits from these methodologies in new ways. It has been a great reinforcement loop. Additionally, there are marketing and other use cases that benefit from visual BI and statistical methods. Here are some of the AI and analytic use cases leveraged by telecom companies:

■ Smarter traffic monitoring and network optimization
■ Predictive churn analysis (predicting the likelihood of losing a subscriber)
■ Price optimization
■ Targeted marketing and attracting new subscribers
■ Preventing fraud
■ Product innovation
■ Performing preventive diagnostics

FIRSTNAME NZ GENERATES ACTIONABLE INSIGHTS WITH GEO-ANALYTICS

Firstname Limited of New Zealand is a small company in Auckland doing some big things for the citizens of the "Land of the Long White Cloud." They advertise themselves as a location intelligence for customer analytics company.

As of this writing, early August 2022, Firstname is monitoring 1.8 million households and helps marketing activities for 226,000 small businesses and thus is getting to know the more than 5 million people in the country.

During our conversation, Stephen Usmar outlined many ways Firstname is using data and analytics to better serve the needs of their customers. Stephen is the founder and managing consultant at Firstname. He has a 30+ year career in data and analytics. More specifically he is a GIS (geographic information systems) and CRM (customer relationship management) professional. He has worked for major organizations in New Zealand, Australia, and Asia Pacific.

"We are a creative geo-analytical team here to generate actionable insights for our clients." — Firstname website: https://firstname.co.nz/

Stephen outlined an agreement that his company has with Spark Telecom for upgrading landline calling and retiring the public switched telephone network (PSTN). The upgrade will move customers onto more modern technology that is already being used by the majority of Kiwis, including landline over wireless and landline over fiber. They use GIS spatial analytics and location intelligence to work with customers that are targeted for the switch in technology. The system works to intelligently optimize human resources to services needed by the community.

During our conversation, Stephen Usmar outlined many of the technologies in AI and analytics that Firstname is employing. These include various data-related technologies, including Microsoft Azure®, Snowflake®, DB2 enterprise data warehouse, and Safe Software® FME data. Geospatial and analytics technologies include Esri ArcGIS platforms. Not everything has to be a sophisticated algorithm, and Firstname uses a combination of more sophisticated techniques as well as less sophisticated techniques. These can be as simple as declarative rules to machine learning methods, such as random forest models. Stephen said that there are always things that will come into a technician's schedule that are not planned for, and therefore there will always be noise in the system that cannot be accounted for. It could be a traffic accident, or it could be a technician taking 20 extra minutes in setting up the system.

The analytics, models, and rules continue to improve with time. Data is continually collected via the company's app on technicians' phones. It collects data every 10 seconds on location, altitude, and time so they can determine time between locations and use and even cross-correlate it with other data foreseeable in the future, such as weather and seasonal differences. This improves the systems' efficiency today and can set the company up with new applications for analytic technologies tomorrow.

https://firstname.co.nz/

5.8 Energy Practitioners

Energy is a very broad field from energy production across new and renewable resources, such as wind, solar, and hydro to non-renewable resources such as hydrocarbon (coal, propane, oil) and nuclear. Then there are energy distributors, energy brokers, and industries that create devices and provide services for more efficient use and cost savings of smart energy consumption. Regardless of application, every energy-focused enterprise can benefit from the use of data in decision-making and business activity.

5.8.1 Major Energy Producer Unites Data Scientists and Subject Matter Experts

Analyzing seismic, drilling, and production data is one of the most strategic tasks an oil and gas company undertakes. Once an initial well is drilled, its production can be modeled, and forecasts can be developed about production. When another well is placed in close proximity to an older well, it can cause an initial increase in production, but eventually it will "cannibalize" production from both the initial well and secondary well. Forecasting production from both wells is an essential input into the decision about where to place new wells and optimize the operation of existing wells. This inter-well analysis increases in complexity as more wells are drilled.

Understanding how to enhance oil recovery from existing wells, help production engineers decide when to make changes in the oil reservoir over time, and when to make changes in their oil lifting methods are all complex decisions. To help make these decisions, data analytic techniques can be used to forecast oil production at wells. If the forecasts do not meet a determined production level for a particular aging well, that well can be remediated.

Subject matter experts (SMEs), or drilling engineers, hold knowledge about the impact of drilling. Data scientists are experts at prediction and forecasting. These functions often belong to different parts of an organization. However, this energy company made sure that data scientists work with these SMEs to apply the knowledge and skills necessary to model the impact of drilling. They have an internal Slack channel (a workplace communication tool) for document management and communication activities. This channel brings order and clarity to their combined work. They also have weekly meetings to discuss their accomplishments and plans.

The SMEs use their knowledge and expertise and analytics tools to explore and visualize the data, developing insights that need to be evaluated through modeling. They then document and share their findings on their community channel. The SMEs and data scientists work together to explore the insights. The data scientists then develop forecasting and predictive models. The SMEs evaluate the data science predictive model for verification of the insight and developing and refinement into a predictive model. These predictive models can then be developed into tools which can be used by SMEs and can also be put into production through development of models which can be deployed to various locations.

By combining each team member's strengths the company is making more informed decisions. Additionally the two teams are learning more about the energy business, and this allows for career advancement and provides job satisfaction.

THIS VALUE ENGINEER HAS COMPELLING CONVERSATIONS ACROSS INDUSTRIES

According to ProjectEngineer (www.projectengineer.net), value engineering is a systematic method to improve the "value" of a product or service that the project produces. It is an integral component of project quality. Value is defined as containing two components: function and cost. A value analysis is undertaken whereby practitioners or subject matter experts gather together to perform the value methodology. The standard job plan consists of six phases:

1. Information. Gathering project information and understanding its primary goals.
2. Function analysis. Identifying the functions of the product or project.
3. Creative. Generating alternative solutions that accomplish the intended functions but add value.
4. Evaluation. Reduce the ideas to a short list that can be implemented.
5. Development. Develop the alternatives into viable, actionable plans.
6. Presentation. Present the results to management or other stakeholders.

My good friend Ben Kim works for TIBCO as a senior value engineer. Ben provided me with his definition of value engineering and what value means to customers. Value engineering, also known as business value consulting, has recently become in demand for many software companies, as customers have evolved in their expectations from vendors and now expect to be sold on the business value of the product or service instead of solely the price, features, and functionalities. Value to a customer can typically be broken down into revenue, cost, risk, and strategy—a value engineer's job is to effectively communicate how their solutions align to the business and IT objectives and goals within those four main buckets.

Ben has the opportunity to engage with clients every week across a broad spectrum of industries and business use cases. However, there is ONE thing that crosses them all—data.

When we spoke, Ben described his conversations with financial service and insurance, healthcare/life sciences/pharmaceuticals, logistics, and energy companies. The problems these companies were trying to solve on the data side ranged from EDI (electronic data interchange), a major movement of data infrastructure from on-premises to the cloud, tracking and tracing data, master data management capabilities, and more. On the analytics side, people are wanting more real-time visual analytics, the ability to incorporate open-source technology, ModelOps (Ben told me that 90% of models are never put in production), and movement to SaaS (software as a service) architectures.

Ben also shared that another common theme he has recognized throughout his experience with customers is that there is a massive disconnect between IT and the business. This is why change management (people, processes, and technologies) is so critical for an organization to be successful in its digital transformation. Once again, all of this hinges on data.

Bottom line—everyone is looking for value from data!

5.8.2 Large Utility Company Adds AI Project to Its Digital Transformation Project

A large American utility holding company based in the Midwest with several million electric and natural gas customers and more than $10 billion in annual revenues, is adding AI to its processes. It is a national leader in carbon reduction and has been moving its coal plants to wind generation. It also has a large amount of hydroelectric generation across several states.

This utility holding company has begun a digital transformation program to transform the way the business has historically been run. One major part of this transformation is to move data storage and traditionally IT data center systems to the cloud. It is also embracing AI across several initiatives. One of these is to understand and model its customer journey—all the data points and interactions the business has with each of its customers. It hopes to build better, smarter apps that customers can quickly use to interact with them. First phase goals are:

1. Easy access on web browsers or mobile devices
2. Available with up to date (near real-time) customer information
3. Collection of user data to understand customer needs

Once these are established the company plans on using an AI ML platform that is currently being used by HR and finance departments to build predictive models to increase revenue and customer loyalty.

5.9 Insurance Practitioners

5.9.1 CEO of Property and Casualty Insurance Company Delivers Analytics Mandate

In 2016, a CEO for a midsize insurance company based in the Midwestern United States attended a national actuarial society meeting in Washington, DC. He returned to his company's headquarters with a mandate. We will develop a corporate analytics program that will help us compete and grow with better use of our data. This is not unlike many stories where an executive attends a national conference and is struck by the promise of analytics for their companies.

> It is not uncommon for a CEO, CFO, or someone in leadership to attend a national conference and see the promise of analytics for the first time.

His company is a direct writer of property and casualty insurance products. The company has a long and successful history and operates in almost every state with several service offices located throughout the country. The company has a top credit rating and a strong financial position, but growth has slowed considerably in recent years. The company had a very strong IT department and actuarial staff. They were statistically savvy and had a good data technology infrastructure, but what they needed was a list of projects they could target to launch the CEO's mandate. Candidate projects were not hard to find once the organization understood that this was a top-down, highly visible mandate. Some proposals included:

Broad Strategic Goals

Establishing/adjusting rates and rating models

Reserve analysis segmentation

Investigating case reserve adequacy changes

Parameterizing an individual claim life cycle model

Reserve analysis segmentation

Price monitoring

Fraud detection

Audit of underwriters

Improving marketing efficiency

Department-Specific Goals

Claims likely to go to litigation (Claims)

Auto-adjudication (Claims)

Predicting losses from motor vehicle record (MVR) data

Predicting large individual losses (Claims)

Marketing—narrow many suspects to top 100 prospects; how to best prioritize those prospects ("prospect score")

Marketing—identify cross-selling prospects

Good audit candidates (Field Services)

Account evaluation (Underwriting)

Correlation of financial difficulties (payment irregularities) to retention, losses, and fraud (Underwriting)

Prospective employee hire scoring (HR)

In the end, three initiatives were selected to prove the value of AI. The initiative that was the signature project and the most difficult was the analytics objective to create a predictive classification model that would detect "sleeping giant" claims trained on historical data and deployed on new claims. These "sleeping giants" are rare events that start small and get very expensive, principally workers compensation claims. What are the proper reserve levels that should be set aside for these claims? If an actuary determines a reserve of $50,000 and the claim balloons to $500,000, this is a major issue for the company.

Because these incidents are rare it created challenges for the team. The team identified 110 predictor (independent) variables for these events, but there were far fewer cases than that for the actual events in the last three years. Thus, there was not sufficient training data to develop traditional ML models. Therefore, a Bayesian hierarchical model was used that incorporated the professional knowledge along with the claim data to determine the likelihood of these events across the claim set.

The company determined that in the initial year, it detected 70% of these sleeping giants correctly; however, the model over-predicted the events, with the model erring on calling something a "sleeping giant" when in fact it never became one. Nevertheless, the project was by far the largest success of all initiatives undertaken with over a 6X ROI in the first year of implementation.

5.10 Other Practitioners

There are many other practitioners applying AI and analytics across every vertical industry. The odds that an organization is at this maturity stage increases with size of the organization, and most large organizations are at this phase. However, we will see that not all leaders are large, nor are innovators. It takes a special commitment to get there.

A MAJOR JOB REQUIREMENT OF ANY TECHNOLOGIST IS BEING A GOOD EDUCATOR AND A TRANSLATOR

During a conversation with a business analyst for a Fortune 500 company with over 130,000 employees, he told me that one of the biggest challenges of the job was getting business leaders to understand some simple analytics. Not visual analytics, but the way some methods are used to forecast anticipated demand and other quantitative metrics. This was not a big surprise to me. I find that for any valued technologist, two of the most important skills are the ability to educate and the ability to translate.

These skills are highly intertwined. Education is the ability to break down complicated concepts into relatable experiences. Simple metaphors are a great way to educate. Translating is closely related. Technologists, or any professional really, tend to develop their own language. The only way to translate is to understand some of the other camp jargon as well. Successful technologists have to be multilingual, understanding the same basic terms as other members of the team.

5.11 Conclusion and Next Steps for Practitioners

As we said previously, the majority of practitioners will stay practitioners and not move on to become leaders. For many organizations, once they arrive at this level they are satisfied with the results, and an inertia has begun to settle in. The thrill of something new and an appetite to creatively innovate that previously pushed them forward has waned. The organization is making good gains with its current program, and there is risk of trying to lead the analytics race against their competitors.

If this is the case, the main challenge for the organization is to maintain their gains and solidify their position using the AI and analytics they have in place and move forward cautiously with new applications and use cases.

If the organization wants to move to the next level of maturity, there will need to be additional investment in time, energy, data, and analytics technology. This is a big step that the majority of practitioners do not make. Some of the challenges they will need to address include:

- What is our strategy for building a self-service, data-driven culture that scales?
- What is our strategy for improving data literacy across all of our business teams to make every challenge data driven?
- How should we be thinking about integrating AI/ML into our analytics infrastructure and work streams?
- How can we create pillars of excellence that support cross-functional decision-making?
- How can we automate some decisions where we eliminate the need for human cognition or human decision-making (human-out-of-the-loop)?
- For decisions we should not automate, how can we provide AI-enabled prescriptive analytics that minimize the time for our people to make a decision or take action?

Reference

Thompson, S., Whitaker, J., Kohli, R., & Jones, C. (2020). Chronic disease management: How IT and analytics create healthcare value through the temporal displacement of care. *MIS Quarterly, 44*(1), 227–256. https://doi.org/10.25300/misq/2020/15085

Chapter 6

The Leaders

6.1 Introduction

> *"A leader is one who knows the way, goes the way,*
> *and shows the way."*
>
> —*John Maxwell*

We continue our journey to climb the data and analytics maturity ladder. Is this an evolution? For most it is, and a slow one. For others in smaller, specialized industries it can happen

> There is no free lunch in AI or analytics.

very rapidly. For a small few, they may jump into the spectrum as leaders. Others do not need to ever become leaders to suit the strategy. One of the authors' favorite theorems is the "No Free Lunch Theorem"; put another way, applied to data analytics, there is no "easy button" that determines the right response to every enterprise. Every enterprise is unique and must decide the maturity level that is best for it.

We cover this deeply in Chapter 8, but the basic point is that each firm needs to match its competencies to its strategy. Doing this allows the firm to execute that strategy. Disregarding it leads to frustration.

There is increasing effort to move from one stage to another. It requires more energy and effort to move a practitioner to a leader than it does to move a novice to a practitioner. And it takes even more energy and effort to move a leader to an innovator.

In this chapter we discuss experiences, AI and analytics use cases, and lessons learned for leaders.

DOI: 10.4324/9780429343971-6

Leaders are in the fourth stage of the AI and analytics maturity continuum. For leaders, data and analytics are within the DNA of the organization. Virtually everyone in the organization has some level of data and analytics, and it is a way of thinking!

THE GOAL—7 KEYS TO ENABLE EVERYONE FOR AI WITH A PLATFORM

I (Scott) had a great conversation with a longtime (almost 20 years) friend. Doug Bryan is an AI strategist with a great career history in AI and ML (like Amazon, Stanford, Accenture, Merkle, and many more). We met at Overstock. Much of the conversation was about his role as AI strategist and what is happening with technology and in the marketplace. However, Doug started speaking to something that immediately caught my ear. I don't think he had formerly thought through all of it, and it intrigued me. So, I had him elaborate and it boiled down to seven points for enabling everyone to effectively use AI. Here are the components needed to make this happen:

1. **Usability**. In the 1980s and '90s with personal computers it was all about usability. However, you cannot have a nice GUI and say we are done.
2. **End to end capability**. You need data sourcing to model management. You need to perform every function efficiently and effectively.
3. **Easy to learn.** This cannot be overstated. Scale and sustainability are extremely important. You cannot do either without this capability.
4. **Easy to remember**. More and more data scientists are frontline domain experts whose day job isn't data science, so platforms need to be easy to remember when they occasionally use them.
5. **Prevent serious errors**. There are things that may too easily occur without sufficient safeguards. An example is collinearity in some general linear models. You have to take care of sharp corners. Overfitting where model performance (e.g., AUC looks great, but the model does not perform well in practice is another example.

6. **Collaboration**. Cannot put citizen data scientists on an island. They will never grow or learn unless they can develop skills with more experienced and knowledgeable data scientists (suggested reading, *The Cathedral and Bizarre* by Eric Raymond, Linux).

7. **Cataloging and governance**. Management must be able to keep an eye on all data assets and all models. You must make ML governance and MLOps easy for stakeholders to manage. Some of these functions should automatically be monitored, like accuracy and data/model drift.

Everyone wants to scale AI across the entire organization. They want their frontline domain experts to have the power to use AI and advanced analytics. This has been the goal of software companies for decades. Sometimes this is called "democratizing" analytics or creating citizen data scientists. The problem is that the people companies want to avail with this power have day jobs, full-time responsibilities. They are not into their elbows in a data science platform. They want the power of AI without the overhead of years of experience. If you can follow these seven platform capabilities, you will be much closer to scaling AI across the entire organization.

6.2 Some Characteristics of Leaders

The most straightforward way to characterize leaders is to contrast them against practitioners. How have leaders evolved, what are they doing differently, how have they matured to the next level? These are "what" questions. But an interesting and important consideration is the "why" question. Let's examine that first.

Organizations vary in many ways, and therefore there is no universal prescription for the way they should approach their analytics projects and programs. Many successful companies that are practitioners have been practitioners for quite some time. There may not be a compelling reason for them to move to the next level. This is also true for explorers and novices. From our experience we would say that the distribution/curve as we define analytics maturity in this book would look something like Figure 6.1.

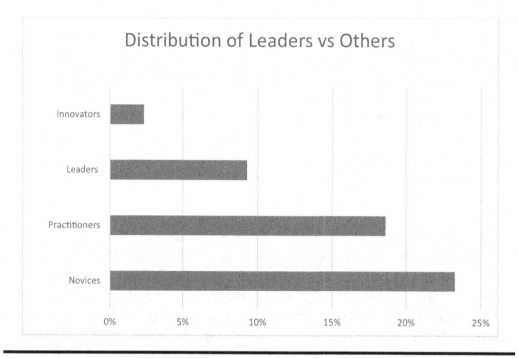

Figure 6.1   Distribution of leaders vs others.

Some organizations will rise to a higher level, some organizations will fall back. Some will move to an initial level of maturity and stay in that position. Not everyone needs to rise to become an innovator. Leadership needs to define the business's strategy based on the organization's ability to execute that strategy. It is aligning strategy to ability that is important. It is not making sure you become a leader or an innovator. Strategy comes first, and developing strategy is circular with the ability to execute it. The best strategy means nothing if you cannot execute. Analytics strategy supports the overall corporate mission and goals. We recommend *The Executive's Guide to AI and Analytics: The Foundations of Execution and Success in the New World* (see Burk & Miner, 2022) for further details on these concepts.

Now that we understand the why, let us return to what separates leaders from practitioners. Here are three top characteristics of leaders that most practitioners do not exhibit:

1. **Organizational and structural differences**. An organization that is structured to allow knowledge sharing across functions, roles, and responsibilities.

2. **Data excellence**. All 5 Vs: **V**olume, **V**ariety, **V**elocity, **V**alue, and **V**eracity.
3. **Self-service**. That enables everyone in the organization.

There are other differences, but these are the top three; next we describe them in more detail and will provide some organizational examples in the industry examples.

6.2.1 Organizational and Structural Differences

While some practitioners may have incorporated some organization design structure to bootstrap its data and analytics capabilities, all leaders have already adopted these philosophies. Some small organizations, for example, tech startups, may not have a dedicated chief data officer or chief analytics officer. These officers may have board functions as well. In small, very tech-savvy companies this is not needed since by their nature everyone is knowledgeable and fluent in the methods.

However, if the organization is medium to large size there will be a central office that is dedicated solely to these responsibilities. There also may be other professionals outside these as well. Most of the large tech companies like Google, Microsoft, and Amazon have both centralized AI and data science departments as well as data scientists that are embedded within functions.

The main purpose of designing the right structure is to ensure continual education, and creative innovation. By bringing people with similar interests together the company can gain the highest value from these professionals. Collaboration is one of the greatest assets of tech companies and why some tech companies are so productive with small staffs. Once the organization grows it must carefully consider ways it can maintain this team spirit and innovative spark.

We mentioned in the last chapter the need for cross-pollination of data and knowledge. These might be a more formal Analytics Center of Excellence (ACE), an Analytics Community of Practice, or some other form of matrix organization that allows data knowledge to be shared across work assignments or job functions. There could be less formal brown bag lunches, or internal conferences for this as well.

6.2.1.1 Notes on Organizational Structure and Design

There is little debate that corporate success or failure relies heavily upon corporate culture. One of the immediate things that any organization can do is to optimize their structure to improve the odds of success. If your organization is very small it is easy to garner an atmosphere of team and shared values. Thus, everyone wins together or dies together. If you are part of a biotech startup with 10 people, people work together because it is either everyone succeeds and becomes wealthy or everyone fails and you are out of a job that you have heavily invested yourself in. Your stake is in the outcome of the entire enterprise; thus, the entire enterprise must succeed. Even if you perform very well relative to others, that does not matter because if the ship goes down, everyone goes down. Furthermore, your peers must deliver and therefore you cheer for them; you do everything you can to make sure they succeed because their success is the collective success, your success. With only 10 people—everyone is important!

What happens in an organization of 10,000 people? First, you typically have lots of layers with staff, department managers, directors, senior directors, vice presidents (VPs), senior VPs, executive VPs. Fancy titles are even created to make people feel more important, because it is easy to get lost in a large organization. Rank matters, ranks matter a great deal.

With rank, politics, posturing, positioning, and games ensue. Life becomes a zero-sum game, meaning for me to win I must take someone down. Backstabbing, turf wars, and petty behavior ensues to make me look better. This is a downside of human nature, but in many organizations it exists as a defense mechanism—the only way for me to win is for you to lose. This creates real problems in many organizations. What is at stake now is my survival, not the organization's survival, so I will forfeit the good of the organization for what is good for me.

For example, suppose everyone in a department knows that their manager, a rising star, is likely to be promoted in the next year and that the manager will be naming their replacement. What is the natural behavior during the next year? The behavior is to try to rise above all your peers, and the easiest way to rise above your peers is not individual accomplishment. No, it is to undermine all your peers.

As a leader, you need to carefully consider options to mitigate the politics and games in your organization. One thing to consider is providing structure within your organization to promote the good of the whole. It will be highly dependent on the size, maturity, and nature of your organization, but consider one example provided by Safi Bahcall:

> Safi suggests that you separate what he calls artists vs soldiers –
> "Artists are the creative types within the organization, the idea

creators, scientists, engineers, designers that are responsible for conceptualization. Artists embrace risk—they want to be on the edge, push the envelope, and develop something radically new. Soldiers are responsible for taking ideas and concepts and turning them into viable products and services. They have practical considerations and therefore are risk averse, they want consistency and control."

Every enterprise has both types of role; the next structure you can provide promotes freedom for each to do their thing and then come together to wed concept to reality for viable innovation. This comes in three parts. First, you separate these camps as much as you can in space and systems to allow for homogeneity. One example for a good system is compensation—you want to reward these camps very differently—the artists should not be punished for product idea failures that do not make it in the market. Their responsibility is creation. Soldiers are responsible for determining if the artist's creation is commercially viable and for the successful launch of the product or service.

Next, you need to allow for systems of transfer that maximize fluidity whereby you maintain the best of each group's contribution. Third, as a leader you honor each group's value to the organization. This often does not occur in organizations, and when it doesn't it

> Steve Jobs, version 1.0, called artists "heroes" and soldiers "bozos."

undermines the capacity of those organizations to compete. For example, Steve Jobs, version 1.0—his first tour at Apple—ended shortly after he alienated so many that it became problematic for him to continue as head of Apple. He called the artists "heroes" and the soldiers "bozos." Artists represented 5% of the company and soldiers represented 95%. In his second tour at Apple, version 2.0, a more mature Jobs realized that everyone was needed as part of the team, and thus he became a much better leader. The point is, if you do not need someone in your organization you should not have them there—if they are there, honor them as key to the organization's success.

6.2.2 Data Excellence

Data is the cornerstone of success with analytics. You can have the best analytics algorithms and models available, but if you do not have good data, efforts will at best be mediocre if not a complete failure. Leaders have made large investments in their data infrastructure and people infrastructure.

Leaders have all five Vs in their data—**V**olume, **V**ariety, **V**elocity, **V**alue, and **V**eracity. The volume of data available is staggering compared to a few years ago. Variety is twofold. First, diverse types of data that the organization can use—structured, unstructured, and semi-structured. Text is an example of unstructured data with much promise (see the next section for more details). The second aspect of variety is technology: leaders have multiple technologies to support their data needs—cloud, on-premises, web-enabled, and purchased data sources from external organizations.

Velocity is how fast the data is available from creation to access. Leaders are using streaming data sources where the data is continually flowing in. They are also using batch and micro-batch data sources. They have a diverse set of tools and use them appropriately for the needs of the firm.

Value is the merit and usefulness of the data. Data is everywhere and may be cheap to acquire. Traditionally, organizations acquired data because it was easily attainable. Leaders understand the data that is needed to drive the greatest potential benefit is often more difficult to attain. Leaders are much more judicious about the data they are acquiring.

Veracity is the quality and consistency of the data. This relates to the credibility of the data. Leaders invest heavily on resources to ensure their users believe the data they are accessing is valid and useful for their designed intention.

6.2.2.1 The Use of Unstructured Data—New Horizon Leaders Are Tapping Into

We spoke in the previous section about how leaders are using all forms of data (the 5 Vs). Data variety is tapping into diverse types of data and data technologies. Text, a subset of unstructured data, is one example of the types of data leaders are using in large measure compared to practitioners. This chapter is full of examples using text data to improve decisions and actions.

Bill Inmon is recognized as the "father of data warehousing." Bill states that if you look at all the data in the corporation only a small percent, depending on the corporation, from 5% to 15%, is structured data.

This structured data is primarily transactional from systems like sales, bank, or clinic transactions where operational systems like ERP, EHR, and HR process them. The actual percentages of structured data vary from one business to the next. The rough proportions of structured data to unstructured data are illustrated in Figure 6.2.

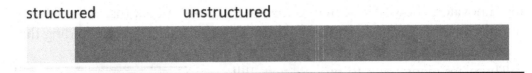

Figure 6.2   Structured vs unstructured data.

A closer examination of the unstructured data in the corporation shows that some of the unstructured data is textually based and some of the unstructured data is not textually based. The non-textual unstructured data is typically sensor or IoT data. Figure 6.3 illustrates this breakdown.

Again, most of the structured data is transactional data. This data is generated by business activities, such as bank deposits, payments made, sales made, telephone calls, and the like and stored in the corporate databases. We have been using these databases for decades to fuel our analytics like BI and visual BI to even ML and AI. There is typically great business value in structured data. In most enterprises, most business decisions are made based on structured data. In fact, if you were to take all of the decisions made across all organizations, 90% of the decisions would be made based on 10% of the data, the structured data. That means there is a huge portion of the data we are ignoring. This is illustrated in Figure 6.4.

Novices and practitioners are satisfied with this ratio and the fact they are making most business decisions based on a minority of the data. Leaders

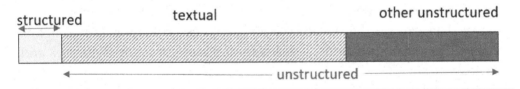

Figure 6.3   Breakdown of structured, textual, and other unstructured data.

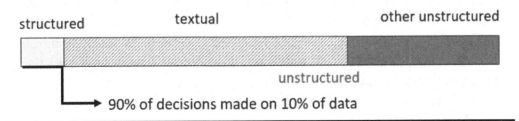

Figure 6.4   90% of enterprise decisions are made with only 10% of the data.

and innovators, however, search to make every use of data that is valuable (another one of the 5 Vs), and text is very rich in value. They are finding that textual data makes all the difference.

There are many ways to process text. Bill states that to handle text, you must address both the text and the context. He says, "Text by itself is interesting. Text plus context is valuable." His company uses a process of textual disambigu-

> "Test by itself is interesting. Text plus context is valuable." —Bill Inmon

ation to create value from operational processes like call centers, internet sentiment, corporate contracts, insurance claims, surveys, applications, maintenance, and parts documentation.

ENTREPRENEURIAL MARKETER MAKES HIS WAY TO AI AND ANALYTICS

Jim Sterne has had a fulfilling career! He has a great story, and he is a great storyteller. You should check out his website and podcasts (at the end of this vignette). It seems to be a consistent theme—people that have careers in data have a variety of experience and I (Scott) could be wrong, but I think it is much more varied than all the career roles most professionals experience. Data is varied, and we have laid out in this book the importance of subject matter expertise. However, that expertise is so much more amenable if you have a common background from industry to industry or professional role to professional role. An understanding of data can be that backbone for analytics professionals that spans across sectors and functions. It is a common core for many industries and professions.

Back to Jim. Jim started his career selling technology equipment. He did extremely well; it was the right time and the right place. Then he realized his company had a gap in marketing, so Jim developed materials to market technology. After commuting to Silicon Valley for a year, Jim decided to find work at home in Santa Barbara where two companies told him, "We can't afford you, but we need your help. Would you agree to be a consultant?" He realized it would increase his income and the variety of work he did. Jim has been a consultant ever since.

He then consulted and keynoted about online marketing in the 1990s, founded a conference and a professional association around digital analytics in the 2000s, and founded the Marketing Analytics Summit (formerly called the eMetrics Summit), chairing 100 conferences around the world.

An internationally known speaker and consultant to Fortune 500 companies and internet entrepreneurs, Jim has spent more than 40 years in sales and marketing and most of that on measuring the value of digital medium for creating and strengthening customer relationships. He's authored a dozen books on internet advertising, marketing, customer service, email marketing, web analytics, and most recently: *Artificial Intelligence for Marketing: Practical Applications*, published by Wiley and SAS Business Series.

Most importantly to Scott (author), Jim has been a great advisor and is becoming a great friend.

Jim's website—www.targeting.com/

6.2.3 Self-Service That Enables Everyone in the Organization

The third and final characteristic that separates leaders from practitioners is the self-service and data and analytics that is part of the XaaS explosion. XaaS is "anything as a service"; it particularly applies to improving business with technologies that improve the way people work.

We mentioned DaaS (data as a service) in the last chapter. AI and analytics *are empowered by services* and in turn power many XaaS services. DaaS means regardless of my location and job function the data the service provides me is commensurate with that location and job function. For example, if I am a sales and marketing person in Germany and I reference a product, the system is smart enough to pull the German version without me having to specify my location or identify a particular database. Using the exact same interface with the exact set of mouse clicks, as an example, a marketing analyst in Texas will be notified that for their role and location that product has been discontinued.

A data scientist will have an entirely different set of capabilities from the same system. They may use the data from DaaS and train an AI model on that data, package that model, and then write it out as an executable web service for business users to run as a service based on their needs. Then the data scientist may monitor the model performance with ModelOps. See the following gray box for more on the "Everything Ops" craze.

"EVERYTHING OPS" CRAZE

XOps has emerged as the umbrella term for defining a combination of IT disciplines, such as DevOps, DataOps, MLOps, GitOps, and BizDevOps. Data scientists and AI developers use these platforms for their AI development and maintenance.

DevOps is a software development approach that allows a team to manage the application development pipeline from development and testing to deployment and monitoring.

BizDevOps, also known as DevOps 2.0, is an approach to software development that encourages developers, operations staff, and business teams to work together so the organization can develop software more quickly, be more responsive to user demand, and ultimately maximize revenue.

DataOps attempts to reduce the cycle time of data analytics projects while improving the quality; it starts right from the beginning of the pipeline and is deployed to various points in the analytics chain and IT operations.

MLOps refers to creating, deploying, and maintaining machine-learning models. It is an umbrella term that involves combining a variety of methods, such as DevOps, machine learning, and handling of data that can simplify and build more efficient ways of deploying machine-learning algorithms. All of this has to be done while keeping the business goals in mind.

GitOps is the practice of managing infrastructure and application systems using Git (open-source version control system).

6.3 Healthcare Leaders

Healthcare covers a broad set of practices from the life sciences and pharmaceuticals to all forms of clinical care—outpatient, emergency, inpatient, post care, long-term care, and hospice. Health insurance is huge in the United States and works hand in hand with the largest healthcare player in the field, the US government, which is pushing an aggressive set of regulations across every aspect of the healthcare enterprise.

Out of all these groups, pharma and biopharma are the largest initiators of taking data into consideration for everything from creating new biologics to streamlining operations to improving the performance of the manufacturing process. Provider organizations are enabling clinicians with AI-assisted mobile devices; these devices provide for AI-assisted care at every point of the patient journey.

6.3.1 Using Regulations and Mandates as a Catalyst for Innovation

Chronic Disease in the United States per the CDC

■ Six in 10 adults have a chronic disease.
■ Four in 10 adults have two or more.

> Source: CDC (see references: www.cdc.gov/chronicdisease/
> resources/infographic/chronic-diseases.htm;
> December 13, 2022, edition of this page)

If you were a healthcare payer in the United States in 2020 you were involved in "meaningful use" requirements. You were responsible for implementing the CMS (Centers for Medicare & Medicaid Services) payer mandate. Many payers viewed this as additional work and expense with more government requirements. However, one solution provider created a way to look at this requirement as an opportunity for payers to use as a path to drive innovation and be part of their value-based care initiatives.

CMS has been pushing interoperability standards for several years. A standard that has broad use and global acceptance is HL7® FHIR® standard (pronounced FIRE, Fast Healthcare Interoperability Resource). What this standard enables is a common data model that users must adhere to when applying the standard so that data is consistent and coherent to a specified definition.

Thinking of the mandate as an opportunity, a large enterprise solution provider created a solution that would leverage HL7® FHIR® as well as other APIs, such as data virtualization, data science, and visual BI platforms. Bringing all this technology together is extremely powerful. The problem they took on was asthma, specifically predicting acute asthma events. Everyone knows someone that has been affected by asthma. It is the #1 chronic condition among children and the #1 cause of school absenteeism among children (>13 million total missed days of school/year). It is a major reason for emergency room visits—one out of four are due to asthma, folks that is 1.75 million a year. It is estimated to cost $82 billion in the United States; and something most of us are probably not aware of, 10 people die from asthma every day in the United States.

If you can reduce 10% of any of those statistics, it means more kids making it to school each day with a cost savings of $8.2 billion per year! It means 200,000 fewer ER visits!

Predicting the likelihood of an acute asthma event (attack) is a very interesting problem because the triggers of asthma are largely due to environmental and social factors. Most of the related data are not held in clinical systems—it is ancillary, environmental, and "disparate" data. This goes well beyond the traditional thinking of clinical researchers who are used to pulling data from charts and medical records. But with HL7® FHIR®, additional APIs, and data virtualization all of this is possible. The solution sources data from weather, air quality, health and demographic surveys, and more. Figure 6.5 is a graphic flow of the base system, but this system can be expanded to consider other data sources.

The system uses public and private APIs. FHIR is used to source EMR data to a FHIR server, which is used to serve the data into a data mesh. At the same time APIs are used to gather information from public APIs for weather and air quality, calendar events, pollen count, and more. Additionally, APIs serve up self-reported data and social determinants of health data into the centralized data mesh. This data is used to train AI and ML models, which are then pushed back into the data mesh to run in production. Every day the mesh creates messaging and event services for case managers via visual BI interfaces, patient's smart phone SMS messaging, and emergency departments via email so that all these parties can take appropriate action on the likelihood of critical asthma events. For patients having the greatest risk,

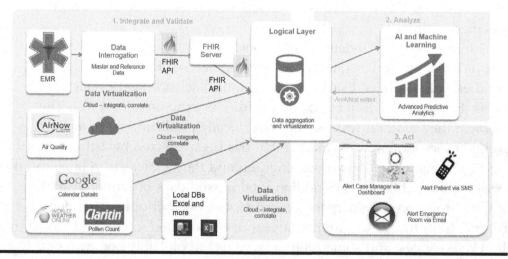

Figure 6.5 Architecture for data flow, AI, and action for critical asthma events.

case managers can contact those patients and help schedule local physician appointments to prevent a more severe outcome. Lower triaged patients can see that they are at a certain risk and take the appropriate measures. Emergency room managers can see expected numbers that might present to the ER and take the appropriate actions on managing staff and resources.

This solution turns HL7® FHIR® + API data into insights that drive down healthcare costs. Once all the data is aggregated, AI developers create predictive models for acute events of asthma that might make a student or employee miss school or work—and forms actions in three ways. The models are fed back in the enterprise systems to:

1. Create visual dashboards for care or case managers
2. Forecast patients coming into ERs to determine staff and resource needs
3. Alert patents via apps or SMS texts

We live in a time of uncertainty. It is not the event itself that keeps us from living our normal lives, but the uncertainty, the likelihood of the event that paralyzes us to fall back and live lesser lives. With predictive and prescriptive analytics, we can live a more fulfilled human experience.

MOBILE HEALTHCARE IN THE PALM OF YOUR HAND

A persisting challenge in healthcare is the fractured nature of personal medical and related information that impacts an individual's health. There are clinic visits to primary providers, clinic visits to specialists, and visits to diagnostics labs, pharmacies, and hospitals. These are parts of the patient journey. Then there are social determinants of health, such as age, sex, education, social support, economic stability, health coverage, and community. There are environmental determinants of health, such as air quality, water quality, sanitation, weather, and climate. With so many factors affecting health it has been a huge challenge to access all the relevant data for actionable medical analytics that will lead to improved care, reduced cost of care, and assured equality in care.

Getting multiple systems to communicate and share information has been a challenge in medical services. It has been a long-term challenge. Interoperability is the ability of computer systems or software to exchange and make use of information. Interoperability has the potential to improve the quality-of-care delivery, improve outcomes, improve operational efficiencies, and reduce costs. Therefore, there have been significant efforts in improving interoperability by many regulatory bodies across the globe. In the United States, the Center for Medicare and Medicaid Services (CMS) sets standards that dictate the practices of the industry.

CMS has been pushing interoperability standards for several years. One standard that has a broad use and global acceptance is the HL7® FHIR® standard. What this standard enables is a common data model that users must adhere to when applying the standard so that the data is consistent and coherent to a specified definition. It allows people to opt into applications so that they can access related medical information. FHIR is an application program interface (API)–based standard, which is what mobile apps and services such as Google Maps, airline ticket search engines, and Yelp are based on. With FHIR, users can access both patient and payment data. New policies (see

www.cms.gov/newsroom/fact-sheets/interoperability-and-patient-access-fact-sheet;

www.cms.gov/Regulations-and-Guidance/Guidance/Interoperability/index#CMS-Interoperability-and-Prior-Authorization-Proposed-Rule) include:

Patient access API
Provider directory API
Payer-to-payer data exchange
Public reporting and information blocking
Prior authorization process improvement

Beth Spears and I (Scott) spoke about how FHIR is enabling patients, providers, payers, researchers, and other industry participants to access and share data more easily and efficiently. Beth said, "It's mobile healthcare in the palm of your hand." That is what this technology offers. You can use apps to book appointments securely. You can look at provider ratings and profiles to determine if this is the right physician for you. You can have all your medical records in one location and accessible, literally, at your fingertips. It is FHIR in the background that is enabling all of this. All API calls. Beth explained the modern technology being used by the industry:

It's all API calls, back and forth using FHIR as the standard. There is no way you could easily exchange and access medical records up until now with the numerous legacy technology and standards used in the industry. It is just like ordering from Amazon, getting directions from Google Maps, or making reservations on Yelp. Now you can manage your healthcare needs just the same, thanks to FHIR! Without FHIR, you could not do that.

FHIR will also enable AI and analytics to improve the quality of care and the efficiency of delivery by sourcing data for advanced analytics, including natural language processing (NLP), prediction of diseases, and outcomes. And, in the end, it could prescribe the most effective treatment or action to be taken.

6.4 Manufacturing Leaders

Manufacturers have had many challenges over the last several years. Things like "just in time inventory," which pushed them to carry near-zero amounts of inventory crippled them when COVID hit because supply lines came to a grind and they did not have raw materials or in-process materials to manufacture. Scenario planning is something that leaders are doing in this space to assess various risk components. They use a combination of historical data combined with human intelligence to formulate simulation models that show upside and downside risks on the impact of their strategic objective planning for the upcoming year. Some other challenges that manufacturers face are:

■ Proliferation of products: more options, shorter life cycles, more complex products
■ Agile, flexible operations
■ Easy accommodation of mixed shifts and new products
■ Investment in quality and reliability
■ Increase productivity, reduce cycle times and costs
■ Maximize value obtained from factory equipment
■ Global market, competition, and supply chains

6.4.1 Smarter Identification of Defects with Text Analytics

A large, global, automotive aftermarket manufacturer needed to better identify problems reported by dealerships on their auto parts. Their three major clients were Chrysler, Ford, and GM. The automotive aftermarket is the secondary market of the automotive industry, concerned with the manufacturing, remanufacturing, distribution, retailing, and installation of all vehicle parts, chemicals, equipment, and accessories after the sale of the automobile by the original equipment manufacturer (OEM) to the consumer.

One of the greatest expenses for this company is manufacturing defects and warranty coverage. If customers are experiencing problems, they bring their cars into the dealerships for service. A technician takes information and if a part is under warranty the technician makes a claim to the manufacturer. Because there are so many things that can go wrong and claims by customers are often ambiguous, much of the claim is categorized and free text.

Suppose there is a problem with a door. A customer can come in and make a complaint. When the technician fills out the claim he may create a category that is ambiguous and likely nonexclusive. Examples are noise, noisy, popping noise, popping/clunking noise, rattle, replace, replaced, debris, and others. Then there are notes for free text identification of the problem. To further complicate the problem, the European market often receives claims in multiple languages, such as English, French, Spanish, and some Portuguese.

Efficient and effective defect identification is critical to get back to the plants that manufacture the parts. Sending defective doors back by themselves does not provide sufficient information to diagnose the problem. It is how the part is performing inside the car that causes claims. And to understand this, they need to understand the information inside the claim. If the manufacturer cannot identify the specific issue then there are no adjustments made in the manufacturing line and it continues to produce problem components.

The company decided to use text analytics to automate and facilitate better working methods of the process. By using automated methods, the service technician's notes could be utilized and processed across the thousands of claims. These findings were moved upstream in the manufacturing process.

The Process Simplified

1. The company uses their client's web portal to download their claim data. Each client, Ford, Chrysler, and GM, has their own portal and format.
2. This data is downloaded, appended with other pertinent data, and loaded into a database.

3. Each claim is run across an AI language classification model to determine the language.
4. Each claim is then run across an AI defect classification model to determine the defect. Claims that do not achieve a sufficient matching probability are written off to a special database. It is these claims that fall out that are often the most informative.
5. The QA (quality assurance) department assesses the information via their BI platform.

6.5 Retail Leaders

Retailers that have achieved a leadership level in analytics maturity are embracing AI and analytics across many of their initiatives. My good friend, Xingchu Liu, is the chief data and analytics officer at Macy's, a retail leader. Xingchu also leads the innovation lab at Black Locus, the retail innovation lab for Home Depot, and he sits on numerous retail advisory boards at Northwestern University, Texas A&M, and Southern Methodist University. To put it another way, Xingchu knows a lot about retail innovation, and it was great to get his insights. He said the three major challenges as he sees it are:

1. Assortment-related challenges
2. Right value proposition
3. Right time, right location, right delivery

6.5.1 Assortment

Xinghu said that data and analytics have greatly changed the way retailers are approaching assortment. Early in his tenure leading the innovation lab for Home Depot, everything was more focused on branding, and you had groups of analysts that would collect various information about suppliers to determine which brands you would have as national brands, private brands, exclusive brands, or white label. This was very labor oriented, as humans had to collect and analyze the data.

Now with social media, Google Search/ Pay, and external sellers of information, everything has changed. Much of the data captured is immediate and machine driven with minimal labor. The analysis is also greatly automated or

"There has been a mind shift in this space. Heavily on science, less on art."
—Xingchu Liu

assisted by power AI and analytic tools. He said: "There has been a mind shift in this space. Heavily on science, less on art."

6.5.2 Right Value Proposition

A value proposition should clearly explain how a product fills a need, communicate the specifics of its added benefit, and state the reason why it's better than similar products on the market. The ideal value proposition is to the point and appeals to a customer's strongest decision-making drivers. This still requires art, but data is helping tremendously. With real-time data and near-real-time data, retailers can be more agile in their approach. With market testing and some tried-and-true, data-driven approaches, they can separate themselves from the competition.

VALUE PROPOSITION OF TWO INNOVATIVE RETAILERS

Xingchu mentioned two emerging retailers with interesting value propositions. These are unique and time will tell if they are worthwhile.

Shein (a global retailer) provides value to its customers by its recognition and reputation, as the company is a leading brand established in China and now is consistently growing internationally. The company also offers its customers trendy and fashionable products at low cost and sometimes offers additional discounts.

Stitch Fix (a global retailer) offers four primary value propositions: customization, convenience, pricing, and brand/status. The company enables customization. Clients use its service by filling out an online survey specifying their size, style, and price preferences.

6.5.3 Right Time/Location/Delivery

This may be the most mature area for leaders. For non-store purchases, Amazon has set the bar for delivery. COVID amplified this need for home deliveries, which drove much more volume, and competition forced the market to excel or die; other retailers, like Walmart, Home Depot, Lowe's, Macy's, and many others were forced to start home deliveries if they had not done so previously. Geolocation analytics have greatly improved over the past few years. Package delivery companies and internal logistics for companies today would not have been conceivable 10–15 years ago.

Shein, mentioned in the previous gray box, is an innovative retailer and is using an AI program that matches local demand at scale. PSFK, an innovation consulting and research services firm, says, "AI engines can quickly pick up a change in demand or interest in new trends, and its supply chain can react in real-time, giving consumers more value and the brand much cheaper operating costs."

For brick-and-mortar stores it has been more challenging. For a time it appeared the days of brick and mortar were over, but now there has been a revitalization for brick and mortar. In today's retail world, you have to offer both. That makes the problem more difficult, and leaders are using data to solve that challenge.

6.6 Energy Leaders

Currently, much of the energy focus is on renewable energy. However, most of the global energy production is still based on fossil fuels. Power generation from coal and natural gas, fuel, and manufacturing components from oil, are still the largest sources of energy and power. Oil and gas companies feel a great deal of pressure and uncertainty. These companies have great pressure to explore new energy sources, while at the same time realizing there will always be a need for these materials, if only in manufacturing. However, with regulation, traditional long-term investments are uncertain. No one wants to invest over a long-time horizon when rapid changes in policies could terminate any return on this investment.

Therefore, we continue to see energy leaders invest in data-driven techniques to discover new methods and make old methods more efficient.

6.6.1 Global Top Five Oil Producer Manages Equipment with Text Analytics

A global top five oil producer had terabytes of equipment information across thousands of documents generating more than 50 TB (terabytes) in a central location. There were hundreds of documents for each piece of equipment. These documents contained text as well as engineering diagrams, risk assessments, project plans, and environmental plans. There was no way to effectively search this information.

The company entered a proof of concept (PoC) plan with a technology company; they developed the following goals:

■ Allow searches for a *<specified name>* equipment item that produces a list of all documents containing information on that item and make that list "clickable" to the source document. Moreover, there would be context information provided for each item.

■ Allow for searches like "list of all the pumps we have that are over ten years old," "list of how many pumps (or which) have pumped more than <specified> barrels in the past year," and similar searches.

■ Provide all this information in a knowledge graph via a graph database.

The PoC was completed in two weeks using a new technology called Textual ETL. The results demonstrated the capabilities of Textual ETL. A nexus of 2,700 documents were incorporated, a graph database was constructed with 7.5 million nodes, with additional metadata containing 22,000 labels. The customer is in the evaluation process at the time of this writing.

6.7 Financial Services and Insurance Leaders

Financial service and insurance companies share some common business challenges. Using data with various AI and analytics methods can help these companies reduce risk, maximize revenue, and decrease costs. One of the major categories both industries face is reducing risk.

Two subcategories of reducing risk are payment risk and fraud. Banks and financial service companies face non-repayment risks on various types of loans. Insurance companies face the payment risk of having to make unexpected or excessive payments on customer claims under existing policies. Another subcategory of risk that both industries face is the risk of fraud. In this section we will examine the use of text analytics, an extension of NLP, to reduce the financial risk of fraud for a major insurance holding company.

Another major category both industries face is streamlining operations and reducing administrative costs. Banks and insurers typically have large labor costs. These industries have been slowly transforming their workflows and services to be more digitally enabled and more automated, but there is still a lot of opportunity for improvement. AI and analytics can help in this next wave of automation.

Claims processing for insurers is a major expense, insurers are using analytic techniques to auto process (auto adjudicate) claims to reduce the amount of human intervention, but labor costs remain a challenge. Banks have streamlined their operations as well and have pushed customers to do more self-service online, but this has opened up risk of customer dissatisfaction and fraud risk as well. While our example in this section was selected to reduce fraud, it also reduced the labor costs.

6.7.1 Insurance Holding Company Reduces Fraud Risk and Improves Operations with Text Mining (Analytics)

A large US-based insurance company, with over $2 billion in annual revenue, is using AI and analytics to reduce the cost of fraud and labor. The company provides property and casualty insurance products and services, alternative risk-management products, and related services to businesses and individuals, and administers flood insurance policies. This company offers policies in almost 30 states.

Fraud is common and costly for the insurance industry. According to the Federal Bureau of Investigation (FBI), insurance fraud is the second most costly white-collar crime in America and accounts for more than $40 billion in losses every year (www.fbi.gov/stats-services/publications/insurance-fraud). The Coalition Against Insurance Fraud's estimates are much higher (https://insurancefraud.org), and the organization states that fraud occurs in about 10% of property-casualty insurance losses.

Insurance companies have SIU (Special Investigation Unit) groups as part of their claims departments. When a claim is flagged as suspicious the claim is sent to this group for a manual review. These manual reviews can be very expensive to conduct, because a lot of human/labor time is involved. Before the company undertook its advanced analytics program there were two primary methods for a claim to be flagged:

1. A rule-based process based upon heuristics. These rules were created by humans and determined to be "rules of thumb." The data run against these rules was structured data from the company's relational data warehouse. These conditional rules were very simple and involved a series of if-then statements. This was an overnight batch process where incoming claims that had entered the data warehouse were run against the IT logic. If a claim was a match it was forwarded to the SIU for further investigation.

2. Secondly, very small samples of claims were manually selected outside the heuristic rules-based process. These reviews were expensive, but often performed as well as the rule-based system, which indicated that the rules were not very effective in finding claims that were fraudulent.

It was this lack of utility identified in #2 that initiated an investigation of alternative methods. If an analytic method could be used to improve the number of claims of even 10% that were truly fraudulent sent to the SIU, the company could save millions. So, an "Automated Fraud Referral" project PoC was funded. The goal would be to:

1. Increase the number of true, fraudulent claims that are found by the process
2. Decrease the proportion of claims that SIU investigates that are not fraudulent
3. Automate the feedback loop to determine true fraud reporting and false positives of suspected fraud
4. Provide visual analytics for all SIU staff to automate the workflow process

6.7.1.1 The Pilot

The initial proof of concept was conducted by building a predictive model based on all available data, especially unstructured data. Important parts of the claim information are notes and ancillary text (this is considered unstructured data). This data was not present in the company's data warehouse. As stated in the introduction to this chapter, 90% of business decisions are made on 10% of the data. The claims department knew that most of the important information that could be used to determine a claim as fraudulent was in these claim notes and text. Therefore, it wanted to create a predictive model that would categorize the likelihood of fraud with all the data available, i.e., the data warehouse and the textual data.

The project would focus on internal model creation and automated ways of referring cases for investigation. A brief overview of the work performed includes:

1. Extraction of notes and ancillary text into a database with certain relevant claim identifiers and metadata included. This would allow for joining the information to the data warehouse and using all data for feature

extraction. Simply put, feature extraction is drawing out all of the useful information from a data column that can be used in a predictive model.

2. Predictive models were created, tested, and validated.
3. Two predictive models were placed into production.
4. A feedback loop was created to mark successful identification of claim fraud, i.e., "true positives," as well as unsuccessful identification, i.e., "false positives."
5. The pilot was considered a success.
6. Continual learning, refinement, and expansion ensued.

6.7.1.2 Results after Two Years

A project study was undertaken on the work and results:

1. The fraud modeling project paid for itself while in development.
2. After two years the project's ROI was estimated between 350% and 500%.
3. Claims referred by the modeling project have an economic impact that averages about 35+% larger than claim handler referral.
4. At current rates, the automated fraud referral project has increased SIU cost avoidance by 35–50%.
5. There are over 40 predictive models in production today. These models include various fraud/risk models as well as being a component in the real-time pricing of some business insurance policies.

RISK MANAGEMENT AND FINTECH—MANAGING FRICTION

Online payments are the lifeblood of modern businesses. Financial technology companies that operate as online payments systems support online money transfers and serve as an electronic alternative to traditional paper methods, such as checks and money orders. They also operate as a payment processor for online vendors, auction sites, and many other commercial users, for which they charge a fee.

These companies must manage several forms of risk. They must stop fraud before it starts with effective authentication. They must effectively prevent fraud without loss of revenue. They must minimize chargebacks and meet all regulatory requirements. To do this there are massive amounts of data flowing through their systems, and they must develop platforms that are lightning quick and intelligent at the same time.

During my conversation with my friend Joe Toner (we worked together at Ebay/PayPal), he mentioned an interesting balancing act that fintech companies must constantly address—a great customer experience balanced with financial risk for the payment platform. And I love the way Joe put it—"you have to manage the friction."

He meant the more controls you put into managing risks for fraudulent transactions, the more likely you are to frustrate a customer by slowing down the payment app or you could be denying a transaction. Worse, you could be shutting down a business because of suspected fraud. All these actions reduce risk to the online payment processor by lowering the probability of fraud or chargebacks. However, they reduce the customer satisfaction with the payment app. Preferred payment systems allow customers to buy and transact personal or business transactions easily and securely. They manage the friction.

6.8 Other Leaders

There are many other leaders in the public and private sectors. Government organizations are often slow adopters of new technologies. However, some state government organizations are moving forward with ambitious data initiatives, like the state of Texas. Ed Kelly, retired chief data officer, is now working with the state as a consultant moving new programs forward. Ed shared with me the Texas Open Data Portal where the public can see data-related initiatives and access data resources. The public can also view the Texas Department of Information Resources's yearly strategic plans through 2026.

HUMANS AND MACHINES WORKING TOGETHER TO EXTRACT INFORMATION FROM TEXT

Thomson Reuters is a Canadian multinational media conglomerate. One billion people worldwide read or see Reuters news every day. Their Reuters business provides trusted business, financial, national, and international news to professionals through Thomson Reuters desktops, the world's media organizations, and directly to consumers via reuters.com and Reuters TV.

Eighty percent of the world's data is unstructured. Extracting information from unstructured data is much more difficult than extracting it from structured data. That is the reason Thompson Reuters Labs was created—to bring together sharp minds of AI-focused engineers, research and data scientists, and designers to make sense of huge volumes of data.

> "Providing legal, tax, accounting and compliance professionals with the tools and information they need to empower people and decision-making, that will shape tomorrow." —Thompson Reuters website

During a call with my friend Josh Lemaitre, we talked about how Josh became a founding member of Thomson Reuters Labs and about some of the things the lab is doing in AI and analytics.

Josh said it was all about text in some shape or form; scanned PDFs that are converted into machine text with OCR (optical character recognition) or XML documents. They build meta layers from this raw data. His team utilizes techniques of auto completion, text summarization, tagging, and entity creation. These entities can be expressed in knowledge graphs and each entity reduced down. This provides great cost savings for editors and improves quality, precision, and accuracy.

Validation of models requires machine algorithm side-by-side human testing. Sometimes the machine algorithm is useful, sometimes it is not. Potentially, the algorithm is good enough to deploy in a semi-automated fashion with some human oversight. At other times, the machine algorithm provides minimal support and humans are still required to do most of the work.

In some domains, the text is more nuanced and difficult to work with than other domains. For example, legal text is very subjective and requires a ranking algorithm, entity match, or text classification. Text summarization is another task that machines are quite adept with, at least for a first pass. However, humans are always required for validation and testing and annotating the text. This requires knowledge of statistical techniques beyond machine learning, like interrater scores and interrater reliability analysis.

Some AI algorithms can be deployed to production systems and run automatically. However, many applications require human insight or human oversight. We speak about this in Chapter 9, "Human Out of the Loop Analytics!—A Major, Uncomfortable Step."

6.9 Challenges from Moving Leaders to Innovators

Most leaders will not move on to become innovators. The move to the next level is quite steep, and the rewards must justify the additional energy and expense. To be an innovator requires hiring and retaining some of the brightest minds in the AI and analytics industry. We will see in the next chapter, our final stage of the maturity spectrum, that very few make it to this stage.

References

Burk, S., & Miner, G. D. (2022). *The executive's guide to AI and analytics: The foundations of execution and success in the new world*. Productivity Press.
CDC. (2022, December 13). www.cdc.gov/chronicdisease/resources/infographic/chronic-diseases.htm

Chapter 7

The Innovators

> *"Creativity is thinking up new things. Innovation is doing new things."*
>
> *—Theodore Levitt*

> *"Innovation distinguishes between a leader and a follower."*
>
> *—Steve Jobs*

7.1 Introduction

We now reach the final stage of the data and analytics maturity spectrum. Innovators are a small group of organizations or pockets within an organization. To be a true innovator means you are approaching problems in new ways that have not been undertaken previously. Often what innovators do, fails. What does not fail may become mainstream to leaders over time. These innovations are done by internal development as they have not been productized in any real fashion. Therefore, with time and success they become the target methods for commercial products.

Innovators are typically agile and adapt quickly to success and failure. They characterize what Safi Bahcall called artists (see Chapter 6, Section 6.2.1.1): "Artists embrace risk—they want to be on the edge, push the envelope, and develop something radically new."

If an entire organization is an innovator, it typically is a small organization because of the adaptation requirements. It could also be part of a large

DOI: 10.4324/9780429343971-7

organization, such as an innovation lab for a major tech company. These labs are measured by much different criteria than established business functions. They are not only allowed to fail at projects but are encouraged to attempt things that will likely be failures knowing that the upside payoff for a truly revolutionary success may be highly significant.

> "There is no innovation and creativity without failure. Period." —Brene Brown

In this chapter, we try to inspire thinking about some of the innovative ideas that have surfaced over the last several years. These may no longer be as cutting edge as they were just a few years ago. We will not get a glimpse of what is truly revolutionary today until the passage of time. We will not make distinctions between an organizational innovator and a departmental innovator.

7.2 Some Characteristics of Innovators

Innovators exhibit all the same characteristics as leaders with respect to strategy development. They are the top spenders for AI and analytics programs. They invest in formal education programs for staff, managers, and executives, including paying for tuition. They also have associations with academic centers that are doing research and development of next-generation data technologies. They hire from the top-tier data science and computer science universities' programs.

They spend a significant portion of their budget on technology as well. They focus on creating an infrastructure that is elastic and rapidly scalable. They have corporate preferred technology but allow for learning and innovation with new tools as well in order to stay open minded to emerging technologies and providers. This allows for quicker innovation and job satisfaction for data engineers, data scientists, analysts, and developers.

These organizations may have progressed through all the previous levels, and those that have gone through all the levels typically have been applying data-driven techniques for decades. Or, they may have leap frogged into a higher level, or may have been chartered as technology disruptors. They have

> "Relative advantage is the degree to which an innovation is perceived as better than the idea it supersedes." —Everett M. Rogers, *Diffusion of Innovations*

distributed in-memory computing like SPARC clusters. And these are large clusters used to train complex AI models via deep learning, a form of advanced neural networks. These SPARC clusters may have thousands of nodes.

Innovators are developing new methods and applications; therefore, they are not using established commercial data science platforms. They are likely using cloud-based open-source platforms as a foundation, but only using a portion of the libraries for AI and ML. They are using Kubernetes and containerization of AI assets. In the next section, we discuss some interesting things that innovators are doing differently.

USING DATA TO BRING BACK THE WOOLY MAMMOTH

I had no idea where my conversation with Joe Nipko, PhD, would lead. Joe and I worked together in a pricing science group. There were about a dozen people with all kinds of backgrounds, all quantitative. These backgrounds included operation research, industrial engineering, statistics, computer engineering, computer science, econometricians, and Joe was a trained physicist. I remember listening to NPR on the way in and there were a couple of times I would have questions for Joe on quantum mechanics or space and he never disappointed. After working for EY (Ernst & Young) and in traditional business, Joe has made a major career change.

He joined the @Form Bio team as the head of AI/ML. He told me that he had been contacted by them and they asked him if he wanted to be part of the team that was bringing back the Wooly Mammoth. No joke. It sounded straight from *Jurassic Park*, but it is real. It is serious. It is AI/ deep learning applied to biology. It requires highly computational infrastructure and very sharp scientific minds.

The process is called "de-extinction," and it is distinct from cloning. There is no living cell from the extinct animal to start the process. So they look for the closest living relative to serve as a host for bringing back the extinct species. They have to use AI to build the genetic sequencing. They are serious about the Wooly Mammoth and have announced their second project, the Tasmanian tiger.

Wow!!!

https://colossal.com/news/

7.3 Hot Topics of Innovators

7.3.1 ChatGPT

ChatGPT, developed by OpenAI, is one of the latest rages in AI. It holds the possibility of fundamentally changing peoples' professional work and personal lives. Many say it could make existing web search engines like Google, Bing, Yahoo!, and DuckDuckGo obsolete. It is a family of large language models and is fine-tuned with both supervised and AI reinforcement learning techniques. When released in November 2022 there was immediately a large buzz created in the AI field and news went viral.

Wow!!!!!!!

On LinkedIn, authors were showing how ChatGPT could create code in programming languages like R and Python with no outside interference. And it was not just any code, it was well-constructed code. A famous AI and ML podcaster, Sam Charrington (the *TWIML AI Podcast*, formerly *This Week in Machine Learning & Artificial Intelligence*) interviewed ChatGPT on his show. Yes, he interviewed a machine on his show. They discussed the background and capabilities of large language models, the potential applications of these models, and some of the technical challenges and open questions in the field (https://twimlai.com/go/603).

In a follow-up, Sam outdid himself. He set up ChatGPT as an interviewer and had it interview a second ChatGPT as a guest. Yes, the machine actually came up with its own questions as a host and the questions were answered by a second ChatGPT just as if it were any other guest. And the host adapted to its responses. Sam titled this episode "Will ChatGPT take my job?" since he is a podcast host (https://twimlai.com/go/608).

The program uses an algorithm that selects words based on lessons learned from scanning billions of pieces of text across the internet, according to InApp (https://inapp.com/blog/what-is-chatgpt-and-here-are-7-ways-to-use-chatgpt-to-your-benefit/). Here are some ways ChatGPT can improve your professional life:

1. **Generate texts**. Useful for writers, marketers, and other professionals.
2. **Answer questions**. Valuable tool for businesses and organizations that want to offer better customer service or support.
3. **Improving machine-learning systems**. This can help machine-learning systems to better understand and respond to human language and to make more accurate predictions.

4. **Improving natural language processing.** This can help NLP systems to better understand and respond to human language.

And your personal life:

1. Use it as a brainstorming tool
2. Automate repetitive tasks
3. Use it as a writing prompt
4. Use it as a personal assistant
5. Use it as a research tool

7.3.2 TinyML

TinyML is the next evolution of the Internet of Things (IoT) or Industrial Internet of Things (IIoT). As the world became full of sensors, cameras, and automated delivery of data from edge devices, data scientists and engineers have been working on creating value from that data. Now enter TinyML. TinyML is one of the hottest trends in the embedded computing field right now, with 2.5 billion TinyML-enabled devices estimated to reach the market in the next decade and a projected market value exceeding $70 billion in just five years.

"We see a new world with trillions of intelligent devices enabled by TinyML technologies that sense, analyze, and autonomously act together to create a healthier and more sustainable environment for all." — Evgeni Gousev

This is a field of machine learning that focuses on the development and deployment of ML models on low-power, low-footprint, microcontroller devices. The microcontrollers that TinyML models are designed for are small and power efficient, capable of running on battery power for years at a time.

At the same time, TinyML is a subset of what is known as edge AI. TinyML is similar to edge AI, but TinyML takes edge AI one step further, making it possible to run machine-learning models on the smallest microcontrollers.

TinyML software is typically ultra-low power; these applications run on a physical hardware device. There are many machine-learning algorithms that are used, but the trend is that deep learning is becoming more and more popular. People that develop TinyML applications are normally data scientists, machine-learning engineers, or embedded developers. Normally the models are developed and trained in a cloud system.

There is a TinyML framework. It is a software platform that makes it easier for developers to develop TinyML applications. It leverages the advantages of edge computing—computing in the local space as opposed to in the cloud, to deliver several key advantages, namely:

- Low latency of local compute for real-time applications
- Reduced bandwidth costs from lower requirements for remote communication
- Excellent reliability that persists even when network connectivity is lost
- Improved security with fewer transmissions and local data storage

7.3.3 Geospatial Machine-Learning Satellite

We have mentioned varying aspects of geospatial, geoanalytics, and mapping. However, geospatial machine learning is getting a new reinvigoration. This new emphasis has much to do with satellite technology; this includes both the types and quantities of satellites available. This new emphasis also takes advantage of the remarkable increase in image resolution and types of sensors being employed on satellites these days. According to Kumar Chellapilla:

> To get a sense of the scale of this, it's not even a linear scale but this is exponential. Just two years ago the number of satellites in the sky that were doing things like capturing imagery, whether it be hyperspectral or even visible imagery off the surface of the earth, was just less than 1000. Now this year (2023) or early next year it'll hit 10 thousand. In another ten years it'll be 100,000 satellites. Their multi-purpose cameras are getting so good that within two years the cameras on the satellite go obsolete. So companies are not even trying to keep them up there, it is OK if they are put in low-orbits and crash down within a few years. And the satellites are like little shoe boxes, they're not these monsters that they used to send out that cost millions of dollars, now they cost 10s of thousands. Or maybe $100,000 to get a little satellite up there and in two years it is ready to come down and when it won't even hit the ground it is just going to burn out in the atmosphere. So you have this capability of sensors everywhere right on the Internet. We talk about the IoT revolution but it is happening even in space.

That is just the number of satellites going up, which is enabling millions of more images available for all sorts of ML applications, such as computer vision, computer simulation, customer location data, point of interest data, and so much more. Then you get the image sizes and resolution improvement on top of that, Kumar continues:

> You won't believe that the scale of data is so large that if somebody wants to work with California data, just all of California, all of a sudden it's like a 10 GB to 10 terabyte image. I can work with four megabytes or five megabytes; on my iPhone pictures are a few megabytes and I can work with that. But a 10TB image? State of the art right now is like 20 megapixels. But, now we are talking about 20 gigapixel to 20 terapixel images and we're like 'oh but then if it's computer vision you have a deep learning model' and you just scan it all the way across. That is a problem.

7.3.3.1 Finally, the New Sensor Suites Are Special Purpose

There are satellites built just for detecting methane. NASA is going to launch one. They will tell how much methane there is for sustainability purposes. Measuring and sensing is way better than modeling and predicting. There are also many applications for hyperspectral imaging, such as soil vegetation and how plants react differently to visible light versus other spectra. If you want to know about moisture in the soil can detect water versus land or whether soil is dry or what kinds of soil and how much nutrition the soil needs, those kinds of things can be detected with hyperspectral imaging, and so specific-purpose satellites are being built for Agtech.

"I think it is time for a radical federalism in this country, where people trust innovation coming from the local level and ramp that up." —Eric Garcetti

These problems are causing the innovators to think of new ways to scale solutions to solve these problems. Furthermore, the number of startup companies doing satellites is exploding.

7.3.4 Flexible, Scalable, Adaptable Architectures for Data, AI, People

Innovators typically use the largest datasets in the world. These datasets are massive and were unfathomable a few years ago. Now, they are commonplace. But the smartest, most innovative users are being very smart about how to dynamically scale their data, their ML, and their people across time and different projects. They do not want to be locked into a static data model or hardware in a data center. That is the reason these innovators have embraced elastic cloud technologies for data storage, data pipelines, model training, and applications. Furthermore, they flex their people and human resource needs whenever possible.

Smart innovators are very careful to weigh out the short-term versus long-term needs. For example, for human resources, it would be most cost effective to limit the scale to a minimum and use contract and short-term resources as much as possible. But smart innovators know there is no persistence of knowledge by constantly changing out people. The technology is a much easier determination, and most cloud environments allow for quick, dynamic scaling of data volumes and computing needs.

AI INDUSTRY CHALLENGES: BEST-OF-BREED OR END-TO-END SOLUTIONS

When I met with Kjell Carlsson, PhD, we spoke about the current state of AI vendor solutions. The market is in a bit of a flux. Many new entrants are offering features, not platforms. For leaders and innovators this is all they need as they select best-of-breed solutions for problem areas. Innovators typically use this as a jumping off step and build their own features. Leaders have longer cycles but are happy to move on as a new "best" becomes available.

Other AI shops, typically practitioners, desire a full-stack, end-to-end solution where their engineers, modelers, citizen data scientists, and developers use the same platform as a single corporate platform. The entire data pipeline from data acquisition to provisioning to insight discovery to AI model development to model deployment and MLOps is done within one platform. And there are additional AI features. This platform may be best of breed in some of these functions, but we have never seen one as best across all important features.

The business must determine the best solution given its constraints and needs.

7.4 Simulation and Synthetic Data

7.4.1 Simulation

There are still fields where data is not readily available or is extremely expensive to acquire. In these areas simulation and synthetic data can help. Simulation is not a new concept. Statistical simulation has been around for decades, but it is being revisited to deal with problems that need to be solved efficiently and cost effectively.

Simulation is a vital tool for the development and testing of AI systems. It allows developers to create virtual environments in which they can train and evaluate their AI models, without the need for expensive and time-consuming physical experiments. This is especially useful when the environments being simulated are complex, hazardous, or otherwise difficult to access.

In addition to its use in training and testing, simulation is also important for the safe deployment of AI systems. By simulating the behavior of an AI system in a controlled environment, developers can identify and address potential issues before the system is deployed in the real world. This can help to ensure that AI systems operate safely and effectively and can help to build public trust in the technology. Overall, simulation plays a crucial role in the development and deployment of AI systems and is an essential part of the broader AI ecosystem.

7.4.2 Synthetic Data

Synthetic data is artificially generated data that is used to train and evaluate machine-learning models. It has some of the same benefits and intentions as simulation. It is an important tool in the development of AI systems for several reasons.

First, synthetic data can be used to train machine-learning models when real-world data is scarce or difficult to obtain. For example, if a developer is working on an AI system that needs to be able to recognize rare or exotic objects, it may be challenging to find enough real-world data to train the model on. In this case, synthetic data can be used to supplement the real-world data and help the model learn to recognize the desired objects.

Second, synthetic data can be used to test the robustness and generalizability of machine-learning models. By generating a wide range of synthetic data points that cover a variety of different scenarios and edge cases, developers can ensure that their models are able to handle a diverse range of inputs and are not overly reliant on a specific subset of the data. This can help to improve the reliability and performance of AI systems in the real world.

Third, synthetic data can be used to protect sensitive or confidential real-world data. In some cases, it may be necessary to train machine-learning models on data that is sensitive or confidential, such as medical records or financial data. In these situations, synthetic data can be used to preserve the privacy of the real-world data while still allowing the model to be trained and evaluated.

Finally, synthetic data can be used to augment real-world data by adding additional diversity and variability. This can be useful for tasks such as image or language translation, where it is important for the model to be able to handle a wide range of inputs and variations. By generating synthetic data that covers a broad range of scenarios and variations, developers can improve the performance and flexibility of their AI systems.

TEXAS POLICE DEPARTMENT CHALLENGES DATA SCIENTISTS WITH EXPLAINABLE AI

Years before explainable AI was a major concern, a Texas police department challenged data scientists with its core task of a predictive model project. Per IBM:

Explainable artificial intelligence is a set of processes and methods that allows human users to comprehend and trust the results and output created by machine learning algorithms. Explainable AI is used to describe an AI model, its expected impact, and potential biases. It helps characterize model accuracy, fairness, transparency, and outcomes in AI-powered decision making.

This police department had problems with officer turnover. There were a variety of contributing factors, and the police department contracted a consulting firm to discover these factors and build a predictive model so it could be proactive and supportive of officers that might be leaving their force in the near future. The data science team developed a predictive model with high accuracy in just a few days with variables across dimensions, such as incidence reports, firing a weapon while on duty, overtime, sick day's usage, age, tenure, and many more. The consulting team thought they were done, they were successful. And they were, initially. The department could bring people in and intervene, but it quickly became apparent that they needed the ability to tell the person in question why they were suspected of appearing to leave in the short term. Why the intervention was needed.

This was an additional requirement and a requirement the data science team had not encountered previously. The project contract was amended, and the work was started. The interesting discovery was that the explanation of why an individual was identified took four times as long to develop as the creation of the initial predictive model!

It is much easier to determine the likelihood of a future event compared to understanding why it will happen for this unique individual, to understand what are the driving factors that determine the likelihood for this individual case.

7.5 Causal Inference

Causal inference is an extremely important topic in AI and analytics. As more and more ML models are created for various purposes there is an increasing probability these models may not be understood. Causal inference is the process of determining the cause-and-effect relationships between variables. It is an important concept in many fields, including statistics, economics, and AI. In AI, causal inference plays a key role in the development and evaluation of machine-learning models.

One of the main benefits of causal inference in AI is that it allows developers to build more accurate and reliable models. By understanding the underlying causal relationships between and among variables, AI systems can make more informed predictions and decisions. This is especially important in applications where the consequences of incorrect predictions or decisions can be significant, such as in the fields of medicine or finance.

Another benefit of causal inference in AI is that it helps to ensure that machine-learning models are transparent and interpretable. By understanding the causal relationships among variables, it is easier to understand how and why a particular model is making a particular prediction or decision. This is important for building trust in AI systems and ensuring that they are used ethically and responsibly.

Following is a simple example of assuming a predictive model can be used for prescriptive action. Using a model for prescription without understanding the underlying mechanisms of the predictors can lead to erroneous and costly results.

7.5.1 Predictive Models vs Prescriptive Models—They Are Not the Same!

It is amazing how many articles written today describe prescriptive analytics as just a different business case of predictive analytics with no additional requirements from the data side or the modeling side. It is absolutely one of the least understood paradigms out here. You cannot simply use observational data and a machine-learning algorithm and declare it to be a prescriptive model. We have even had conversations with people that know that causation is not correlation but still think there are no requirement differences for answering the question "what is the probability this event will happen?" vs "why did it happen?" or "how can we make it happen?" The following is a very simple example of why (there are many reasons) you cannot take a predictive model and then declare it as a prescriptive model. Consider a simple five-variable model to predict obesity by measuring BMI (body mass index). BMI is a weight-to-height ratio, calculated by dividing one's weight in kilograms by the square of one's height in meters and used as an indicator of obesity and underweight. Suppose we use the following five variables to predict BMI:

1. Gender (male/female)
2. Number of hours per week in the gym or fitness center
3. Amount of diet soda intake per week
4. Age
5. Geographic location (place of current residence)

Those five factors would do a decent job predicting BMI via a machine-learning model, given that we can train the model correctly and with enough data. This model will likely generalize, meaning that it will predict BMI of individuals with future data (given ordinary, common assumptions). Good predictive model—PASS! Now, if you believe the many posts, articles, and misdirections out on the internet and in some books, you can use this model to *prescribe* actions to lower your BMI. No, you cannot relocate someone to Colorado or Hawaii and expect it to have a practical effect. Colorado and Hawaii have lower BMIs on average due to culture and genetics—not geography. Culture and genetics are confounding variables (they relate to location and BMI), and they are more likely to be causal mechanisms; the causal mechanism is NOT geography. Good prescriptive model—fail! This is just one reason a predictive model may not be prescriptive.

This example is simple and straightforward; moving someone from Mississippi to Colorado will not likely change his or her BMI, at least in the near term. It is much more difficult to understand the underlying associative mechanism in medical models; therefore, practitioners must be careful and understand the difference between association and causation.

GENOTYPES, PHENOTYPES, AND CAUSATION VS CORRELATION

I almost titled this vignette, "Two Nerds and an Hour." Elliot Layne and I covered a gamut of AI, ML, statistical, and other topics in less than an hour. Elliot is a doctoral student and is coalescing a great deal of knowledge from his previous studies, previous work experience, and new studies. It provided for a very interesting discussion.

Elliot mentioned that there is much to be understood between genotypes (the actual genetic constitution) and phenotypes (the expression of the genes). Two individuals can have the same genotype, and each express the genes (phenotypes) differently. He is working on this problem to better understand it. This took us into an area that I have a big interest in, causal inference.

This is a highly nonlinear problem, and you can take single-nucleotide polymorphisms (SNPs) and feed them into an algorithm to train a ML model. They may be highly predictive for the expression without being causal of the expression. How? These SNPs are just highly correlated with other SNPs that actually are the causal mechanism for the expression.

We spoke about the confusion of predictive versus prescriptive models and that so many people do not properly understand the requirements for determining causation. We have much more to talk about.

7.6 Healthcare Innovators

According to my friend Joe Nipko, PhD, there are fantastic applications of AI in genomics that will revolutionize the health and sustainability of the world:

7.6.1 Genetic Diagnostics

Advanced AI algorithms can be leveraged to diagnose cancers using cell-free DNA fragments, for example, classify metastatic versus primary prostate cancers from patient molecular data, predict how a certain type of cancer will evolve based on a tumor's spatiotemporal gene expression patterns, profile cardiovascular diseases, and classify inflammatory bowel disease—facilitating not only diagnoses but improving the development and implementation of efficient, patient-centered treatments.

7.6.2 Integrated Genetic-Phenotypic Diagnostics

In parallel, next-generation phenotyping (NGP) technologies have leveraged deep-learning algorithms to collect, structure, and analyze physiological data, including faces, to develop precise genetic diagnoses and shed light on actionable clinical insights. AI-facilitated genotype- and phenotype-informed identification provides a comprehensive snapshot of unique clinical cases—with syndromic genetic conditions affecting 8% of the population, the benefits are invaluable.

www.nature.com/articles/s41591-018-0279-0
https://pubmed.ncbi.nlm.nih.gov/30617323/

7.6.3 Drug Discovery and Development

One of the reasons the cost of drug development has grown so much despite massive efficiency improvements is the reliance on reductionist models, especially for very complex diseases. Unrivaled in its power to match up to the complexity of the path mechanism of disease, AI, however, can be leveraged to discover drugs specifically tailored to individuals' genetic backgrounds—buoying the development of next-generation individualized therapies and ushering in the new era of precision medicine.

7.6.4 RNA Therapies

Meanwhile, an estimated 100 petabytes of data have been generated related specifically to RNA—the biological workflow of which is particularly well understood (including RNA splicing, polyadenylation, and microRNA targeting).

7.6.5 Infectious Disease Profiling, Epidemiology, and Therapeutics

AI applications to infectious disease have further shed light on pathogen genome sequences, epidemiological dynamics, drug-development strategies, and vaccine discovery. Of tangible benefit in the context of the COVID-19 pandemic, thousands of manuscripts have been published combining ML and sequencing data, such as specifically to uncover SARS-CoV-2's evolutionary origins, design antibodies, or probe host cellular responses.

7.6.6 Agricultural Biology

In parallel, AI methods for plant genomics and phenomics have galvanized the next-generation plant-breeding revolution—from helping to pinpoint the genetic bases of key traits to identifying microRNAs associated with stress-related conditions.

7.6.7 Conservation

The computational capacity of deep-learning models have been critical to advancing a panoply of conservation efforts. First, ML is helping predict how poorly adapted a given genetic strain of species would be to a certain set of environmental conditions (anthropogenic or not) by combining known genetic and environmental information. Second, ML is advancing species engineering and de-extinction efforts in particular—harnessing its computational prowess to fill gaps in the genomes being reconstructed from often highly degraded and fragmented remains of ancient DNA.

7.6.7.1 Medical Innovators Using AI and Sound for Better Care and Outcomes

7.6.7.1.1 AI and Medical Devices Improve Care Outcomes, Patient Satisfaction, and Efficiency of Care

Healthcare is interesting. Many functions are far behind most industries in quality and efficiency. However, there are impressive innovations coming on the clinical side of medicine. I have had the pleasure of working with several people at the University of Iowa Health Care (UIHC). UIHC is one of the nation's leading academic medical centers and is affiliated with many clinics and hospitals. One of the most innovative physicians I have met is Dr. John

Cromwell, Associate Chief Medical Officer and Director of Surgical Quality and Safety. He is also an entrepreneur who is engaged in three companies that are changing the way medicine is practiced.

He led the development of an AI/ML platform that reduced the incidence of surgical site infection (SSI) and readmission rates for surgical cases early in the advent of AI for predictive analytics in medicine. SSIs are the leading and most expensive cause of hospital-acquired infections, increasing the cost of an encounter by greater than $20,000. AI systems present an opportunity to markedly reduce these costly infections. Dr. Cromwell's company, DASH Analytics (www.dashpredict.com), provides real-time decision support in the operating room, which allows surgeons to change the wound-management strategy based upon objective risk-stratification data personalized to the patient on the operating room table. Use of this system at UIHC reduced SSI in the target population by 58–74%. This system is not static, but constantly re-calibrating to changes in patient populations, surgical selection criteria, the procedures being performed, and the hospital environment. Active use of the SSI module would be expected to drive down direct costs of care and readmissions while improving patient satisfaction. Downstream effects could include improved reimbursement through cost containment programs such as CMS Pay-For-Performance.

Dr. Cromwell's blood management programs are well-documented to lower costs of healthcare delivery and improve outcomes. With transfusion of a single unit of blood costing more than $1,000, most hospitals that implement blood management programs will reduce transfusion costs by 20–30%. In parallel, they will reduce transfusion-related complications, such as transfusion reactions, lung dysfunction, infections, and kidney failure. Perioperative blood transfusion is a common source of blood utilization and may be recognized and treated preoperatively, reducing the need for blood transfusion. Such a program is highly data driven and requires robust analytics and support at the point of care.

More recently Dr. Cromwell has focused on medical devices that assist clinicians in decision-making. The first device was based on the problem of delirium. The cumulative effect was of post-surgery delirium in patients 70 and older that has led to an estimated national burden of $32.9 billion yearly, reported Tammy Hshieh, MD, MPH, of Brigham and Women's Hospital, Boston, and co-authors, in JAMA Surgery. Delirium costs rival those of cardiovascular disease and diabetes.

Because delirium is nearly universally under-recognized and under-treated, hospitals and their patients are already paying for the cascading effects of delirium but failing to capture the available reimbursement. Additionally, the failure to identify and surface the presence of delirium results in an inappropriately low case mix index, negatively affecting risk adjustment in pay-for-performance initiatives, according to DASH Analytics. Their system provides a systematic approach to screening, documentation, and early intervention for delirium, which can result in better patient outcomes, improved reimbursement, and decreased financial penalties.

Another medical device company that Dr. Cromwell has started is Entac Medical (https://entacmedical.com). Entac Medical is a digital health company developing wearable devices. Their technology applies predictive analytics/AI to biological acoustic signals to predict downstream patient adverse events, improving patient outcomes, preventing hospital readmissions, and reducing the cost of care. Their current device, PrevisEA™, is a noninvasive, easy-to-use device that analyzes intestinal sounds for a validated acoustic biomarker of digestive health which is displayed as the Previs™ Index. The device is placed on the patient's abdomen within one hour of surgery completion. At postoperative hour 12, the Previs Index displays "High Risk" or "Low Risk." "High Risk" indicates that digestive health is likely insufficient to support early oral refeeding and the patient is likely to develop gastrointestinal impairment (GII), mostly commonly associated with postoperative ileus or less frequently due to other causes. "Low Risk" indicates that digestive health can likely support early oral refeeding without subsequent GII. In PrevisEA clinical trials, GII was defined as vomiting, need for nasogastric tube insertion, or a physician-ordered reversal of diet greater than 24 hours after completion of surgery. They also offer PrevisCDP; this is a clinical documentation consulting program offered freely as a companion to the PrevisEA device. Also available is Previs™ CDO that provides hospital support for accurate coding of postoperative ileus.

UIHC and Dr. Cromwell are providing innovative solutions that will improve care outcomes, patient satisfaction, and efficiency of care, thus lowering healthcare costs.

7.6.7.2 Artificial Intelligence Could Soon Diagnose Illness Based on the Sound of Your Voice

There are all types of AI projects using body sounds. NPR reported on October 10, 2022, that the National Institutes of Health (NIH) is funding a massive research project to collect voice data and develop an AI that could diagnose people based on their speech.

Voice sounds and vibrations contain a very large set of information. And according to Dr. Yael Bensoussan it can even help diagnose an illness; researchers are working on an app for that purpose. Everything from your vocal cord vibrations to breathing patterns when you speak offers potential information about your health.

Someone who speaks low and slowly might have Parkinson's disease. Slurring is a sign of a stroke. Scientists could even diagnose depression or cancer. The team will start by collecting the voices of people with conditions in five areas: neurological disorders, voice disorders, mood disorders, respiratory disorders, and pediatric disorders, like autism and speech delays.

The project is part of the NIH's Bridge to AI program, launched in 2021 with more than $100 million in funding from the federal government with the goal of creating large-scale healthcare databases for precision medicine. "We were really lacking large what we call open source databases," Bensoussan says. "Every institution kind of has their own database of data. But to create these networks and these infrastructures was really important to then allow researchers from other generations to use this data."

The ultimate goal is an app that could help bridge access to rural or underserved communities by helping general practitioners refer patients to specialists. Long term, iPhones or Alexa could detect changes in your voice, such as a cough, and advise you to seek medical attention.

7.6.7.3 Large Academic Medical Center in Texas Uses Simulation for Outcomes

Simulation was mentioned as one of the key technologies being used by innovators. UT Southwestern Medical Centers is assessing kidney transplant evaluations based on AI and simulation.

Living donor kidney transplantation is the treatment of choice for patients suffering from advanced renal failure. Frequently donors do not have two identical kidneys. Instead, there can be asymmetrical differences between the two organs' size and efficiency in filtration abilities. When a donor has kidney asymmetry, physicians will use the smaller, less efficient kidney for transplantation. When there is more than a 10% size difference between the two kidneys, doctors typically perform an additional test to measure the function of each kidney, known as a split renal function test as a guide to select which kidney to use for the transplant.

Most transplant centers arbitrarily consider size and functional asymmetry of less than 10% as clinically insignificant (meaning either kidney can be used for transplant), and asymmetry of more than 20% as a cut-off for transplantation, with the concern being that the smaller kidney may not be healthy enough to be desirable for donation.

Texas Southwestern Medical Center wanted to examine kidney transplant asymmetry. It conducted a retrospective study of 100 kidney donors who had asymmetric kidneys, gathering three measurements from each patient: the kidney size (volume), kidney split function, and semi-quantitative implantation biopsy scores. "We combined these three in an effort to define what the true level of acceptable asymmetry is without danger to the patient, and to determine which of these factors has the greatest impact on recipient outcomes," says Dr. Tanriover.

The team created a linear regression model and Monte Carlo simulation to predict the outcome of those patients. Simulation was critical, as researchers only had 100 patients' data in the system. As Dr. Tanriover pointed out, "Using regression coefficients, I could do a simulation as if I had 10,000 kidney donors to visualize how much each variable impacted recipient kidney function after one year." Using simulation in the model was important, as there are a limited number of living kidney donors, and the low number can make it difficult for a study to differentiate small differences.

The model showed a clear correlation between donor kidney size and recipient outcomes. In fact, the model showed that kidney size was the only variable that truly mattered when it came to the three measurements. Researchers found that the results from the split renal function test should not necessarily be part of the clinical decision criteria. In fact, they found that the split function test and the biopsy should be eliminated as part of the kidney evaluation process.

Researchers also used simulation to answer another clinical question: what if the kidney in question is of adequate size but its split function level is well below what is considered acceptable for transplantation? Would you still take that living kidney immediately, or would you instead wait to accept a kidney from a deceased donor at the expense of prolonged wait-time and possible increased risk of dying? Currently there is no standardized protocol on how to approach this decision.

To answer this question, the team conducted a sensitivity analysis with simulation. In the model, they kept the size of the kidney at the transplant-worthy level but varied the functionality. "We wanted to know what recipient outcomes would be in a year with these different levels of split kidney function," says Dr. Tanriover. "How do you optimize outcomes, and what should be the limiting level of kidney transplant function?"

Running the simulation 10,000 times, the team found that even with very low kidney function levels, there was only a small incremental risk of a recipient having less than ideal outcomes one year later. The researchers wrote:

> In our opinion, the risk of receiving a preemptive living renal transplant with any extreme split function difference, as long as adequate donor kidney volume is transplanted (2 ml/kg), outweighs the benefit of waiting for a deceased donor renal transplant that has higher function. The reason for this is that preemptive kidney transplantation offers lower mortality and allograft failure risk as compared with patients who received a transplant while on dialysis.

With this probabilistically determined information, doctors now have a clear and simple answer to complicated clinical questions around kidney transplantation. "It's clear that everything pretty much comes down to the size of the donor kidney—higher kidney volume equals better patient outcome," says Dr. Tanriover. "It's helpful to know that the split renal function test results and implantation kidney biopsies don't add any necessary information in the overall big picture."

7.7 Manufacturing Innovators

A leading manufacturer of automotive parts had been struggling with a high rate of defects in their manufacturing process for some time. This was causing significant delays and disruptions in their production, as well as increasing costs due to the need to rework or scrap defective parts.

Determined to find a solution, the company's management team decided to invest in AI and ML technologies to help them better understand and address the root causes of the defects. They worked with a team of data scientists and engineers to develop a deep-learning algorithm that could analyze data from various sources, including sensors on the manufacturing equipment, production data, and quality-control records.

The deep-learning algorithm was trained using a large dataset of past production data, which included both defective and non-defective parts. This allowed the algorithm to learn to identify patterns and correlations that might be contributing to defects in the manufacturing process.

After analyzing the data, the deep-learning algorithm was able to identify several factors that were contributing to the defects, including variations in the raw materials being used, fluctuations in the manufacturing equipment, and errors in the production process.

Based on these insights, the company was able to make several changes to their manufacturing process to address the root causes of the defects. They implemented a new supplier quality management program to ensure that the raw materials being used were of higher quality and more consistent. They also increased the frequency of equipment calibration and maintenance and introduced new quality-control procedures to catch defects earlier in the production process.

In addition to these changes, the company also used the insights provided by the deep-learning algorithm to continuously optimize their production process and identify new opportunities for improvement. They were able to identify bottlenecks and inefficiencies in the process and implement changes to address these issues. Specifically, the company applied four AI frameworks:

1. **Real-time monitoring**. By using sensors and other IoT technologies to collect data from their manufacturing equipment and production processes in real time, the company could use AI algorithms to continuously monitor and analyze this data for patterns and trends. This helped them identify problems or inefficiencies as they occurred and make adjustments to the process in order to improve efficiency and reduce waste.

2. **Predictive maintenance**. AI algorithms were used to analyze data from sensors and other sources to predict when equipment would likely fail or become less efficient. This helped the company schedule maintenance and repairs at optimal times, reducing downtime and improving overall efficiency.

3. **Optimization of production schedules**. AI algorithms were used to analyze data on demand patterns, production capacity, and other factors to optimize the production schedule. This helped the company better match production with demand, reduce waste and overproduction, and improve overall efficiency.

4. **Process optimization**. AI algorithms were used to identify bottlenecks and inefficiencies in the production process and suggest changes to improve efficiency. This involved optimizing the use of resources, identifying opportunities to automate tasks, and improving the layout of the production facility.

Thanks to these efforts, the company was able to significantly reduce the rate of defects and improve the overall efficiency of their manufacturing process. They were also able to increase their production capacity and reduce costs, which helped them remain competitive in a challenging market. The success of this project demonstrated the power of AI and ML technologies to drive significant improvements in manufacturing operations.

THE COW ON A BEACH PROBLEM

Another interesting problem that Elliot Layne and I discussed (see the other vignette in this chapter, "Genotypes, Phenotypes, and Causation vs Correlation") was the problem of domain adaptation in deep learning, AI. I was familiar with the general problem, but Elliot had a great example.

To put it simply, this is a form of bias and is truly a basic statistical sampling problem. Elliot's example is so illustrative. As a data scientist in agriculture, you are training a deep-learning model to recognize cows. You want to sell your image-recognition model as an API call in a smartphone application. You train the model with thousands of images of cows, and the model learns well and is highly predictive of identifying cows. You think your job is done. Your APP is selling like hotcakes and reviews are good. Life is great.

Then complaints start coming in. The software is failing! You are getting dozens of reports of poor accuracy. You ask customers to send you images of the failures, they do. They send you dozens of images of cows on beaches that your system fails to recognize. What? Cows on beaches? Where?

It turns out there are lots of cows on beaches in Africa. You did not train your algorithm outside the United States, where all the cows are in fields or holding pens. And your deep modeling did not focus on the cows, it learned their domain, their surroundings, not the cows themselves.

By not providing a representative sample, the deep-learning model failed.

Back to basics.

Back to statistics.

7.8 Retail Innovators

Retail is a highly competitive industry, with retailers often competing on factors such as price, product selection, convenience, customer service, and brand reputation. In order to succeed in this environment, retailers must be able to effectively identify and meet the needs of their customers, while also managing their costs and operations efficiently.

One way that retailers are trying to stay competitive is by adopting AI and other digital technologies to optimize their operations and improve the customer experience. For example, AI can be used to personalize the shopping experience, optimize inventory management, and identify opportunities for cost savings.

However, retailers also face challenges in implementing and effectively using AI and other technologies. These can include the need to invest in new infrastructure and equipment, the need to train staff on new technologies, and the risk of disruption to existing business models.

Overall, the retail industry is constantly evolving and adapting to new technologies, consumer preferences, and market conditions. Those retailers that are able to effectively harness the power of AI and other technologies to meet the needs of their customers and improve their operations will be well positioned to succeed in this competitive environment.

Retailers are using AI in a variety of ways, including:

Personalization. AI algorithms can be used to analyze customer data, such as purchase history, browsing behavior, and demographic information, to personalize the shopping experience and make recommendations to individual customers.

Inventory management. AI algorithms can be used to optimize inventory levels and replenishment, helping retailers better match supply with demand and reduce waste and excess inventory.

Price optimization. AI algorithms can be used to analyze data on customer demand, competition, and other factors to optimize pricing strategies and maximize profits.

Fraud detection. AI algorithms can be used to identify fraudulent activity, such as fake returns or fraudulent credit card transactions.

Customer service. AI-powered chatbots and virtual assistants can be used to provide assistance to customers, such as answering questions or providing product recommendations.

Marketing. AI algorithms can be used to analyze data on customer behavior and preferences to create targeted marketing campaigns and improve the effectiveness of advertising efforts.

Overall, AI is helping retailers better understand their customers, optimize their operations, and improve the efficiency and effectiveness of their business.

7.8.1 Large US Retailer Improves the Customer Experience with AI

The large US department store chain was a well-known and respected brand, but they were facing increasing competition from online retailers and other brick-and-mortar stores. They knew that they needed to find a way to improve their operations and enhance the shopping experience for their customers in order to stay competitive.

After conducting a thorough analysis of their business, the management team decided to invest in AI technologies to drive efficiency and improve the customer experience. They worked with a team of data scientists and engineers to develop and implement several AI-powered solutions.

One of the first areas they focused on was inventory management. They collected data on customer purchase patterns, store traffic, and other factors, and fed this data into an AI algorithm. The algorithm was trained to identify patterns and trends in the data, and to use this information to optimize the store's inventory levels and replenishment schedules.

This helped the store significantly reduce the amount of excess inventory they had on hand, which reduced costs and improved their bottom line. It also helped them improve the availability of popular items for customers, which in turn helped to increase sales and customer satisfaction.

In addition to this, the store also implemented an AI-powered chatbot on their website to help customers. The chatbot was able to answer a wide range of customer questions and provide personalized product recommendations based on the customer's past purchases and browsing history. This helped improve the customer experience and increase online sales.

The store also used AI algorithms to analyze customer data, such as purchase history and browsing behavior, in order to personalize the shopping experience and make targeted recommendations to individual customers. This helped to improve customer satisfaction and loyalty.

Overall, the implementation of AI technologies helped the store streamline their operations, reduce costs, and improve the shopping experience for their customers. This allowed them to better compete with other retailers and remain successful in the highly competitive retail market. The store's management team was pleased with the results and committed to continuing to invest in and utilize AI technologies in the future.

"NO INCENTIVES TO TELL THE TRUTH, JUST CLICKS"

"No incentives to tell the truth, just clicks." That is what Geoff Pofahl said that resonated with me. We had a different, but very rich conversation. Geoff and I met doing pricing optimization on the commercial side of the world. Geoff has returned to academia, and we spoke about the lack of transparency and bias in the media these days. I really appreciated the candid and insightful interview. One thing that Geoff would like to see more in books these days is discussions about ethics. He also has an honor student working on the idea of criminal justice being more algorithm driven. I am not convinced, but it is an interesting professional and open discussion.

7.9 Energy Innovators

There are a wide range of players in the energy industry. Some of these include:

Energy producers. These are companies that extract, process, and produce energy, such as oil and gas companies, coal mining companies, and renewable energy companies.

Energy utilities. These are companies that generate, transmit, and distribute electricity and other forms of energy to consumers.

Energy traders. These are companies that buy and sell energy and energy-related products, such as oil, natural gas, and electricity, in the wholesale market.

Energy service companies. These are companies that provide services to the energy industry, such as engineering and consulting services, drilling services, and environmental services.

Energy equipment and technology providers. These are companies that produce and sell equipment and technology used in the energy industry, such as drilling equipment, pipelines, and renewable energy technologies.

> **Energy investors**. These are individuals and organizations that invest in the energy industry, such as hedge funds, private equity firms, and venture capital firms.

There is not a single area of the energy industry that is not being positively affected by the explosion of data and the use of AI and analytics in the industry. Some of these are:

7.9.1 Predictive Maintenance

ML and AI algorithms can be used to analyze data from sensors on equipment, such as wind turbines or oil rigs, to predict when maintenance or repairs will be needed. This can help to reduce downtime and improve the efficiency of operations.

7.9.2 Optimization of Energy Generation and Distribution

ML and AI algorithms can be used to optimize the generation and distribution of energy from sources such as solar panels or wind farms. This can help to increase the efficiency and reliability of energy systems.

7.9.3 Data Analysis and Visualization

ML and AI algorithms can be used to analyze and interpret large datasets, such as data on energy consumption patterns or weather patterns, to identify trends and insights that can be used to optimize energy systems.

7.9.4 Cybersecurity

AI algorithms can be used to monitor energy systems for cyber threats and anomalies, helping to protect against cyberattacks.

7.9.5 ML Modeling Wind for More Efficient Energy Use

A large energy company was looking for ways to improve the efficiency and reliability of their wind farms. They decided to implement AI technologies, including ML algorithms, to optimize the performance of their wind turbines.

The company collected data from sensors on the wind turbines, including information on wind speed and direction, turbine performance, and maintenance records. They fed this data into an ML algorithm and trained it to identify patterns and correlations that might be affecting the performance of the turbines.

The ML algorithm was able to identify several factors that were impacting the performance of the turbines, including variations in wind conditions, the age and condition of the turbines, and maintenance issues. Based on these insights, the company was able to make a number of changes to improve the performance of their wind farms.

For example, they were able to optimize the placement of the turbines to take advantage of more favorable wind conditions, and they implemented a more proactive maintenance program to address issues before they became serious problems. They were also able to identify opportunities to upgrade or replace older turbines with more efficient models.

As a result of these efforts, the company was able to significantly improve the efficiency and reliability of their wind farms. They were able to generate more electricity with the same number of turbines, and they experienced fewer outages and other issues. This helped to reduce costs and increase profits for the company, and it also helped to reduce their environmental impact.

The success of this project demonstrated the power of AI and ML technologies to drive significant improvements in the energy industry. The company was pleased with the results and committed to continuing to invest in and utilize these technologies in the future.

PHYSICIST TURNED ENERGY DATA SCIENTIST

Adam Sroka started as a physicist and Photon Scientist, getting a doctorate in engineering. But he also has a business background and understands the value of data in the energy sector. He now has his own data science practice serving the energy sector. He offers a great, practical balance. Adam says:

> Many organizations aren't getting the most out of their data and many data professionals struggle to communicate their results or the complexity and value of their work in a way that business stakeholders can relate to. Being able to understand both the technology and how it translates to real benefits is key.
>
> Simply hiring the most capable people often isn't enough. The solution is a mix of clear and explicit communication,

strong fundamentals and engineering discipline, and an appetite to experiment and iterate to success quickly.

If this is something you're struggling with—either as an organization finding its feet with data and AI or as a data professional—the approaches and systems Adam has developed over his career will be able to help so please reach out.

Well said, Adam.

7.10 Financial Services and Insurance Innovators

Insurance companies need to brace for a profound change in a business model that has been around for centuries. As the Internet of Things and machine learning reduce the amount of insurable risk in the world, then insurers need to find new revenue streams to offset the reduction in premium income. This is likely to see a fundamental shift in what it means to be an insurance company, moving insurance from a "just-in-case" grudge purchase that promises compensation should the worst happen toward a partnership approach,

> "Wouldn't it be great if rather than sending a team of people to clear up after a flood, we were able to tell somebody they are beginning to have a leak? That technology already exists." — David Williams, AXA

working with customers to help them make better decisions to reduce the amount of risk in their lives and improve their safety and well-being. Connected devices are all about prevention, and this is a game changer for insurance companies. In the past, insurers would take money from a customer and then hope to never hear from them. Now, insurance companies can partner with customers and collect real-time data from connected devices. They can use this data to minimize risk by alerting customers when needed, and moreover provide benefit by communicating with customers using visual BI. This makes customers happier, and customer retention rises.

A QUOTE ON REALITY OF SPEED OF INNOVATION ADOPTIONS

"While consumer innovations like mobile telephones or VCRs may require only a few years to reach widespread adoption in the United States, other new ideas such as the metric system or using seat belts in cars require decades to reach complete use. The characteristics of innovations, as perceived by individuals, help to explain their different rate of adoption."

—Everett M. Rogers, *Diffusion of Innovations*

7.11 Where Do Innovators Go from Here?

Innovators have a simple trajectory; they keep moving forward and innovating. Or they fall back into a leader role. The trajectory has less to do with technology than with the value of the innovation. Industries and business models mature, and at some point cutting-edge innovation is not what separates the winners from the losers. Once again, strategy is king.

Chapter 8

Data and Analytics Readiness

"Plans are worthless, but planning is everything."

—*Dwight D. Eisenhower*

8.1 Introduction

Some people would like you to think that data and analytics readiness has much to do with the money spent on technology or the investments you have made in people to transform your organization into a data-driven, analytics company. That is only a small portion of what it takes for your organization's data readiness position. This determination is much more nuanced than taking inventories of capabilities or looking at budget sizes.

A requirement for any business interested in digital transformation is the match of people and technology to fit the businesses' strategy and operations.

In the previous chapters we have examined the five stages of data and analytics maturity, and we also pointed out that some organizations should stay at the first level. For most organizations, however, they will mature into higher levels over time, but they will not continue to climb through all five. They will mature to a place and find balance, the correct fit. They will find the right amount of investment to make and where technology and methods fit their strategy and operations. This is key—the match of people and technology to fit their strategy and operations.

DOI: 10.4324/9780429343971-8

There is no one size fits all. As we have said, there is no "easy button" that determines the right response to every enterprise. Every enterprise is unique and must decide the maturity level that is best for it.

What is critical is that every organization measures its AI and analytics capabilities against its goals and specific objectives. It needs to align its data and analytics strategy to its business strategy. It then needs to determine its current capability against the abilities required to achieve those strategies.

Aligning strategy to ability is what is really important. It is not making sure you become a leader or an innovator. Strategy comes first, and developing strategy is circular with the ability to execute it. The best strategy means nothing if you cannot execute. Analytics strategy supports the overall corporate mission and goals. We recommend *The Executive's Guide to AI and Analytics: The Foundations of Execution and Success in the New World* (see Burk & Miner, 2022) for further details.

8.2 Sources of Failure

We pointed out in Burk and Miner (2022) that most enterprises do not understand the sources of failure of AI and analytics programs. Most people do not realize that leading corporations are failing in their efforts to become "data driven" (Bean & Davenport, 2019). A survey conducted by NewVantage Partners polled very large corporations such as American Express, Ford Motor, General Electric, General Motors, and Johnson & Johnson. Results of the survey (New Vantage Partners, 2019) included the following statistics:

- 72% of survey participants report that they have yet to forge a data culture
- 69% report that they have not created a data-driven organization
- 53% state that they are not yet treating data as a business asset
- 52% admit that they are not competing on data and analytics
- FURTHER: the percentage of firms identifying themselves as being data driven has declined in each of the past three years—from 37.1% in 2017 to 32.4% in 2018 to 31% in 2019.

These numbers have not improved. In fact, some studies show they are declining. What is the problem?

Is investment lacking? No. Companies now are spending more than ever in data, analytics, and AI technologies. AI investment in the United States is growing 36% per year, and it is growing faster in some other countries, with China growing over 300%. In healthcare 74% of executives said their organizations would invest more in predictive modeling in 2021.

Is it a lack of technology? No. There are fascinating breakthroughs occurring on all fronts, with image, voice, and streaming pattern recognition methods on the forefront. These technologies are driving investment and leading many initiatives with applications from radiology to autonomous vehicles.

Is it a lack of technical talent? Not really. While some studies cite that we need to train more data scientists, developers, and related professionals, the curve of demand by supply is dampening. And some experts are suggesting the increasing popularity of data scientists may cause an oversupply of talent.

Is it the lack of creating an executable strategic plan? Yes. While there has been a lot of strategic wishing, organizations lack meaningful strategic plans, specifically, the development of executable strategies and the leadership to see these strategies brought to fruition. This is the missing element. The critical element that many organizations lack.

Those companies that have digitally transformed themselves are 26% more profitable than their average industry competitors. But this has required an investment in leadership as well as in technology. Research across the five global industrial revolutions point out one common element of companies that were successful vs those that were not—top leadership was involved at every level of the organization and this leadership firmly focused on success.

> What is a data and analytics readiness assessment? A requirement for any business interested in digital transformation (www.itsallanalytics.com).

We divide this chapter into two parts.

The first part is an assessment process for those organizations that have developed a business strategy and want to assess their data technology, their analytic technology, and their people capability to execute that strategic plan with a data and analytics strategy.

The second part is for organizations that are rewriting their strategic plans based on market shifts brought by the AI and analytics revolution. If you are an organization that is reinventing itself to compete in this new revolution, we offer some guidelines for co-developing your business strategy with an accompanying data and analytics strategy to support it.

WHY SHOULD WE DO A READINESS ASSESSMENT?

- Businesses that use data to improve the speed and quality of decisions will survive. Those that don't will not.
- Data-driven decisions are necessary for today's success, but not sufficient.
- Most organizations have grown their knowledge and infrastructure in a modular fashion.
- Most organizations do not have an impartial assessment of their strengths and weaknesses.
- Prevention vs poor health

8.3 Determining an Organization's Readiness to Execute with Data and Analytics

Data and analytics strategies are not meant for their own ends. They complement and support your business strategies. And this is further complicated because business strategy, data strategy, analytic strategy, and organizational and people strategy are interconnected and should be considered simultaneously. If you already have your business strategy in place and you want to determine whether you can support this strategy by performing a data and analytics assessment, the following three points are high-level questions you should be asking to determine your ability to execute these strategies:

- Do we have the right people and knowledge to support these strategic initiatives?
- Do we have the right data and related technology to support these strategic initiatives?
- Do we have the right analytics technology to support these strategic initiatives?

CAN YOU ASSESS DATA AND ANALYTICS READINESS WITH A QUESTIONNAIRE?

Scott was asked this question in a data-driven digital marketing podcast. Following is Scott's response:

No, I do not believe that you can effectively do this. It might provide efficiency, but it does not provide effectiveness. There is a difference, and many people confuse the two. You can be efficient and get to the wrong place very quickly. Getting to the right place is effectiveness. Ideally, you would like to be efficient and effective, but I don't think there is any way to be effective in gauging an organization's readiness with questionnaires—yet there are many out there!

You must assess data and analytics readiness with extensive conversations with leadership followed up with interviews of many people across the organization. No organization is the same. No set of goals are the same. It has to be a dynamic flow. Would you want to assess someone's mental health with a questionnaire? Again it may be very efficient, but I don't think it is very precise.

Why are podcasts popular? Can't a host send a questionnaire to a guest? No, there is so much information provided through the dynamic flow of the interview process!! The same is true with a readiness assessment.

Can you start with a questionnaire? Yes, this can offer a jump start and overall improve the process.

Moreover, an initial questionnaire can lead to whether a further assessment is likely to be fruitful. It may be that the organization needs to do some very basic things before a deeper dive is even taken.

8.3.1 Conducting a Data and Analytics Readiness Assessment

Conducting the assessment begins as a top-down process. You must assess data and analytics readiness with extensive conversations with leadership followed up with interviews of many people across the organization. No organization is the same, and therefore the process is not a set formulation. It needs to be dynamic in nature and adapt to the organization and its people. Obviously, there is a loose framework to follow as best practice, which we cover in future sections. We now provide the major steps of this framework and then describe each step.

8.3.1.1 The Framework Overview

1. Meetings with senior leadership to understand
   a. Business strategy, goals, objectives
   b. Budgets—past, present, and predicted
   c. Culture—especially the agility and willingness to adapt
   d. Historical innovation appetite and any indication this is going to change—is there a future appetite for innovation?
   e. Key players. Business leaders outside of senior leadership that will drive the strategy.
   f. Key players that are involved with projects and transformation initiatives, corporate initiatives (HR, project managers, and ancillary staff)

2. A second set of meetings with the key leaders in 1e. and 1f. to
   a. Onboard and educate the goals of the readiness assessment
   b. Confirm or clarify the message received in conversations with senior leadership.
   c. Develop a communication process—time line, mode of delivery, content.
   d. Determine high-priority staff to interview.

3. Execute the communication process.
4. Conduct interviews with designated leaders, managers, and high-priority staff.
5. Provide a written questionnaire for remaining designated staff.
6. Perform an extensive analysis of findings.
7. Create a written report with detailed study findings.
8. Present to leadership summarizing the report findings.
9. Work with leadership to determine next steps. This could include:
   a. A gap analysis and remediation plan
   b. A presentation/communication presentation to staff on assessment findings

SHOULD WE DO OUR OWN ASSESSMENT? USE OUR IT VENDORS? OR OUR IT CONSULTANTS?

You should not use internal resources, your IT vendors, or your IT consultants to perform your assessment for the following reasons:

Internal assessments carry biases and a lack of knowledge. The lack of knowledge is easy to see. Why would your organization pose the knowledge to be able to critically examine its capabilities to perform one? Second, there are strong biases inside any enterprise. An internal assessment carries the risk of organizational bias, i.e., "pride." It also carries an attachment to existing technology that may not be the best technology for the job. Third, stakeholders do not want past decisions criticized, so there is a tendency to think everything is right with the state of the organization to succeed.

There are many reasons not to use IT vendors, let us focus on two. First, they are financially incentivized for you to use their solution. Why would they recommend a competitor? Second, a more innocent reasoning is that their knowledge is tied to their own technology. They are experts in what they engineer. They have much less understanding of the broader technological field.

There are many reasons not to use IT consultants. For one, many IT consultants or system integrators have partnerships with enterprise technology/software providers.

So, based on the previous gray box on what not to do, what is a better choice?

A neutral, independent technology agnostics consulting firm that provides one service, performing data and analytics readiness assessments. They are not partnered with specific technology companies. They do not share revenue in any way with IT consultants or tech firms. They are independent, third-party providers.

8.3.1.2 Goals of Meetings with Senior Leadership

In this section we have assumed that the business strategy is in place. Too often this strategy is created without a plan to determine whether the enterprise has i) access to the data to support the strategy, ii) the related data technology to support the strategy, iii) the AI and analytics technology and knowledge to support the strategy, and iv) the right culture. So, it is important to align all these dimensions so that the business strategy can be executed. This starts in the C-suite.

The goals of these meetings are multifaceted and multilevel and vary greatly depending on the size of the organization. And it is possible to perform an assessment for a specific line of business (LOB). To make things simple, we will outline a process for a $5 billion manufacturing company that produces construction equipment, a manufacturer.

First meetings are between the independent assessment consulting company and the internal project management team (JTF, joint task force) to align and set the agenda with the CEO's strategy meeting. It is paramount to start these meetings at the highest level of the organization. In this meeting the JTF expresses the goal of the project and gets signoff from the group with a commitment to

1. Communicate the project initiative in writing and with a corporate kick-off meeting
2. Make available all resources in a timely manner for the program
3. Confirm the next level of leaders that will be interviewed by consultants
4. Commit access to hierarchical business strategy, goals, and objectives
5. Commit to budget access for specific investment categories of staff and technology can be determined—past, present, and future (so that level and trend of engagement may be determined)

Interviews with senior-level staff begin to cascade down through the organization to determine cultural agility and willingness to adapt. Concepts of concern here include:

> "Building a visionary company requires 1% vision and 99% alignment." — Jim Collins and Jerry Porra

- The historical innovation appetite within the organization
- Any indication this historical innovation appetite is going to change
- The future appetite for innovation
- The level of data literacy and knowledge across departments and staff
- Departmental goals and the determination of data, AI, and analytics technology to support those goals

After the senior-level staff interviews, then the next round of interview candidates (key leaders) is determined across all departments.

8.3.1.3 Meetings with Key Leaders

The key leaders identified in the meeting with executive leadership will begin. These meetings will focus on educating key leaders on the goals of the readiness assessment, onboarding them, and seeking commitment to the project's success. Additionally, they want to confirm or clarify the message received in conversations thus far.

The JTF will develop a communication process, which includes a time line, the mode of delivery, and its content. They will also determine the next round, high-priority staff to interview.

8.3.1.4 Execute the Communication Process

This step is delivering the plan developed by meetings with key leaders and the JTF. It may include video and live presentations by leaders. It will include a rollout timeline. It may also include written documentation and other material on the program.

8.3.1.5 Conduct Interviews with Designated Leaders, Managers, and High-Priority Staff

The cascade for information continues with interviews of identified staff to assess readiness across the dimensions already discussed. As this process moves into more dedicated, granular levels, the information gets more voluminous and at the same time, often higher quality. Leaders and managers are sometimes removed from the frontline battles that staff face. It is in these frontline engagements that data-driven technology makes all the difference.

WHY DO YOU WANT TO PERFORM HYBRID INTERVIEWS, LIVE, AND QUESTIONNAIRE?

Each method provides benefits. Web entry questionnaires afford the ability for more people to give input, while live interviews allow for immediate clarification and diving deeper into areas that can prove very meaningful. A conversation allows for a more effective discovery of pertinent facts. Some areas within the business are more amenable to direct categorical response. For example, what databases, data, BI, AI, and analytic technologies have been deployed by IT. Whereas the types of analysis that are being done, by whom, and the approach taken is more of a directed conversation.

8.3.1.6 Provide a Written Questionnaire for Remaining Designated Staff

This is optional but highly recommended. People always want to feel part of the process and part of the solution. And while questionnaires are not as dynamic and fluid as interviews, they can provide insightful information.

8.3.1.7 Perform an Extensive Analysis of Findings

A mountain of information has been taken by this point. The assessment consultants take the intended business strategy, the level of past and projected commitment to execute on data strategies, and the current state of knowledge and technology and perform an in-depth analysis.

8.3.1.8 Creation of a Written Report with Detailed Study Findings

Based on the analysis of findings a written report is developed. An accompanying presentation is constructed as well. This is intended to present the most important findings to leadership. A few important sections that should be included in this report are:

- **Executive summary**. This section provides an overview of the assessment, including the purpose, scope, and key findings.
- **Background**. This section provides context for the assessment, including the organization's business strategy starting at the highest level and then cascading down to the goals of the different business units and departments to support it. It will explain how best practices in data, AI, and analytics can support these objectives. It also shows what competitors are doing with data-driven practices and will include any relevant industry or market trends.
- **Current state assessment**. This section describes the current processes, systems, and capabilities that were evaluated as part of the assessment. It should include data and analysis that supports the evaluation of the current state.

- **Desired state assessment**. This section describes the desired outcomes, goals, and objectives that the organization hopes to achieve with data-driven processes and technologies. It will include the criteria used to evaluate them.
- **Gap analysis**. This section identifies the gaps between the current state and the desired state and provides an analysis of the root causes and impact of those gaps.
- **Recommendations**. This section provides a plan for closing the identified gaps, including specific actions, time lines, and responsibilities.
- **Implementation and monitoring**. This section outlines the plan for implementing the recommendations and monitoring progress toward closing the gaps.
- **Conclusion**. This section summarizes the key findings of the gap analysis and provides recommendations for future actions.
- **Appendices**. This section may include additional data, supporting documents, or material that was used in the assessment but is not included in the main body of the report.

8.3.1.9 Present Findings to Leadership and Determine Next Steps

The JTF presents to leadership, summarizing the report findings, and works with leadership to determine next steps. Based on the meeting outcome the JTF will develop a presentation for senior leadership to present the findings and plans for the program.

8.3.1.10 Presentation to the Organization

It is recommended that the CEO and their staff deliver this presentation.

WHY NOW?

The authors are sometimes asked, "Why should we do an assessment now? We are very busy and it seems like a lot of work." We have three short responses:

- **Your competition has started or will soon.** Business strategy must change in response to changing markets and economic conditions. Are your competitors capitalizing on new data and analytic methods? How will you respond?

■ **Time value of your investments.** Companies have been making large investments in people and technology over the years. However, many companies do not understand their return on investment of these expenditures. Should you be shedding some of these investments? Where should you be making greater investments?

■ **Can you afford to wait?** With the pandemic, inflation, and a recession, massive changes have been created in the way businesses operate. Technology, if applied correctly, makes organizations run more efficiently and more effectively. *If applied correctly.*

8.4 Redesigning an Organization to Execute with Data and Analytics

Some organizations are redesigning themselves to be more data- and process-centric. This started decades ago with the first wave of digital transformation, which included the integration of digital technologies into all areas of a business, fundamentally changing how businesses operate and deliver value to their customers. Now companies are undergoing a second digital transformation by applying various forms of analytics into all areas of a business, fundamentally changing how a business operates and delivers value to its customers.

The data and analytics used to support these initiatives vary greatly. Some are designed to assist human decision-making by taking data and making it relevant for business personnel to make quicker and better decisions and the corresponding actions. A great example of this type of technology are visual BI dashboards. Humans navigate and interact with these dashboards and then make decisions based on what they see.

ML and AI can also assist in decision-making in a more machine, less human cognition process. An example of this would be the creation of a predictive model for breast cancer for a radiologist. The radiologist's productivity is greatly enhanced by the machine determining that this specific patient has breast cancer. Then there are fully automated, 100% machine-driven actions. An example of this would be AI-enabled autonomous vehicles.

The goal of any digital transformation is to improve operational efficiency, increase revenue, and enhance customer engagement and satisfaction. If you are an organization that is reinventing itself to compete in the data revolution and have the option, we offer some guidelines for co-developing your business strategy with an accompanying data and analytics strategy to support it.

In a previous book, which we have mentioned (Burk & Miner, 2022), we go into detail on creating executable strategies based on AI and analytics. However, in this section we present a few key ideas.

DEVELOPING A DATA AND ANALYTICS STRATEGY INVOLVES SEVERAL KEY POINTS, INCLUDING:

1. **Identifying business goals and objectives**. A data and analytics strategy should align with the overall goals and objectives of the organization. It should clearly define how data and analytics will help the business achieve its desired outcomes.

2. **Understanding the data landscape**. It is important to understand the data landscape, including where the data is coming from, how it is stored, and how it is used. This will help identify any gaps in data collection and storage, and determine what data is needed to support the business goals.

3. **Prioritizing data and analytics projects**. Prioritizing data and analytics projects will help focus efforts on the most important initiatives and ensure that resources are allocated effectively.

4. **Building a data-driven culture**. A data-driven culture is essential to the success of a data and analytics strategy. It involves creating a culture where data is valued and used to inform decision-making at all levels of the organization.

5. **Investing in the right technology**. The right technology is essential to a successful data and analytics strategy. This includes not only the tools and platforms used to collect, store, and analyze data, but also the skills and expertise needed to make the most of these tools.

6. **Governance and security**. It is important to establish governance and security protocols to ensure that data is collected, stored, and used in compliance with legal and regulatory requirements and that data is protected from unauthorized access and breaches.

7. **Continual monitoring and improvement**. A data and analytics strategy should be continually improved and updated over time to reflect changing business needs and advances in technology.

Developing a data and analytics strategy addresses the fundamentals of people, culture, strategy, and execution for leaders and decision-makers. Getting these fundamentals wrong makes for the primary gaps between having an AI and analytics program that fails and one that succeeds. These are what we call the six foundations as illustrated in Figure 8.1.

Leaders have two principal jobs:

1. Developing the strategy
2. Executing the strategy

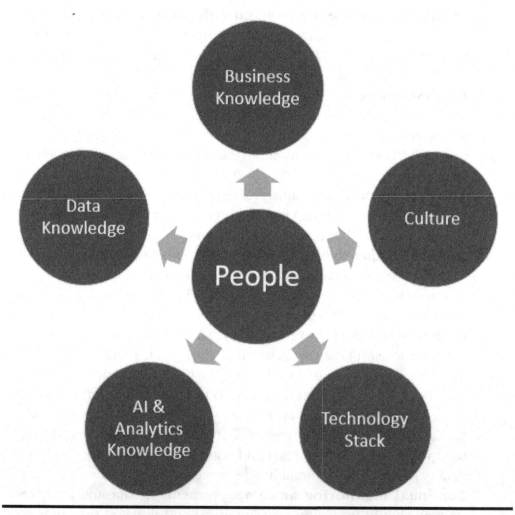

Figure 8.1   The six foundations of the success of AI and analytics programs.

That's it. That is why an executable strategy is so important. Too many leaders focus on #1 and not on #2.

Larry M. Miller, Institute for Leadership Excellence, defines an approach to align levels and leaders of the organization. Summarizing this approach in an abbreviated fashion: Senior leadership is responsible for defining strategic goals, core processes, future culture, and capabilities. Senior leadership writes a design charter and assigns to design teams. The design teams discover the current states and dreams for ideal states, and they convert these into a technical and social system plan that they pass on to the business units and distributed leaders. These business units and distributed leaders assign implementation tasks and teams that create action and accountability plans. They then discuss these at an "alignment conference" where all levels of the organization attend and identify new design requirements. See Figure 8.2, adapted from Larry's work.

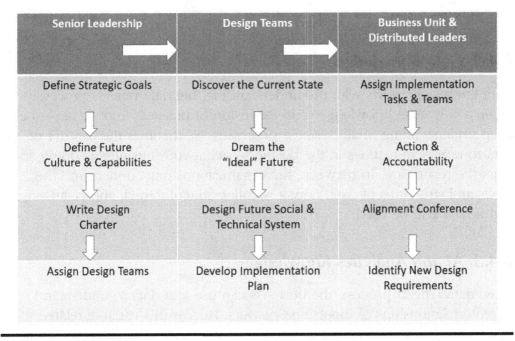

Figure 8.2   Strategy alignment for execution, adapted from Larry M. Miller.

Note that strategy often defines the future business and economic performance, but not the means to get there—the future processes, culture, and capabilities. This must be tailored to your unique organization. Also, note that strategy execution is too often a vertical, silo-ed, performance review process and does not create horizontal alignment.

We now briefly describe the six foundations that form the success of your AI and analytics program, as presented in Figure 8.1.

"The loftier the building, the deeper must the foundation be laid." —Thomas A. Kempis

8.4.1 Business Knowledge

Business knowledge describes the intimate and deep understanding of the operations and critical success factors of your business. What factors contribute most to the success or failure of the enterprise? This includes an intimate knowledge of past, current, and future states of your business. Which core capabilities led to organizational successes, and lack of which capabilities led to organizational failures? What are the anticipated needs for success in the future?

8.4.2 Data Knowledge

Data knowledge starts with the understanding that data reflects processes. So, in a way, data knowledge is an extension of business knowledge—the deep understanding of all business processes. Next comes the capture of data to represent realities in the business—what your business is doing and what the results are. In between, the organizations must understand the types and structures of data; how it is collected, combined, and cleansed; and how it will be used.

8.4.3 AI and Analytics Knowledge

Since data reflects process, the business can use that data to understand the interrelationships of inputs and outputs. How is this variable related to that business result? If I change this part of the process, what is the result? Based on history, what should I expect next year's demand to be? If I enable my organization with interactive visual dashboards, will they make better decisions? Can I build a machine-learning model to predict what will happen if I manipulate all of these inputs? Can I create "what-if" scenarios and thus see different models that provide trade-offs? Can it tell us the inputs that will optimize our margin?

These are the types of questions leaders can answer by combining these first three foundations.

One key component of these forms of knowledge is "literacy." Specifically, data and analytics literacy. AI and analytics program success requires many in the organization to have deep understanding and literacy in these topics. Furthermore, you cannot build a culture without people speaking the same language. Therefore, everyone must have a basic literacy of your business, data, and analytics. This is an important example of how these six foundations are interdependent.

8.4.4 Technology Stack—Architecture, Platforms, Systems

To turn business, data, and analytics knowledge into results effectively and efficiently, you need to design the right data and analytics architectures. You need to purchase and develop the right technologies.

8.4.5 Culture

Culture has been one of the four principal focuses of this book—people, culture, strategy, and execution for leaders and decision-makers. As stated, "Organizational culture is the shared values, customs, traditions, rituals, behaviors, and beliefs shared by the members of that organization." We have spoken a great deal about culture. Culture has a major impact on your program's success, as it influences the reception of knowledge and the use of that knowledge.

In this book we have provided insights on how leaders affect culture and the idea that structure and culture may be equally important to innovation.

8.4.6 People

The reason that "People" is in the center of Figure 8.1 is that people influence everything. Who you hire, train, nurture, promote influences everything. Your people are your organization. That is the reason we have spent so much time on this foundation.

Our focus in this book has been primarily on two of these six foundations for AI and analytics program success—people and culture and the structure and processes that support them. We have also emphasized strategy and execution. These are the hardest elements to get right and implement. These are the elements that leadership, from the CEO to all levels of leadership and management, must be involved in to ensure success.

You will need the other four foundations. You will need data and analytics knowledge/literacy, data architecture, and the technology to support your analytics/AI architecture. Finally, it is crucial you develop your use cases and target your AI and analytics efforts.

In summary, all six foundations are necessary for AI and analytics success. People and cultural challenges are the hardest to get right. You also must execute, so you need to create your strategy with everyone involved, as everyone needs to be responsible in its execution.

> "Before anything else, preparation is the key to success." —Alexander Graham Bell

Finally, don't worry about getting it 100% correct the first time. Planning is meaningful in that it clarifies and educates, but all plans must be abandoned or altered as internal and external environments shift. Be a hands-on leader that is willing to experiment, fail, and learn. Encourage and reward that through the organization. Good luck!!

8.5 Conclusion

This chapter was about assessing your organization's readiness to execute a data and analytics program based on your current business strategy, people, and technology. We also provided some considerations if you have the opportunity to redesign your organization to accompany a new wave of digital transformation based on data and analytics.

References

Bean, R. & Davenport, T. (2019, February 05). Companies are failing in their efforts to become data-driven. *Harvard Business Review*. Retrieved from https://hbr.org/2019/02/companies-are-failing-in-their-efforts-to-become-data-driven

Burk, S., & Miner, G. D. (2022). *The executive's guide to AI and analytics: The foundations of execution and success in the new world*. Productivity Press.

New Vantage Partners. (2019, January 07). Big data and AI executive survey 2019. *The Data Analytics Report*. Retrieved from https://dataanalytics.report/whitepapers/big-data-and-ai-executive-survey-2019

Chapter 9

Additional Stories on the Data Front

"Simplicity has great value. So find the balance."

—Steve (Liqin) Tao, Analytics Lead, Accenture

"Many people think cloud growth has been slowing as it is maturing, but I think it is just getting started and there is a lot of room for growth."

—Aryl Kohrs, Technology Strategist

There were so many rich conversations and interviews we conducted over the year and a half we were writing this book. Scott spoke with well over 100 people in more than 10 countries across the globe. We are grateful, and we mentioned our thanks to these people in the Introduction. We have included many of the takeaways in the vignettes (gray boxes) across the preceding chapters. However, there were just too many and some did not fit nicely in context. But there are valuable lessons in these stories, so we wanted to include them as a compendium of sorts in this chapter.

9.1 Managing the End-to-End Process of Patient Experience—Two Case Studies By Carol Maginn

Following are two case studies that my friend Carol Maginn wrote up after we had a mixture of personal and professional experience in healthcare.

DOI: 10.4324/9780429343971-9

We are all in the world of healthcare, not just to use new technology, but to leverage data to make life better. Putting data and analytics to work for patients requires taking a holistic approach to data management. Organizations looking to "use predictive analytics" find that their greatest challenges are not in the algorithms but rather the access to useful and usable data. The Covid-19 pandemic has pushed healthcare employees to the limit, and burnout is a huge problem. Staffing shortages and employee strikes are also pushing healthcare organizations to find the most efficient ways to make data insights actionable.

Leading healthcare providers have found that putting effort and rigor into laying their data foundation is the most important component of a data strategy that provides efficient access to patient insights in real time across the enterprise. Leveraging standard data models, managers, and processes is critical to ensure that we have connected all the data and have a complete patient view. Data foundation rigor will pay back dividends to providers and payers in their quest to have the most comprehensive view of a patient's care, billing, follow up, and outcome.

I have had the opportunity to audit, from the patient perspective, various medical procedures, processes, and surgeries at various healthcare systems. My conclusion is that information gaps during the pre-surgical process, the actual surgery, the follow up, and finally the patient's continued care plan can lead to very poor patient outcomes.

9.1.1 Patient Case A

In one example, I observed a patient who expected to undergo a robotic sigmoid colon resection. Based on multiple pre-surgical appointments, the surgeon concluded that the patient was a good candidate for robotic surgery and recommended this procedure. This patient went into surgery, and hours later, after beginning the robotic surgery, the surgeon determined that he was unable to resolve the colon issues robotically. The patient then underwent a traditional invasive surgery that took almost twice the time as planned. Recovery from this surgery was extremely difficult, resulting in a longer hospital stay and recovery. This patient almost died due to multiple complications following discharge from the hospital. Pain was also higher, and multiple medications were used for pain management. The patient was discharged to the rehab on a weekend without the prescriptions for drugs being given at the hospital. Multiple days passed before the physician at the rehab called in the necessary prescriptions that the hospital had been prescribing; during this delay the patient developed a temperature. A urinalysis was run for suspected infection, and it was determined the patient had acquired a potentially life-threatening urinary infection (pseudomonas) from the hospital. Fortunately, the patient responded to a seven-day treatment of IV antibiotics but was still low on red blood cells. The red blood cells were not regenerating, and the patient was close to requiring a blood transfusion. The rehab physician was concerned that perhaps there was internal bleeding causing the low hemoglobin count. The patient's PA ordered that the patient be sent back to the hospital emergency room for an MRI of the gastrointestinal area. Upon arrival, the chief nurse at the emergency room of the hospital determined that an MRI was not needed and rejected the orders of the PS and sent the patient back to the rehab (both trips required the patient to be transported via van as she was unable to even sit up for long. The patient spent eight hours in the emergency room until 2 a.m. that day, exposed to many sick patients in the emergency room, and the MRI was not completed. The next day the physician again ordered the MRI, which was completed, and the patient was returned to the rehab. This exposed a very sick patient to the hospital twice after already fighting a major hospital infection and in a compromised immunity state. Imagine if the emergency room nurse would have simply had all of this information about the patient available rather than having to make a poor judgment call (a.k.a. guess), which could have cost the patient her life had there been internal bleeding. Why would the data from the same hospital where the patient had this major surgery not be available in their own emergency room? What if that emergency room had quick access to the patient's risk of internal bleeding score, a risk of infection score, and a patient experience score? Imagine the difference these insights would have made in an instant when the wrong decision was made.

After this patient returned to the rehab, approximately a week later, she became infected with Covid-19 and had to be sent to yet another rehab since the rehab she was initially sent to didn't accept Covid-19 patients. Once again, given the high risk of patients over the age of 80 getting Covid-19 in a rehab facility in Florida, would it not have been prudent for the hospital or physician to recommend a rehab that had facilities for Covid patients, rather than being transported again to get to the second rehab? Being readmitted twice to the same hospital in under 30 days resulted in that hospital losing thousands of dollars due to poor quality of care.

Risk scores for these types of events are constantly being run by the more data-savvy healthcare providers.

A top hospital in Phoenix, Arizona, is using smart wristbands to gain access to data and to communicate with their patients throughout the healthcare procedure process. There is no requirement for the patient to have to log in to a portal (though that is encouraged). The smart band provides the data to the healthcare professional about their patient on a continual basis so that they know where they are in their procedure process, and so that they know who to reach out to for any questions or concerns. Had each of the facilities that the aforementioned patient had access to the smart band data and risk score alerts, the hospital may have kept the patient longer, discharged her to a better-equipped rehab facility, or had access to patient prescriptions by date. These are all things that the healthcare system that gets five-star ratings can do.

Here is additional information about the smart band technology:

https://ehrintelligence.com/news/how-banner-health-modernized-clinical-communications-collaboration

https://mhealthintelligence.com/news/banner-healths-new-telemedicine-platform-enables-in-patient-monitoring

9.1.2 Patient Case B

In another case example, a different patient was sent to the same hospital for an emergency colorectal surgery. That patient's physician deemed the patient to be a high risk and so instead of a traditional surgery closure, the patient's wound was closed with a negative pressure wound therapy (NPWT) closure. This process is not used in every colorectal surgery but only for those patients who are at high risk of infection based on predictive analytics models. This patient also got a major hospital infection. His white blood cell count was over 40,000, and his surgeon was extremely concerned as he had "coded" twice following surgery. The physician reached out to family in Texas and urged them to come to Florida to be with the patient and other family members. His outcome did not look good. While the patient still acquired a hospital infection, imagine what could have happened had the traditional approach for wound closure been utilized. Thanks to the physician's accurate risk assessment, good communication, fast action, and competent nursing staff, this patient survived the surgery and passed away nine years later at 87 years of age for a condition unrelated to his surgical procedure.

Predictive models for infection risk assessment have been utilized at many healthcare providers that use the NPWT process, including the University of Iowa Hospitals.

9.1.3 Pricing Offers an Intuitively Simple Problem That Provides Use of the Most Complicated Mathematical Models

Reeto Mookherjee, PhD, and I were senior pricing scientists together at Zilliant, a B2B pricing optimization company. We had fun working on some challenging problems together. Pricing is a cool problem to work on because everyone understands some of the basics of pricing, although there are many misconceptions. In general, if you as a seller lower your price, the more likely someone is to buy, but the less money you receive. Ideally, you would like to sell all your products at the maximum price you can get, but what is that price? If your price is too high your products may sell very slowly or not at all. If your price is too low, you might be leaving money "on the table." You could have asked for more, and thus made more money.

In real life the problem is not nearly as simple. There is a lot of psychology in pricing, take for example luxury brands or cannibalism of other products you offer. There are supply-chain issues, inventory costs, changes in regulations. What are the competitive pressures? Are your competitors willing to create a price war to gain market share? The problems become very complicated.

Therefore, from a mathematical solution standpoint the problem is "very rich," meaning you can approach it in some extraordinarily complex ways. You can use ensemble modeling techniques. You can mix the econometric models with optimization models and statistical segmentation models. Following is the first few sentences of an abstract for "Pricing, Allocation, and Overbooking in Dynamic Service Network Competition When Demand Is Uncertain" by Reeto and Terry L. Friesz:

> We study the problem of combined pricing, resource allocation, and overbooking by service providers involved in dynamic noncooperative oligopolistic competition on a network that represents the relationships of the providers to one another and to their customers when service demand is uncertain. We propose, analyze, and compute solutions for a model that is more general than other models reported in the revenue management literature to date. Previous models typically considered only three or four of five key revenue management features that we have purposely built into our model: (1) pricing, (2) resource allocation, (3) dynamic competition, (4) an explicit network, and (5) uncertain demand . . . we prove existence and uniqueness of a

pure strategy Nash equilibrium for dynamic oligopolistic service network competition described by our model.

That is a lot to unpack. Reeto has done a much better job in documenting much of his work. I think this is an important lesson. He has published in academic journals, and he and the Ingram Micro team were named finalists for the prestigious 2015 INFORMS Edelman Analytics Award.

9.2 Textual Extraction, Transformation, and Learning

Bill Inmon is the father of data warehousing. Bill has written many books, published in nine languages, and has sold over 1,000,000 books worldwide. Bill and I are friends and have been supportive of each other's projects as well as swapped stories about the Republic of Texas.

> "We process natural language using our unique, advanced, and adaptive technologies to help our customers 'See the Knowledge' captured in modern compositions of data." —ForestRim Technology website

Bill developed textual disambiguation technology—Textual ETL (extraction, transformation, and learning) at ForestRim Technology. It is a groundbreaking solution that automates the transformation of large volumes of textual artifacts, by creating metadata—data about data—to isolate what's relevant and identify meaningful relationships, what we might call pure knowledge.

In most corporations today, the vast majority of business decisions are made on a distinct minority of the data. Most business decisions are based on structured data. But structured data is only a small part of the data that passes through the corporation.

Ninety-five percent of corporate decisions are made using only 5% of the data.

Bill mentioned some key areas where text is critical for making important decisions. Some examples:

■ Emails
■ Internet conversations
■ Corporate contracts
■ Call center conversations
■ Medical records

- Warranty claims
- Insurance claims
- And a whole lot more

The problem is that classical data models do not work well (or at all) on textual data. There are a lot of reasons why data models are inappropriate for text. For example, context. Consider the word "boxing." What does boxing refer to? It may refer to a fistfight with gloves on. Or it may refer to a way of packaging some retail goods. Or it may refer to a military maneuver. Or it may refer to a holiday that is held in England the day after Christmas.

9.2.1 Some Sources of Textual Data

9.2.1.1 Voice Recordings

Typical sources of voice recording are hospitals and video recordings. It is normal to use VTT technology—voice-to-text transcription technology—to convert recordings to electronic text. It is possible to transcribe voice manually. But manual transcription of voice is normally prohibitively expensive and time consuming. In addition, it is still possible for voice transcription done manually to contain errors. It is much more efficient and much less expensive to simply play the voice recording into VTT technology, and VTT technology converts the voice to electronic text.

9.2.1.2 Printed Text

Printed text can be ingested and placed in an electronic format as well. Much text ends up in a printed format. OCR (optical character recognition) technology is used to transfer the text from the paper into an electronic format.

9.2.1.3 Internet and Social Media

A third viable source for the collection of text is the internet and social media. There are many sites on the internet where people talk about their experiences with a company, its products, and its services. As such, the internet is a wealth of information for a company that wishes to hear about what their customers are thinking.

9.2.1.4 Email

Another excellent source of text is email. Text in email is already in an electronic format. But email has its own limitations. The first limitation is that emails often contain spam. And spam is not what anybody needs to be analyzing. Spam needs to be removed from the email stream.

9.2.1.5 Electronic Texts as a Source

In some cases, the text that is desired is already in the form of electronic text. In these cases, there is no need for the physical conversion of the data into an electronic format. But there are other considerations to the electronic text that is found.

9.2.1.6 What Is a Taxonomy?

In its simplest form, a taxonomy is just a classification of objects. The objects can be anything—trees, cars, houses, grasses, animals, birds, etc.

9.2.1.7 What Is an Ontology?

A related form of a taxonomy is an ontology. An ontology is nothing more than a related collection of taxonomies. For example, there might be a taxonomy of countries. Then there might be another taxonomy of states, where a state is shown being related to a country. And there might be another taxonomy of cities, where the cities are shown to be related to a state. Together the related taxonomies form an ontology.

9.2.1.8 Language and Taxonomies

So why are taxonomies and classifications useful in doing textual analytics? The answer is that in using language, people do classifications all the time, and they don't even realize that they are doing classification. When you speak or write, classifications are done subconsciously, without even knowing you are doing it. Doing classifications is just a normal part of communication.

For example, take the simple sentence "He parked his car outside." This sentence is filled with classifications. The word "he" more specifically could have been "Jim Smith." The word "car" could have been "Porsche." The word "outside" could have been "on Eudora Street." So, the sentence "he parked his car outside" could have been, in an unabstracted, unclassified format, "Jim Smith parked his Porsche on Eudora Street."

9.2.1.9 Textual ETL and Taxonomies

So how does Textual ETL use taxonomies in converting unstructured text to a structured format? Textual ETL does what is called taxonomical resolution. Textual ETL reads the raw text, finds the words that have taxonomies related to them, and then selects the word to go into the database and supplies the hierarchical resolution to the database.

9.2.2 Two Examples of Analysis Types

There are two basic types of analytics that can be performed on the databases of text that are produced. Those two forms of analytics are:

- Correlative analysis
- Sentiment analysis

9.2.3 Correlative Analysis—An Introduction

Some types of text lend themselves to different kinds of processing. For example, in doctors' notes there is almost never any sentiment. Doctors' notes express things such as medications, procedures, and symptoms. Doctors treat patients whether they like or dislike the patient. So, sentiment is not something that is done on doctors' notes. Instead, correlative analytics is done on doctors' notes. In a correlative analysis, the occurrences of different occurrences of text within a record are analyzed. For example, suppose the medical records of 10,000 patients are accessed. The analyst wants to find out:

- Out of the 10,000 people, how many have had COVID?
- Of the people that have had COVID, how many are smokers?
- Of the people that have had COVID, how many are cancer patients?
- Of the people who have had COVID, how many are overweight?
- And so forth.

9.2.4 Sentiment Analysis—An Introduction

On the other hand, retail business and the hospitality industry are very interested in the sentiment of customers and prospects. Retailers and hospitality industries are most interested in both the good and bad things that people say. Listening to the customer is the basis for increasing business and increasing revenue flow. In sentiment analysis, you look for the expression of sentiment. In addition, you look for the object that is the source of the expression of sentiment.

Sentiment analysis is typically done where people are talking about their experiences with a company, its products, and its services.

9.2.5 The Semantic Layer

A semantic layer is a business representation of corporate data that helps end users autonomously use common business terms. A semantic layer maps complex data into familiar business terms such as product, customer, or revenue. With a semantic layer there is a unified, consolidated view of data across the organization.

Semantic, in the context of data, means "from the user's perspective"; which sounds like a nice, clean solution to a nasty unbounded complexity problem. The semantic layer is not entirely new.

www.forestrimtech.com/

9.3 Less Tech Is Often Better than More Tech in Pricing Solutions

I had a great catchup with my old colleague Joe Leyva; it had been 15 years since we had spoken. Great relationships, even professional ones, stand the test of time. We both worked at Zilliant, and Joe is still there. Joe told me about many of the changes in the revenue and pricing analytics space. Things have changed quite a bit. Pricing optimization and revenue optimization were the gold standard 10 years ago. These are highly technical solutions with applications from statistics and operations research—segmentation and mathematical optimization. Today that is no longer the case for several reasons.

Joe said that pricing management, a form of BI and analytics, has taken the primary role in B2B operations these days for a few reasons. For one, optimization models require much attention and must be refreshed based on changing market conditions. Things like high inflation trends erode these models quickly. Second, customers want to be in control, they want to use their knowledge coupled with system recommendations to set prices. Third, these are not versions of older BI systems. The analytics and visibility allow users to make powerful and agile decisions.

9.4 Data + Planning Is the Key to COVID Vaccine Center

Brett Dixon told me in an interview, that after college, data-driven decision-making just became the way he approached decisions, both in his personal as well as his professional life. When I asked Brett if he could think of any stories where he used data to improve decisions, one immediately came to mind; it was the COVID vaccine hub for Collin County (part of Dallas, Texas). He led the IT part of that COVID hub; the team used six sigma processes and data-driven approaches to get the center started in minimal time.

The team evaluated the floor layout, performed time studies, and optimized the flow of patients through the various checkpoints. Once they had preliminary data, they set an ambitious goal to vaccinate 2,000 people per day. Working backward they set the center up for 10 hours a day. They needed to vaccinate 200 per hour. This forced them to remap the space, streamline the process even further, but they got there. Brett called it "Data + Planning."

Patients were registered in EPIC (a national EMR solution). The process kicked off in early February 2021. Brett added that you must get everything just right. Even at the end of the day you must monitor exactly how many patients you can vaccinate with the remaining vaccine in a vial. Once it is opened, it cannot be stored, and the state of Texas was tightly monitoring effective usage.

9.5 Data Science Provider–Partner Relationships Greatly More Productive than Adversarial

In an enjoyable conversation with someone I had worked with for years providing data science strategy and solutions, an important success factor came to light. This person preferred not to be named. However, this is one of the most successful sales professionals that I have worked with. When I asked about what key principles they had learned, the response was, "It is very clear. When we are brought in as partners, these engagements are very successful. When we are brought in as adversaries, it is not successful." And he was not speaking about his success or his company's success. He meant the company they were providing solutions for was successful when the client wanted a partner that provided an environment of trust, mutual effort, and success. When the client saw them as someone wanting to just make money, it failed.

9.6 A Data Day in the Life of a Software Development Manager

In his role, my friend Venu, a software development manager for a large software company, outlined a number of systems that he uses in his day-to-day operations. We will not go into names of systems in this vignette, just Venu's intention for using them.

1. First a platform portal for software features. An internal company request or an external request from a customer on the company portal or ratings site may say, "I would like this feature added." It bubbles up to product development and product management for review and consideration.
2. There is a sales support system where account representatives, sales engineers, and related staff can enter feedback from the field on current functionality and performance issues, desired enhancements, and more.
3. There is a web-based bug tracking system for enhancement requests, features, high velocity fix time, and features for most critical issues.
4. An internal system for bugs, source control, programmer's collaboration, and customer success.
5. Then there are activities in the broader corporate systems, like an HR tracking system for hiring and his team's performance metrics, job resource tracking, and broader HR.
6. There are internal communications systems for knowledge management, communication, and scheduling.
7. He uses external developer boards for collaborating with the broader developer community. To contribute and to resolve issues.

These are some examples of managing a day in the life of a software development manager. Or, the data life of Venu.

9.7 A Digital Marketing "Grinder" Knows There is Value in Analytics

A Los Angeles–based digital marketer and I spoke about this track record and what excited him about marketing analytics, particularly digital marketing. He is a high-performing analytics professional with a passion for digital marketing and 14 years of experience impacting positive organizational outcomes. He is a bridge connecting the right resources and communicating analysis requirements. While he was a director, he called himself a "grinder," He is confident in his ability to collaborate with cross-functional teams to solve complex, high-stakes problems. And he is committed to continuous improvement and contributing to team success.

He said that you must determine whether you have the right data available to achieve the desired goals. And you may not have what you need to answer the original question or be successful in the initial project, but in the process you will come up with new candidates that will add value. It is a process of discovery. And, once again, we agreed that companies do not have to be analytics superstars to achieve valuable results.

9.8 Taming Unstructured and Semi-Structured Information

Ross Leher and I met late in the process of writing this book, but I am very glad we had a chance to talk so I could include the information he shared with me. His company, WAND, has developed curated taxonomies to improve the way our clients search and organize unstructured and semi-structured information. After 20 years, they have become the premier source for industry vertical taxonomies, business taxonomies, and specialty domain-specific taxonomies. The breadth and coverage of their taxonomy library is vast and has been used by thousands of companies around the world to organize information.

Different companies employ the use of taxonomies differently. One use case might be classification of internal documentation. Running the raw text against a taxonomy hierarchy allows organizations to identify their document by type of document. This allows for more intelligent retrieval of a given document for various business purposes.

On the other end, taxonomies enable Textual ETL. Here an entire corpus of documents is run against a nexus of taxonomies. The result is a database that contains not only search text but contextual information about the text. Searches and insights can then be gleaned that are just not possible on text alone.

1. Imagine being able to perform a simple search to return all records where John Smith was the admitting physician.
2. Another simple search to return all records where John Smith prescribed beta blockers.
3. Another simple search to return all records where John Smith billed a level 4 visit.

These searches are not multipart searches where "John Smith" is indicated in a different place. For Textual ETL, the database is constructed by all the different contexts inside the text for John Smith, and the system can use these contexts to intelligently determine what John Smith's involvement has been.

9.9 Data Sharing Drives Citizen Engagement

When I spoke with Ed Kelly he offered some interesting perspectives on data uses for the state of Texas. Ed was the chief data officer for the Texas government. He said that open data not only fosters transparency but also yields economic benefits. Public-sector agencies recognize the need to show their work to the constituents they serve. Open-data sharing and government transparency are fundamental expectations for our citizens.

Cities, counties, and states provide many critical services to the community that often go overlooked, undervalued, or represented poorly by a single incident. By boosting visibility and transparency through open-data initiatives, agencies can better earn respect from citizens who recognize the value that agencies contribute to their quality of life.

Smart governments interact with their citizens to form partnerships to address city or statewide challenges, whether that means identifying a pothole that needs to be fixed or monitoring statewide spending on IT products and services. Fostering transparency by providing open data on a self-service basis doesn't only provide goodwill and engage citizens, but also delivers business value. Opportunities include reduced transactional and service costs, increased customer satisfaction, greater operational efficiencies, and private-sector development of new uses for data.

Providing open data can be challenging. Governments must decide what data is important and ensure that it's accurate and free of any personally identifiable information to protect an individual's identity. And once they decide to engage, they must keep the stream of data flowing and current to maintain the public's trust and confidence. In addition to focusing on reliability and accuracy, open governments must also make information easily accessible in a machine-readable format, provide extensive high-value datasets for public consumption and publish data that has both breadth and depth of granularity.

By showing their work, local and state governments can not only highlight the great effort and service that they provide, but improve their operations and standing in the community, including with the individual citizens that they support.

9.10 The Onion Peel, Everyone Uses Data

I have known Craig Digby since we were in first grade. That is a long time! I had two motivations for our call. First, I wanted to catch up. Second, I wanted to know how he was using data in his professional life. The first goal was easily satisfied. The second began with Craig not thinking he had much to offer. But we started to peel the onion. So, I prodded and the conversation looked a bit like this:

> **Me**: Craig, you are in sales, how do you determine who you should approach with your offering?
>
> **Craig**: Well, ten years ago, I would travel to a place that I thought our equipment would sell and I would check in, go to my room, and actually start a contact list from a phone book.

We then discussed the progression of how he acquired leads and interacted with prospects. Now, he is using the internet in a variety of ways to determine a qualified prospects list. He then researches each company he will interact with and knows what they are doing, their basic financials, their market, customers, and much more. In other words in less than 10 years he went from having a company name and an address to a customer portfolio of targeted information. The difference, data, and technology. Craig is not using sophisticated analytics, just smarter, data-enabled techniques to provide products to customers.

Me: Craig, are you doing a presentation, a demo, or something in the sales cycle?

Craig: Primarily, it is a discussion, and we have a nice corporate portfolio. I can show the corporate website and compare it to the competition. It is a dynamic conversation.

It appears the "right tech" for the intended business use. Not over-engineered and seems to be working quite well for Craig.

Me: Craig, once you get an order, what do you do with it?

Craig: We have an internally developed CRM program to record the full sales cycle activity across the spectrum, all conversations and interest through the order. Once a quote is made the order is sent to manufacturing, which ensures every bolt and part is in the pipeline and verifies the quote is acceptable. Then the contract is available for signing.

We went on to other areas. Returns? Rare, but there are systems in place. Then Craig told me that since COVID he travels a great deal less, but his sales are just as high or higher. He really enjoys using his phone and iPad anywhere, anytime. He said, "you know, I am using data all the time."

Yes, peel the onion, we are using data all the time.

9.11 Constraints of Federal Regulations Tie States Ability to Provide Important Services

In a conversation with an IT consultant for the state of Texas, it was quickly apparent that rules and regulations at the federal government level can hamper a state's ability to provide meaningful services to its inhabitants.

An example, he pointed out, was the Texas Special Supplemental Nutrition Program for Women, Infants, and Children (WIC) program. This is a nutrition program that helps pregnant women, new mothers, and young children eat well, learn about nutrition, and stay healthy. If the state had access to the Medicaid database, even if it was deidentified, it would be able to cross-reference its inhabitants with mothers, infants, and children that could benefit from this program. However, according to federal law, most databases the government uses have to be isolated and independent pools of data, i.e., you cannot blend the data with other agencies.

Other examples that could promote health are AIDS, mental health, and subject abuse. These are often diseases and conditions that are highly correlated and yet there are not effective ways to cross-reference much of this information. If they could be, it would allow governments to provide services more effectively. The code of federal regulations, CFR Title 42, is the principal set of rules and regulations issued by federal agencies of the United States regarding public health. And you cannot cross-reference any information by these standards.

However, this is fully possible using modern master data-management capabilities, an independent, external identifier that would preserve confidentiality with the benefits of accessing the information and offering important services. Privacy is very important, and it should be preserved, but with technology it is possible to preserve confidentiality and offer useful resources to citizens at the same time.

9.12 Oncology Decisions Based on More than Clinical Factors—Quality of Life Matters

I was encouraged by a conversation with Ray Hall. He has experience in healthcare that I know very little about. He started working in oncology on web development and said the mission of this company was education and to create a bridge between the medical community and the personal lives of their patients. Too often clinicians try to optimize their therapies solely on the clinical outcomes. However, there is much more to life than clinical outcomes.

How will these therapies affect one's life? What about a woman that has breast cancer, and her only daughter is getting married in six months. It is one of the most important events of her life. Does she want to lose all her hair or be physically incapacitated such that she cannot be involved in one of the most rewarding experiences she will have—planning the wedding with her daughter?

Clinical decisions should not be made outside the context of one's life. In medicine we do not want single-factor optimization. We need to balance the outcomes based on a unique individual. For some, it will be mere survival, for others it will be a more complicated equation. Person-centered healthcare is the answer (Miner et al., 2023).

9.13 The Greatest Successes in Analytics Are Often the Simplest

I had a great conversation with a new acquaintance from Denmark, Aurelie (Lily) Giraud. Lily is a self-described self-made data scientist. Our conversation was rich and very conforming of a few points that I have heard in conversations with other data scientists and analytics professionals.

In her journey, Lily has discovered the power and importance of data. More importantly, she aims to connect with people and get at the problems and pain points they are experiencing and translate those difficulties into a data-driven solution for them. I (Scott) think this is one of the biggest missing gaps for most data scientists. Data scientists are great with data, but oftentimes they are not able to bridge the gap from the business problem to the correct problem solution, a design that will ease the pain and solve the problem.

Lily said that often analytics people go too quickly to build up a solution without pausing to understand the real need. As a result, they create a solution of poor value for the business. One of her techniques is to go in with a blank slate, no preconceptions. She then listens and asks many, many questions. She asks for clarification to make sure she is getting it right. She takes nothing for granted.

We spoke about some of the reasons for analytics project failure, and she said one of the biggest reasons is that the organization is not ready. They just do not understand basic data properties, limitations, and how to formulate questions that can be answered with data.

When I asked her about her most successful projects, she hesitated. I think she was thinking I might be expecting the most sophisticated answer. She paused and spoke about a very successful visual BI project that offered great gains. We exchanged this as a common phenomenon. Anyone reading or applying technology gravitates to the more sophisticated, but that is not where the value lies most of the time. It lies in easy-to-understand, simpler solutions rather than whiz bang and fireworks.

Three success tips she would offer:

1. People are often skeptical of the benefits of data-driven technologies and analytics. The best way to overcome these doubts is to "up the data literacy," improve the data communication skills and what analytics can

do for them and their problems. People need to be a part of the data journey from the very beginning no matter which background they come from. The more we engage them at the beginning the more likely the project will succeed.

2. You need well-interpreted data. You need to get a repeatable architecture going as soon as possible. You cannot do any meaningful analytics unless you have:

   a. Enough data—> the right quantity is business dependent and tied to the question/challenge we want to solve.

   b. Clean data—> the quality should be taken into account at the very beginning. Too often we see companies with huge amounts of data that are simply not useful.

3. Before you start with data solutions, pause and take the time to frame the problem you are trying to solve. What do you want from data? What are the challenges? What do you expect to solve with data? Start right, with the right questions. Too often we see projects failing because along the process we realize that they are not answering the real problem because it hasn't been framed properly.

9.14 Three Simple Truths with a Seasoned Actuary and Data Scientist

Several things were very interesting about my conversation with Avraham (Avi) Adler. His core training and expertise is in actuarial practice, yet he has an immense knowledge of mathematics, statistics, and quantitative and computation methods. Actuaries are to be respected for their in-depth training and consistent practice over many decades. Their roots are in the centuries of practice. However, Avi and a growing number of actuaries are learning AI and machine-learning techniques to move beyond traditional forms of closed-form analysis.

9.14.1 As Posted by Scott (Author) on LinkedIn, November 21, 2022

I just had a very engaging conversation with Avraham Adler. My neurons were firing, really firing! We talked about so much for the final book in the series, BUT three simple truths seemed to be at the top of our thoughts:

1. Try to learn from experts
2. Be humble
3. Understand the question

Very discerning truths that every professional should work toward. Avi qualified that these are not the end all, but a great start. I wish you could have heard the conversation. We spoke about GLM, Bayesian, Poisson, exponential, stochastics, TensorFlow, and so much more. None of these compare with the three simple truths.

9.15 Once Again, the Most Sophisticated or Complex Models Do Not Always Win

Humans have a natural gravitation to the biggest thing, the sexiest thing, the most complicated or sophisticated thing. While it often is the newer, more complex technology that outperforms the older, less complex technology it is not always the case. In fact, you would be surprised how often the simpler model or method outperforms the more complex algorithm or method. This phenomenon was exhibited again in a conversation with an analyst for a large airline.

We were talking about forecasting models. I had many questions about data sources and some of the methods, and I threw out some statistical and ML techniques that are used in forecasting and he replied that they were using much simpler methods. In fact, a consultant came in and provided a great presentation on their sophisticated modeling process. My friend said they had a head-to-head competition of the existing, "simple" methods versus the "novel" ML methods; the simple methods won. The point of the story was twofold:

1. Just because something is newer, more expensive, more complicated, or more "whatever" does not mean it is better than the simpler, less expensive alternative.
2. Test, test, test. Do not take someone's word for it. You will not know what is better until you perform the test yourself.

9.16 One Success a Pattern Does Not Make; AI and Analytics Are Not Plug and Play!

A veteran in healthcare and life science learned over a period of many years that people are attracted to shiny objects. He knows it well. He has spoken with hundreds of leaders across many industries, but he is an expert in healthcare. That would be my prior colleague and friend Carleton Jones. Carleton and I have shared the boardroom with executives who are trying to determine solutions to their analytics challenges. We have also spent time apart in different companies and perspectives, so it was great to compare notes once again.

A favorite quote of mine goes something along the lines of "asking the right question is more important than getting the right answer," or maybe I made it up, but I like it. People sometimes know what they want, but often they just tell you that they want what someone else has. Suppose a physician group has an interest in automating their office with voice technology, automatic transcription, and other automation systems. They have heard or read about other successes. However, they may not think about how they are going to incorporate such a system and the operational process it will require into their practice, their unique office environment. Even if a pilot is successful, can they scale and deploy with success?

This is getting complicated. Why should we need to think through all of this? We know that the Alpha Physicians Group has had great success. We just want to mimic what they have. Can you please provide us with the tools and analytics that made them successful?

We live in a complicated world. In data science and software engineering there is a concept called extensibility. In software engineering, extensibility is defined as "the quality of being designed to allow the addition of new capabilities or functionality." It is a measure of the ability to extend a system and the level of effort required to implement the extensions.

9.16.1 One Success Does Not Ensure Future Success

How will you know if something that has worked for someone else will work for you? First, you must be willing to fail. You must be willing to test it against critical success factors on a small scale. You must also define how you will integrate it into the larger system and how it will scale economically. You also need to ask if you can sustain it? AI and analytics are definitely not plug and play!

9.17 Does the Data Support the Allegations?

Dr. Jim Overdahl has had a rich career in answering tough questions with data as an economist and financial expert. He was formerly the chief economist for the US Securities and Exchange Commission (SEC) and the US Commodity Futures Trading Commission (CFTC) and is a specialist in financial markets and the US regulatory environment. He has worked on several high-profile, complex financial litigation cases, including the GM bankruptcy.

We had an interesting conversation about applications of data for proposed legislation and rules, the use of data in legal arguments and cases. His use of analytic techniques ranges from data and economic analysis to assist the SEC, to data-mining techniques applied to commodity for the CFTC.

However, it is a deep knowledge and degree of incisive unraveling of the truth that has provided Jim with a high degree of success. There are bona fide experts and purported "experts." Purported experts try to cut corners and stand behind jargon. This often works for them in many cases where someone is not asking the right questions, sorting through the garbage. However, incisive questioning can remove the veneer from a witness purporting their analysis was done on "big data" or trying to hide behind academic degrees.

I really enjoyed our discussion of determining causation. This is a topic I am extremely interested in, and Jim shared interesting perspectives on the topic. There is much more to understanding causation than simply distinguishing it from correlation, but that is a book for the future.

In the end, much of the complicated work that Jim does boils down to a simple question: "Do the data support the allegations?"

9.18 Precision Analytics and the Internet of Things (IoT) Bolster Life Science and Lifesaving Products

We have all seen the scene in an engaging TV show or movie. The helicopter lands atop a medical center and a medical team runs toward it. A helicopter door opens, and a crew member passes an Igloo® cooler to the medical team. In it is lifesaving plasma or a heart for a patient that is minutes away from death. It has been flown thousands of miles on multiple carriers, we just hope it makes it to the patient in time!

As a technologist, that helicopter scene always seemed a bit low tech and a slight bit disturbing to me. After talking with Balaji Jayakumar, co-founder and chief operating officer of MaxQ, I found out there is indeed a better way. MaxQ is revolutionizing the logistics behind temperature-sensitive biologics. They are at the forefront of several technologies and cover several types of analytics. One is the Internet of Things (IoT). They are monitoring sensor and location data, performing geo-analytics, capturing historical data, and using that data to build predictive and prescriptive models. However, the models they build are developed with specific uses in mind. It is not the "what can we do with data" that drives the data scientists and engineers at MaxQ, but instead it is "we have this problem, or our customers have this problem, how can we use data and analytics to solve it?"

The company's customers develop and sell expensive and sensitive life science products—whole blood, plasma, platelets, medications, vaccines, and medical devices. These biologics are heavily regulated, and the company helps carriers show compliance and adherence to thermal specifications.

The analytic capabilities MaxQ employs ranges from simple descriptive analytics to the sophisticated uses of real-time data and prescriptive models. Description might include basic temperature loggers and historical data. Predictive models might include real-time location, weather, traffic, layover, and other information that informs the carrier of specific actions to take to avoid losing millions of dollars in product.

SOMETIMES COMPANIES NEED TO PIVOT

Entrepreneurs often found companies for a business that is not ripe for the times or maybe the market economics don't play out as originally planned. Or, it could be the market has collapsed due to a change in government regulation or the creation of a new technology. There are many reasons a company may need to pivot to a new strategy to be successful (see *Forbes* article). This happened with MaxQ (preceding story). Balaji Jayakumar told me that the original plan for his company was utilizing microgravity. Balaji was trained as a mechanical and aerospace engineer (PhD Oklahoma State University).

Microgravity is often simulated underwater and on reduced-gravity flights. They came up with the idea of using drones, and NASA was an early customer. They were successful, but the business model did not sufficiently scale due to the limited size of the market.

A "pivot" was necessary, and Balaji and his team switched the focus to biologics and now takes a scientific approach to innovating thermal packaging.

Pivots are not always successful, but what improved the odds for Balaji and his team were the understanding of data and its application combined with identification of an addressable healthcare market and the development of the accompanying strategy.

References

www.forbes.com/sites/jasonnazar/2013/10/08/14-famous-business-pivots/?sh=3286c4e65797

https://packmaxq.com/

9.19 Using Data and Evidence to Improve Federal Programs

The US Government Accountability Office is trying to improve the image of the government in its data use return on investment made by the taxpayer. According to its website (September 10, 2022):

> Each year, the federal government spends trillions of dollars to deliver goods and services to its citizens and address various national issues. For example, Congress appropriated $2.6 trillion in 2020 to help people, businesses, the health care system, and state and local governments respond to the COVID-19 pandemic.
>
> Evidence—which includes information such as data, statistics, and rigorous studies known as program evaluations—can provide important insights that could improve the federal government's performance. Federal agencies have taken some actions to ensure they have sufficient evidence to inform their decisions.

It will take years to analyze the government's COVID-19 response. This single expense was not the only expense the government made. In fact, it made many investments on the pandemic, and it will take years to determine the ROI of the government initiatives.

www.gao.gov/using-data-and-evidence-improve-federal-programs

9.20 Healthcare Leaders Save Face at the Expense of Data Accuracy

I spoke with a healthcare executive that has leadership responsibilities in data extraction for a very large healthcare enterprise. He expressed concern that senior leadership is wedded to a data warehouse because they were responsible for the decision to make that "data warehouse" that cost tens of millions of dollars. Even when the data use is suspect for the application or usage, leadership says that everyone must use "the single source of truth," the enterprise data warehouse (EDW).

The EDW is a great technology and is the right place to go for many applications. Should it be the only source of data in an organization? No. Why? Because data in an EDW is highly transformed, static/batch, and relational. There are times when reporting and analysis require data directly from the source systems. This has created problems for this healthcare enterprise. Senior leaders do not want to admit the EDW does not fulfill every need.

NOTE: There are technical ways around the EDW bottleneck. However, both require much care and caution. One is a mirroring of the production system. When deployed in a production environment, the principal database is the production database. Database mirroring involves redoing every insert, update, and delete operation that occurs on the principal database onto the mirror database every few minutes or hours. Another is the concept of a data lake. A data lake is a centralized repository that ingests and stores large volumes of data in its original form. The data can then be processed and used as a basis for a variety of analytic needs. The authors have heard about successful data lakes and very unsuccessful ones. Be careful.

9.21 Healthcare Data Requires Subject Matter Expertise, Not Just Technical Skills

What is the most important, technical skill in pulling data and being a SQL expert or understanding the business operations behind the data? Well, you need some of both to be sure. However, my good friend for more than 25 years, Matt Ueckert, said of the two, the understanding of the business is the most important. And Matt would know. I cannot recall the number of times in a conference room when someone said, "Let's get Matt in here."

This agrees with my experience as the person pulling the data. Is it easier to acquire the knowledge to write SQL or to understand all the nuances of internal data? Especially in Matt's world of healthcare and dominating health plans. There are the rules—that is SQL, write the code and you can expect it to behave the way you wrote it. The business data on the other hand? "Well, back in 2022, we had a SQL software version change, so when you query you have to understand that the blah, blah, and blah changed. So, if you don't do blah, blah, and blah when you query the data sources, your data will not represent reality." Let me repeat that—your data will not represent reality. So, you as a subject matter expert must know the blah, blah, blah. And many times that gets overlooked.

Matt said, "SQL or any data extraction code will do what you tell it. But you have to know what to tell it."

9.22 Work Satisfaction, Improving Lives

Work can be a whirlwind of activity and challenges. Most professionals do not have time for a long breath, much less time for reflection. That is why it was refreshing to hear how rewarding it was for a professional working in the pharmaceutical/biologic space to see his work; he was improving lives.

That is my friend Danny Stout; he has had multiple roles at a global top 20 pharmaceutical company. The company is focused on metabolic disorders, gastroenterology, neurology, inflammation, as well as oncology. Danny has worked in digital and data science doing good clinical practice (GCP), and more broadly, GxP. GxP is a set of regulations and quality guidelines formulated to ensure the safety of life sciences products while maintaining the quality of processes throughout every stage of manufacturing, control, storage, and distribution. He now is involved in plasma and biologic forecasting for the company.

We spoke about technology, statistics, data science, and things that we both find cool. But in the end, Danny said he finds a great deal of satisfaction knowing that his work is improving lives. I find that pretty cool.

9.23 National Restaurant Change Uses Data for Planning Initiatives

I had the opportunity to speak with Kristen Dixon-Prater on her use of data in the food industry. Kristen mentioned several analytics tools she uses to manage her responsibilities. Two major responsibilities she has are to work with her store managers and to develop initiatives across her district. These initiatives are data led, but employee-informed ideas on how to improve the day-to-day business of operations complete their development. There are three primary areas she covers:

1. Employee
   a. Engagement and satisfaction

2. Customer satisfaction
   a. Time of delivery
   b. Food quality
   c. Meal value
   d. Overall experience

3. Corporate strategy and objectives
   a. Cost effectiveness
   b. Market share
   c. Product marketing

Kristen uses a balance of data analysis, employee input, and her expertise of many years in the business to determine the initiatives she creates.

9.24 Global Chip Shortage May Encourage Cloud Migration, but the Cloud Is Not Impervious to Interruption

Global cloud providers have been encouraging companies to migrate more computing assets to cloud technologies for many reasons. However, a painful reason that is being felt recently is the global chip shortage. Cloud technologies can easily scale up or scale down based on demand, and thus firms do not have to make big capital investments in fixed physical assets. One type of semiconductor in particular that is making data centers more expensive is graphics processing units (GPUs). GPUs have seen a significant rise in prices with significant reductions in supply. We previously provided a section on cloud benefits and drawbacks in Burk and Miner (2020).

However, even cloud technology is not impervious to interruption. Clouds do go down. There are four large native international public cloud providers—Amazon, Microsoft, Google, and Alibaba. Yes, there are other cloud providers, but they often use one of the big four for their infrastructure for public clouds. In 2022 almost everyone had an outage. So, while cloud technology can afford great statistics for their dependency and uptime, they are not bulletproof. That is why some companies have mission-critical applications running in multi-cloud environments. That could be with one provider accessing multiple geographic environments, it could be having contracts with multiple cloud providers, or it could be a failover provided by a traditional data center.

9.25 Do Not Trust Data Just Because It Comes from a Web App or Browser

We have credibility issues, and one reason for those is that data is sometimes trusted because it comes from a technology we trust, like a web app or browser. The world is full of dirty data, and there are several reasons the data could be dirty. A simple example is the data is propagated from an unreliable source. How many times does this happen? Someone says something in social media that is not true and it is shared over and over and becomes part of the data lore. One of Scott's (author) favorites is that you would need to do 250,000 crunches to lose a pound of fat. He has seen this propagated over the internet for over a decade, hundreds of times, with no scientific backing. "According to the experts, it might even take 250,000 active crunches to effectively burn a specific pound of belly fat." What experts?

An issue with this is the source of the data. If you were told something like that on the street, you might question it. However, with a web app or phone app, you may or may not. Unfortunately, too many times people not only accept it, they propagate it; by passing it on to others, it gains traction and myth becomes legend and legend becomes accepted reality.

9.26 The Value of Domain Knowledge Is Critical to AI Success!

Call it subject matter expertise, domain knowledge, or business knowledge, this has been a recurring theme in many of the conversations I have had. Several people have told me that domain expertise is critical for project success. A data scientist at a top five global tech company told me that he believes his company would not do well with a centralized AI and analytics structure for this reason. He believed for their company, domain knowledge trumps data science skills. They have many smart people and best practices built into their systems and methods when tackling an AI project. It is the knowledge of their products and their business that is key to success. It is the subject matter expertise that makes the difference.

While he did not explicitly state it, I believe he was saying that without the domain knowledge the engineers would not know the right questions to ask. Even if you can get someone to state it in business terms, the engineer must have enough information to formulate the question correctly. It is the framing of the question that is so important, and you cannot do that without specific domain knowledge.

I think this is one reason so many AI and analytics solution providers are pushing the concept of citizen data scientists and the democratization of data. Part of it has to do with the lack of supply of data scientists, but even if there were enough they would have to get beyond technical expertise and gain business insight to effectively know what the most rewarding questions were to ask, they should not know how to frame them.

9.27 We Want to Minimize the Amount of Data Collected

Unlike most corporate entities there are areas of the US government that are working on minimizing the amount of data collected. Please see, The Federal Register published in 2019, *Proposed Information Collection; Comment Request; National Institute of Standards and Technology (NIST), Generic Clearance for Community Resilience Data Collections (The Federal Register, 2019)*.

NIST will limit its inquiries to data collections that solicit strictly voluntary opinions or responses. The results of the data collected will be used to decrease negative impacts of disasters on society and, in turn, increase community resilience within US communities.

I learned all of this from Angela Waner, who is involved in government policy and trends around data, uses of data, and analytics. It was refreshing. When asked in business, "What data should we store," you get the response, "everything." Most of that data sits for years or decades without use and is a continued burden. Data is not free. It costs money to collect it, it costs money to continue to store it, and it is a legal and ethical liability.

9.27.1 Interesting Government Websites Related to Data and Analytics

www.nist.gov/
https://analytics.usa.gov/
https://strategy.data.gov/

9.28 AI Demand Must Scale to Costs, Entrepreneurial Lessons

Tobias Zwingmann is a data scientist with a high entrepreneurial bias. He is the author of *AI-Powered Business Intelligence* and a frequent podcast and online seminar speaker. He is an educator, and he utilizes small and big data to create value. As an example, he has a proven record of accomplishment in turning analytical insights into better customer experiences and higher customer engagement.

When we spoke, we talked about his recent book and his entrepreneurial experience. He shared that the original product for his company was to develop an API platform. It operates as a SaaS (software as a service) product with built-in AI. It takes still and video (CCTV) images of events, conferences, or street crowds (any large social gathering) and then provides attendance levels. It is a really cool idea, and Tobias has a formal education in event management. The company also extended the use case to counting cars in images that could be used in a variety of ways.

They have been successful. However, since API platforms charge an exceedingly small fee per API call, the revenue is limited due to the number of calls and a limited market size. As with many entrepreneurial efforts there is a need to continually adapt and generate additional revenue streams. Tobias shared with me many things they are working on, and I believe the future will be bright!

9.29 Human Out of the Loop Analytics!—A Major, Uncomfortable Step

We have written about how the major advantage of any analytics is to augment human intelligence; to pass some of the cognition to the machine rather than have a human interpret it. Over the decades of data analysis, we first started with tables. Then, with classical statistics, it took much effort to work through all the variance and trends in these tables of data. Then in the latter half of the 20th century, when computers gave speed and power, we used visualization to see the patterns easily (descriptive analytics). Then, in the 1990s), we went to interactive visualization where we could brush, drill, and query. Then, as the 21st century came about, we added machine learning where we could input data and have machines tell us what would happen with what likelihood based on that data (predictive analytics). Then we took the next step and had those algorithms tell us what the best action for us to take was (prescriptive analytics). If we agreed then we took that action. All of these examples are "human in the loop analytics." The decision-making is enhanced via data, but the final action is made by a human.

When Justin Fickle and I spoke, we talked about automated actions taken with no outside interaction, "human in the out-of-the-loop analytics." This is a major step for most organizations and is done in limited pilots until the organization can recognize:

1. Some problems should never be fully automated.
2. It takes time for the culture to get comfortable with this shift.
3. There needs to be tight controls and feedback on the efficacy of auto-mated decisions.

There should be very tight feedback loops on the success of automated decision-making with fallback plans in place if models quickly degrade. There are major considerations outside of predictive power. For example, radiology for women's breast cancer. Machines outperform humans dramatically in efficiency and accuracy. However, humans are trained in underlying systems well beyond machines. Therefore humans are more likely to interpret edge cases. For this type of radiology, have the machine make the initial evaluation, then let a radiologist certify it.

9.30 The Last Mile of AI and Analytics

Alex Fry and I had a very interesting conversation about organizations struggling with the last mile in AI and analytics program success. Very often this is the most difficult step for organizations to get right. We spoke about the ability of many organizations to do this for an individual project basis. However, repeatability and sustainability is a real challenge.

Alex and I have much in common. Alex is a seasoned AI/ML specialist, focused on enabling businesses to make automated, intelligent decisions throughout their organizations using machine learning and artificial intelligence. He has been helping customers for decades. Alex says:

> The goal is to help customers activate their insights

> My ultimate goal is to help our customers activate their insights by taking their machine-learning models and deploying and integrating them effectively into their business and customer-facing applications. By operationalizing what were previously offline insights, I've helped build data and analytic products that turn insights into action and achieve massive business value across my customers' organizations.

We discussed some of the gaps that exist in deploying insights into operational systems so that users can quickly access and act upon them. This is the last mile. Moreover, we talked about the business needs for feedback loops and KPIs for business executives. Data scientists, developers, and technical leaders tend to monitor model accuracy and precision metrics. However, business leaders are asking questions like:

- Have we recouped our investment?
- What is the ROI in this project?
- Are project results meeting expectations?
- What is the lift from last week?
- Where are we outperforming/underperforming?
- What should be our next strategy?

Only by completing the last mile with the right business metrics and the proper feedback loops can these questions be answered.

9.31 Public Data Enables Anyone to Be a Real Estate Expert

My friend Francisco "Cisco" Arroyo and I have something in common. We both own some real estate to provide some passive income, specifically rental houses. It is a nice alternative to investing everything in traditional assets like stocks, bonds, gold, and other categories. It is a nice, simple way to diversify with a greater amount of control. Cisco lives in a more metropolitan area, while we live in a more rural area.

I think Cisco is more sophisticated and savvier in investing in this area than I (the trained statistician, data scientist) appear to be. In a call in late 2022, Cisco told me about all the data he uses to make real estate decisions. He triangulates across several types of data and determines value for decision-making, whereas we go to a few commonly used websites with estimates that aren't always very accurate and add that info to gut feeling.

He has been very successful and has an impressive plan moving forward. This has all been made available by publicly available data, marketplaces, and data aggregators. Taking that data from a variety of sources and combining it with knowledge of the specific locations and markets has made it possible for him, and he says "anyone," to be a real estate expert.

9.32 AI and Analytics Should Not Be Done in Isolation—Sepsis Failure

I was told a story by someone working for a mid-sized hospital system that had developed a predictive analytics platform for sepsis (the body's extreme response to an infection). They had good data, great technology, and AI knowledge. Yet, the results they hoped for never materialized. The model was efficacious, but it was not well adopted.

The problem? They did not receive broad physician buy-in at the beginning of the project. Physician leadership was missing. Therefore, by the time the system was made available there was a bias against it. Adoption has been very slow. It will never gain the potential return on investment it could have achieved even if it does gain wider adoption. The upfront fees for licensing and consultants were significant.

It is a lesson in human nature. People need to be invested in the project to drive adoption and use of the project results. "Build it and they will come" is not a successful strategy.

9.33 Today's MLOps Platforms Are Much More Powerful

MLOps is a portmanteau for machine learning and IT operations. When I spoke with my former colleague, Karan Nisar, we spoke about the importance of MLOps. Karan is an ML engineer and is far more knowledge-able on this subject than I am. In fact, in my work MLOps has been an addition to the end of the ML process. We used the same AI platforms that data scientists use for model building to handle the MLOps capabilities. But I learned in talking with Karan, that we were just using a minor portion of the capabilities that exist.

In the classic paradigm, data scientists use a platform or limited set of tools to provision the data, perform analyses, perform feature extraction and selection, build models, deploy those models, and then do simple MLOps functions, like track performance and health of the models and tune or retrain the models. There was also model lineage and version control and some other functions. However, after talking with Karan, I learned that dedicated MLOps platforms today can do so much more. So I asked Karan what were the key functions in MLOPs today, and he provided a long and detailed feature set. First, he suggested that your MLOps platform be inde-pendent of your ML creation. In the end, you want your platform to aid you in building better models faster with experiment tracking, dataset versioning, and model management.

9.34 Executive Has an Epiphany in 2011 on Compute, the Cloud, and Open Source

Imagine being a leader involved in cutting-edge solutions for some of the global Fortune 100, in other words, architecting technical solutions for some of the world's largest companies, but then realizing the plans you have con-structed will soon be antiquated. My friend Pramod Singh was that leader and architect. He was involved in some of the largest massively parallel pro-cessing (MPP) systems for Hewlett Packard. He held global assignments and was a global technologist. Then in about 2011 something struck him; it was all about to change. In the future, it would not be centralized data centers, but distributed cloud processing that would rule the day. Furthermore, it would not be commercial BI, statistical, and data science (a new term at the time) platforms that would be the main tools for data-driven decision-mak-ing. It would be open-source languages and coding tools instead.

He had it right. For a number of reasons, the world is changing. It is a big world. So, there are still plenty of data centers, and there will be many more years of running on servers. And there are plenty of commercial data science platforms. But the most successful software companies are those that embrace open source and become open and extensible to these tools. The dinosaurs, and soon to be extinct providers, are the ones that are sticking to their belief that they know better than everyone else. Have you heard of "short sell"?

On the compute side, there are reasons to stay on premises. But those reasons are dwindling. Cloud allows you to shift your capacity from month to month. Imagine you are a vacation booking agency in the middle of COVID; did your computing needs go down? Or imagine you were an internet retailer, your needs would go through the roof. You can scale your needs in cloud dynamically. Outages do happen; it happens for both on-premises and cloud systems, but more often on-premises. And multi-cloud can add redundancy and security (see Burk et al., 2021).

Tightly controlled propriety commercial systems are dead or will be soon. Academic programs support open-source systems. Self-taught technologists are getting trained with massive open online courses, YouTube, blogs, and web searches. No one wants to spend hundreds of thousands or millions of dollars on licenses that lock them into a restricted set of user knowledge, constraining contracts, or limited functionality with declining research and development.

"The Times They Are A-Changin'," said Bob Dylan. So did my friend, Pramod.

References

Burk, S., & Miner, G. D. (2020). *It's all analytics!: The foundations of AI, big data, and data science landscape for professionals in healthcare, business, and government.* CRC Press.

Burk, S., Sweenor, D. E., & Miner, G. D. (2021). *It's all analytics-part II: Designing an integrated AI, analytics, and data science architecture for your organization.* CRC Press.

Miner, G., Miner, L., Burk, S., Goldstein, M., Nisbet, R., Walton, N., & Hill, T. (2023). *Practical data analytics for innovation in medicine: Building real predictive and prescriptive models in personalized healthcare and medical research using AI, ML, and related technologies* (2nd ed.). Elsevier-Academic Press. (Hardback ISBN: 9780323952743)

The Federal Register. (2019, February 26). Proposed information collection; comment request; national institute of standards and technology (NIST). *Generic Clearance for Community Resilience Data Collections.* Retrieved from https://www.federalregister.gov/documents/2019/02/26/2019-03243/proposed-information-collection-comment-request-national-institute-of-standards-and-technology-nist

Chapter 10

Wrapping Up

> *"Begin at the beginning and go on till you come to the end; then stop."*
>
> —*Lewis Carroll*

10.1 What a Ride—In the End, It Is All Analytics

We will add one thing to the Lewis Carroll quote at the beginning of the chapter.

> *Begin at the beginning and go on till you come to the end;* ***REFLECT,*** *then stop.*

That is what we are doing now in this series, stopping. But, before we do, let's reflect!

Reflecting on the Series, Book 1. *It's All Analytics!: The Foundations of AI, Big Data and Data Science Landscape for Professionals in Healthcare, Business, and Government* (Burk & Miner, 2020).

The initial reasons for writing this book were that people are confused about what data is, what methods and technologies exist, and how they differ. How can we separate reality from hype? Why are people making up new terminology and peddling it as new for last week's soup? Who can you trust? We said in the first book:

> Why do you need this book! No other book has a comprehensive view of the landscape. Yes, you can get a lot of information from

the internet, but it is not curated or validated. Is it someone's blog post who is trying to promote themselves as an expert? Anyone can write a blog and there are many analytics websites which are platforms for marketecture (promotion of product or service over capability).

We previously cited Kasey Paneteta (2019):

> Imagine an organization where the marketing department speaks French, the product designers speak German, the analytics team speaks Spanish, and no one speaks a second language. . . . That's essentially how a data-driven business functions when there is no data literacy.

The rise and speed of technology innovation has created a lot of stir in the media, the press, universities, businesses, and governments. Some of the information is accurate and useful. Some of this information is inaccurate and confusing. Some of it is beyond the reach of the average professional or student because it is either too narrowly focused or too technical without the necessary background. Our first book was about simplifying the subject for an interested reader in a non-threatening, non-technical, broad viewpoint. We considered the information presented in that text as what we would cover in a course titled "Creating Value from Data 101" taught at a university, what some would call a survey course.

Our societies have spent hundreds of billions of dollars collecting data, but most of it sits in silos. Silos of data never analyzed, never touched again. Not only the initial cost to acquire, but also the cost to maintain, backup or archive, and keep secure! The cost is tremendous. Everyone has talked about monetizing data, but few are successful. We have talked about using it for decades, but we have barely scratched the surface. To be clear, it is not technology that is hampering progress. It is a lack of vision, human capital, and execution. The purpose of that book was to help increase knowledge, enable execution, and squeeze dollars from data by informing professionals on how to create value from data.

We covered many of the analytical areas at a high level. The world's countries/societies continue to increase our collection of data exponentially year over year. However, we actually analyze very little of what we collect, but there are big efforts to change that. We explored these advancements for the professional who desires to understand the big picture of analytics, data science, AI, and related fields.

There is a HUGE overlap in the areas where value is created from data. This is not by accident, as we explained. Take a look at the dizzying list of overlapping subject areas:

- Business intelligence (BI)
- Visual BI, analytics
- Visual analytics
- Business analytics
- Data analytics
- Predictive analytics
- Prescriptive analytics
- Advanced analytics
- Text analytics
- Geospatial/GIS/location analytics
- Social/network/graph/knowledge analytics
- Sports/media/banking/energy/logistics/hospitality analytics
- Healthcare/financial/marketing/accounting analytics
- Statistics
- Optimization
- Data mining
- Data modeling
- Machine learning (ML)
- Big data,
- Data science
- Decision science
- (Enterprise or business) decision management
- Business process management
- Data engineering
- Artificial intelligence (AI)
- Computational intelligence
- Auto ML
- Management science
- Linear and mathematical programming
- Deep learning, informatics
- Decision science
- Among others

We think there is a need for simplification. Statistics applies to many forms of analytics. AI applies to many forms of analytics as well (neural networks, deep learning, NLP, chatbots, large language models, and more). So do business intelligence, visual BI, and corporate dashboards. Management science, decision science, and operations research all produce various forms of analytics. Analytics are knowledge specific, domain specific, functional specific, and use specific. The simplification we need is "It's All Analytics"!

Reflecting on the Series, Book 2. *It's All Analytics—Part II: Designing an Integrated AI, Analytics, and Data Science Architecture for Your Organization* (Burk et al., 2021):

The thought for this book was: we hope people are now speaking the same language and have basic data and analytics literacy after reading book one. However, we recognized many firms were failing to succeed even with this knowledge. We reflected on our own experience, talked with other professionals, and did a great deal of industry research. We determined there were three needed components for analytics success, three foundations to analytics success. So we wrote the book that addressed these foundations:

Foundation #1, Organizational Design for Success. We presented the need for a complete organizational alignment of the entire enterprise and its analytics team for making its analytics program successful. This means attention to the culture—the company culture!!! To be successful, the CEOs and decision-makers of a company/organization must be fully cognizant of the cultural focus on "establishing a center of excellence in analytics." Simply, company culture is the most important aspect of a successful analytics program. The focus must be on innovation, as this is needed by the analytics team to develop successful algorithms that will lead to greater company efficiency and increased profits.

Foundation #2, Data Design for Success. We wrote that data is the cornerstone of success with analytics. You can have the best analytics algorithms and models available, but if you do not have good data, efforts will at best be mediocre if not a complete failure. This foundation also dove deeper into data with descriptions of things like volatile data memory storage and non-volatile data memory storage, in addition to things like data structures and data formats, plus considering things like cluster computing, data swamps, muddy data, data marts, enterprise data warehouse, data reservoirs, and analytic sandboxes, and additionally data virtualization, curated data, purchased data, nascent and future data, supplemental data, meaningful data, GIS (geographic information systems) and geo-analytics data, graph databases, and time series databases. Part II also considers data governance, including data integrity, data security, data consistency, data confidence, data leakage, data distribution, and data literacy.

Foundation #3, Analytics Technology Design for Success. This presented the concept of analytics maturity and aspects of this maturity, like exploratory data analysis, data preparation, feature engineering, building models, modelevaluation, model selection, and model deployment. Foundation #3 also went into the nuts and bolts of modern predictive analytics, discussing such terms as AI, machine learning, deep learning, and the more traditional aspects of analytics that feed into modern analytics like statistics, forecasting, optimization, and simulation. This section also went into how to communicate and act upon analytics, which includes building a successful analytics culture within your company/organization.

Reflecting on the Series, Book 3. *The Applications of AI, Analytics, and Data Science: An Overview for Professionals in Healthcare, Business, and Government*:

After you have read the first two books, you have two cornerstones to build your analytics success upon. These are necessary, and if you follow them they can greatly improve the likelihood of your analytics program succeeeding and can increase your program's ROI. Now comes a fun evaluation.

The fun part includes a lot of questions, such as:

■ What can we learn from people at our same analytics maturity level?
■ What are the people at the next analytics maturity level doing? What should we be doing to prepare to move ahead? Or does it really make sense to try and move ahead? Maybe based on our market position, external forces and corporate strategy, should we stay here?
■ What are other industries doing? Can we cross-pollinate ideas from other industries and solve some of our problems? Would this allow us to leapfrog the competition?

The evaluation part:

■ Do your data and analytics capabilities match your corporate objectives? Do you have the right knowledge, the right data, and the right technology to meet your goals?
■ Should you think about conducting a data and analytics assessment? What is that in the first place? What is the process and would it be worth it?

That is our purpose of this book, answering these questions and getting the creative juices going to explore the art of the possible, personally for you, in your unique situation.

We would be remiss if we did not mention that in the creation of this three-book series we determined another unmet need. The need for high-level executives and leaders to understand their role in all of this. That is, the critical need that they help design and align an executable analytics strategy around their business strategy. So, we wrote another book. We recommend what we believe in. We took the time to write it down, *The Executive's Guide to AI and Analytics: The Foundations of Execution and Success in the New World*, so please consider Burk & Miner, 2022.

Wishing you the best,
Scott and Gary

References

Burk, S., & Miner, G. D. (2020). *It's all analytics!: The foundations of AI, big data, and data science landscape for professionals in healthcare, business, and government.* CRC Press.

Burk, S., & Miner, G. D. (2022). *The executive's guide to AI and analytics: The foundations of execution and success in the new world.* Productivity Press.

Burk, S., Sweenor, D. E., & Miner, G. D. (2021). *It's all analytics-part II: Designing an integrated AI, analytics, and data science architecture for your organization.* CRC Press.

Paneteta, K. (2019). LinkedIn. https://www.linkedin.com/in/kasey-panetta-98115313/

Index

Printed in the United States
by Baker & Taylor Publisher Services